# THE LAST BRITISH DAMBUSTER

# THE LAST BRITISH DAMBUSTER

One man's extraordinary life and the
raids that changed history

## GEORGE 'JOHNNY' JOHNSON

EBURY
PRESS

3 5 7 9 10 8 6 4 2

First published in 2014 by Ebury Press, an imprint of Ebury Publishing
A Random House Group company

MIX
Paper from
responsible sources
FSC® C015829

Printed and bound in Great Britain by Clays Ltd, St Ives PLC

ISBN 9780091957742 (hardback)
ISBN 9780091958596 (trade paperback)

To buy books by your favourite authors and register for offers visit
www.randomhouse.co.uk

In memory of the 55,000 aircrew of Bomber Command who lost their lives in World War II and in particular the 53 of my colleagues who died on that fateful night in May 1943.

And in loving memory of Gwyn, who made this life possible.

# CONTENTS

FOREWORD                                                                ix

CHAPTER 1   CHUCK-CHUCK AND A             1
FAMILY AT WAR

CHAPTER 2   MERLIN MUSIC AND THE      19
GREAT ESCAPE

CHAPTER 3   JOURNEY INTO DARKNESS   45
AND THE BABBACOMBE
BOMBSHELL

CHAPTER 4   NIGHT FIGHTERS AND A      71
FIASCO IN FLORIDA

CHAPTER 5   BOMBS GONE AND MY       95
WAR BEGINS

CHAPTER 6   HEADING HOME AND       123
TOASTING THE BRIDESMAIDS

CHAPTER 7    SMOOTH LANDINGS AND THE          151
             DAMS RAID

CHAPTER 8    THE DEBRIEF AND A RETURN         183
             TO THE SORPE

CHAPTER 9    NORTH AFRICA AND THE             201
             LEMON RAFFLE

CHAPTER 10   FROZEN POTTIES AND              221
             CAREER SUICIDE

CHAPTER 11   SINGAPORE, SWORDS AND           245
             MISSILES

CHAPTER 12   TEACHING AND THE TORY           267
             PARTY

EPILOGUE                                     287

ACKNOWLEDGEMENTS                             303

GLOSSARY                                     305

PICTURE CREDITS                              306

# FOREWORD

Shortly before 9.30 on the evening of Sunday, 16 May 1943, the first of 19 Lancaster bombers of 617 Squadron took off from RAF Scampton in Lincolnshire to attack the major dams in Germany's Ruhr valley, and the legend of the Dambusters was born.

At 3.23 the following morning, Lancaster ED 825, 'T-Tommy', piloted by Flt Lt Joe McCarthy, returned safely. Amongst his crew was the bomb aimer, George 'Johnny' Johnson. My father.

At the heart of this audacious attack on Germany's industrial heartland lay technical genius, the remarkable skill of some of Bomber Command's best pilots, and the outstanding bravery of the aircrews. Of the 133 airmen who set out on the raid, 53 were killed and three became prisoners of war, two of whom were badly injured. In any battle, a 42 per cent loss rate would seem unthinkable, and, in contrast to the public euphoria at the success of the mission, the mood in the squadron was sombre. Everyone knew several people who had failed to return. Barnes Wallis, the scientific wizard who had made the raid possible, was said to have been in tears, blaming himself for 'sending so many young men to their deaths'.

Within four months, following two disastrous nights over the Dortmund–Ems canal in September 1943, where 617 Squadron suffered heavy losses, 11 of the original 21 crews that had founded the squadron less than seven months earlier were gone. By the end of the war, only 44 (one in three) of those who took part in the Dams Raid were still alive. Today, 71 years later, only the last three survive – Les Munro in New Zealand, Fred Sutherland in Canada, and Johnny Johnson in Britain.

It is impossible to overstate the sheer courage of these young men, most of whom were in their early twenties. In Bomber Command, over 55,000 airmen out of a total force of 125,000 (44 per cent) lost their lives in World War II. Of course, they knew the risks. It did not take a degree in mathematics to work out the odds of survival. Yet night after night they climbed into their bombers and took their chance. They were all volunteers, young men from all walks of life and from many different parts of the globe, united in their belief that somehow they had to win this war.

The origins of this book lie in a series of conversations I had with my father beginning in late 2007. My mother, whom he had adored for 65 years, had recently lost a long fight with liver cancer. A couple of years prior to that, there had been a resurgence of interest in the Dambusters' story. As my father was one of the surviving originals, he had regularly been asked to appear in television programmes and to give press interviews. He largely declined. We, his family, had heard some of the stories about his wartime experiences over the years. After a glass of wine at a family gathering or under questioning he would relate a little anecdote or two, but not much else. After my mother died, however, and with no let-up in interest from the media and the memorabilia business, he changed tack. He appeared in a number of television documentaries, gave any number of speeches, and signed many hundreds of autographs. Most of the payments for these activities found their way to various RAF charities. The reason for this change of heart was obvious. It gave him a reason to live, and to live a life he could enjoy.

When he then said, completely out of the blue, 'I would quite like to write the story of my life,' I was considerably taken aback. I could see that, given the interest that was being shown in him as a Dambuster, his personal account might be something that people would want to read. But with so many hours having been given over to film and television programmes, together with so many millions of words in books and articles, would there be anything new to say? It would, of course, be a unique personal account of a young man going to war with the RAF and of a remarkable six weeks culminating in a piece of RAF history, but would my father's version really provide significant new insights?

As we continued talking over the following months and years, during long hours of conversation, he revealed stories I had never heard before. It became clear that the answer to my question was yes – he did have something new to say. He talked in depth about his childhood, his RAF training, what it was really like going to war in a Lancaster bomber and his life after leaving the RAF in 1961. As he did so, it became clear that this was indeed a remarkable tale but for different reasons than either he or I might originally have envisaged. Gradually, I began to realise that his stories had something to offer on a number of different levels.

He was born in November 1921, the sixth child of an impoverished farmworker. Today, at the age of 92, he lives alone in a small apartment in a well-run retirement village in Bristol. He suffers the inconveniences and indignities that old age inevitably brings but he is well supported locally and by a large and devoted family. Had it not been for those six weeks in 1943, his life would probably have gone by unnoticed by anyone apart from our family and a few close friends. Yes, he is a 'war hero', and, like many many others who served in Bomber Command during World War II, he deserves to be recognised as such. But this is also the story of a young child who, in today's world, would be called 'neglected' or 'abused' and might even be taken into care. His is the story of someone who, through a series of accidents or twists of fate, was able to serve his country in a number of different ways and whose life has been far more fulfilling than anyone could possibly have imagined in those early years back on the farm. Throughout his life, a number of events, totally outside his control, have shaped his destiny. At first, he wanted to call this book *How Lucky Can You Get?*, and I understand why he would want to use this wartime expression. But there was far more to the way my father's life took shape than mere luck.

This is not a technical history book. It is a personal story of a young man growing up, beginning to make his way in the world and then fighting for his country, devoting himself to serving his country both in uniform and, in later years of public service, either through teaching or through caring for people with mental health problems. It is the story of a young man leaving behind a beleaguered beginning and embarking on a quest for happiness and fulfilment. It is also a record of what it was like to live through most of the twentieth century and illustrates just how much our society has changed in one man's lifetime.

Morgan Johnson
January 2014

# CHAPTER 1

# CHUCK-CHUCK AND A FAMILY AT WAR

I was never frightened. Not when I was standing right there by her side. I knew that she would look after us, no matter what. She was a real beauty in her own purposeful way, and truly inspirational. I felt a great glow of confidence and enthusiasm when I leaned against her. I certainly wasn't scared – not when I was standing next to Chuck-Chuck. I don't think any of us were at that point. Later, when we were up there in the darkness with German fighter pilots and flak gunners trying to seek us out and kill us, there would be plenty of time to be frightened. Chuck-Chuck, you see, was our Lancaster, our state-of-the-art warplane – the pride of RAF Bomber Command and the envy of every air force in the world in 1942.

Having just spilled out of the crew transport at our dispersal area, we had a few moments before we were due to climb aboard, the chat and banter flowing seamlessly from the cramped confines of the truck or bus that had brought us across the airfield to the patch of grass where Chuck-Chuck was parked. Inevitably, cigarettes were fished out of pockets in our bulky flying gear and matches were struck. It never occurred to us that we shouldn't have one last fag before getting on with the job. Thinking back, it might indeed have been more sensible for us to have refrained. The Lancaster's four Rolls-Royce Merlin engines were notorious for leaking oil, and Chuck-Chuck's were no different. The ground crew used to cover the tyres on the undercarriage with tarpaulins to make sure that they weren't corroded in any way or made slippery by dripping oil. So, lighting up while standing on dry, oil-stained grass next to an aeroplane filled with more than 2,000 gallons of fuel and loaded with over 6 tons of high explosives and incendiaries might not have been entirely safe – but then, neither was flying off into the night to bomb Berlin. Even if it had been forbidden for us to stand there having a smoke, I daresay we'd have sneaked one in anyway. What could they have done about it? Told us we couldn't go?

The banter amongst the crew was always quite buoyant, exactly as you would expect with any group of seven lads in their early twenties – girls, beer, girls, football, girls, cricket, girls. I have to admit that I wasn't one of the most talkative of the bunch. For reasons that will become clear, I was a bit quiet, a bit of a loner. By no means did that mean that I was considered an outsider. I was very much part of the crew, one of the team, and that was the major contributing factor in the feeling of confidence that we all shared. We were a team and we knew that we could rely on each other. To say that your crew on a Lancaster was a 'family' is a much-used analogy, but it is much used because that's what it was like, that's how close we felt to one another. For me, coming from a background that was sadly lacking any real family bond, the affinity that I felt with the rest of the crew was something new and intense. I treasured it, and still do.

I pitched into the chat from time to time and enjoyed my smoke, listening to the other lads taking the mickey out of each other. You might think that the chat was just bravado – young men putting up a front to hide their fear from each other, maybe even from themselves. I don't believe it was that sort of bluster at all. It was just the way that we did things.

I've heard a lot of stories about aircrew being so scared before setting off on a raid that they could hardly zip up their flying gear. Like most airmen, I flew with a few crews before finally being assigned one specific outfit, but I never saw anyone losing their head. Some authors over the years have delighted in telling tales about how young men who flew on bombing raids were regularly reduced to quivering wrecks, terrified of what lay ahead of them in the night sky over Germany. I flew on 50 operations during the war and I never saw anyone behaving in that way. You heard stories, but it was always something that seemed to have happened to a friend of a friend in another squadron, on another base. I know that the legendary Guy Gibson said that he found the time just before take-off to be the most stressful part of any operation. That was the time when he felt most afraid. I've always been quite surprised by that, yet Tony Iveson, a pilot who joined 617 Squadron a year or so after the Dams Raid, said much the same thing when he was once interviewed for a television programme. I suppose that, as pilots, they had so much to think about once they were strapped into their seat in the cockpit that their focus was then solely on flying the aircraft and their responsibilities as captain. While they were still on the ground, maybe they had too much time to think about other things. Gibson certainly wasn't the sort to stand having a natter with the rest of the crew before take-off. Joe McCarthy was.

I was proud to be part of Big Joe's crew. To say that I looked up to Joe would be true on every level. He was a big man – 6 foot 3 inches – so I barely came up to his shoulder, and he had a personality to match his size. Born in New York, he had worked as a lifeguard and competed in swimming races, using his pay and prize money to fund flying lessons. Then, in May 1941, when the American Army Air Corps dragged their feet over recruiting him, Joe and his friend Don Curtin headed for Canada and joined the Royal Canadian Air Force (RCAF) to train as pilots. By the summer of 1942, Joe was in England, posted to 14 Operational Training Unit (OTU) at Cottesmore, flying the Handley Page Hampden medium bomber. While he was still in training, on the night of 31 July/1 August, the Hampdens were called on to take part in a raid on Dusseldorf. Joe's first operation as a pilot, therefore, had come just a week before my first operational trip as a gunner. A superb pilot, Joe instilled unshakeable confidence in us. With Joe in charge when we set off on a raid, none of us ever doubted that we were coming back.

As an RCAF pilot serving in the RAF, Joe had shoulder patches on his uniform with the word 'Canada' arching around the top of the sleeve. As an American in the RCAF, he also had 'USA' just below, he and Don Curtin being two of almost 9,000 Americans who had headed north, crossing the border into Canada to sign up with the RCAF. Anyone joining His Majesty's armed forces was expected to swear an oath of loyalty to the King, but the laws of the United States prohibited Americans from doing so, the penalty being loss of their American citizenship. Until December 1941, of course, America was officially neutral, a non-combatant nation, and their government could not condone the actions of young men like Joe. To accommodate their American volunteers, therefore, the RCAF changed the rules, allowing them to swear to adhere to the rules and discipline of the RCAF instead of taking the oath of allegiance. However he managed it, we were glad to have Joe, and not having sworn loyalty to the King didn't seem to bother either Big Joe or King George VI when the two eventually met!

Chuck-Chuck was Joe's Lanc. From time to time a pilot and his crew would be given a new or different Lanc to fly and the way to personalise it was, of course, with a patch of artwork on the port side of the nose, beneath the pilot's position. Joe's nose art was Chuck-Chuck, a panda that was variously depicted driving a Jeep, carrying a Tallboy bomb or, to symbolise the British/American connection, wearing a top hat decorated with the American flag and a vest bearing the Union Jack and carrying a cigarette in a holder to represent President Roosevelt while smoking a cigar to represent Winston Churchill. Chuck-Chuck also appeared on a largered maple leaf to represent Canada.

Joe wasn't the only member of the crew with Canadian insignia. Bill Radcliffe was the rarest of things in Bomber Command – a Canadian flight engineer. Around a third of all aircrew on bombers were Canadian, but the vast majority of flight engineers, for some reason, were British. Bill Radcliffe's family had emigrated to Canada when he was a child but he had returned to England to live with his grandparents while he was at school. In March 1939, with war looming, he had joined the RAF, training as a flight mechanic. That was a ground crew job, giving Bill hands-on experience of working with Merlin engines long before he was put through the flight engineer's course. There wasn't much that Bill didn't know about the Merlin and Joe had a great deal of respect for him. Even though the pilot is the aircraft's captain and the man in charge in the air, no matter whether there are any higher-ranking officers aboard, and no matter how forceful Joe could be when he wanted, when he called for more power or more speed, Bill would refuse to push the engines too hard, making sure that they were in good shape to get us home and that we had enough fuel. Lancasters had six fuel tanks in the wings capable of taking 2,154 gallons of fuel, giving the aircraft a range of around 2,500 miles. They weren't always full, of course. They gave us only enough fuel to get to the target and back – any more was a waste. There was no point in giving us fuel we shouldn't need because the weight of the spare fuel might just as well be taken up by more bombs. There wasn't much allowance for contingency and some Lancs made it home only to find that the bases they could reach with the fuel they had left were fogbound. When their fuel ran out, they crashed. It was part of Bill's job to switch between tanks, eking out the fuel to get us to the target and back, hopefully with a little to spare.

On every flight, Bill used to carry a small Chuck-Chuck panda bear toy tucked into his flying boot. I was never the superstitious type and I don't think that we were a particularly superstitious crew, but Chuck-Chuck was always with us and must have worked well as a mascot because we were to enjoy a healthy portion of good fortune on all of our trips. We had more than our fair share of luck.

We also had more than our fair share of Canadians. Dave Rodger was another. The son of an immigrant Scotsman, Dave had been a steelworker and served in the Canadian Militia before training as an air gunner. He was the comedian of the crew, generally at the centre of the banter and always game for a laugh. When he joined the crew in January 1943, a flying officer and our only other officer apart from Joe, he had already been in one crash and had had a spell in hospital with a smashed knee. Dave was our rear gunner.

Our third Canadian was Don MacLean. A teacher from Toronto, Don joined us on our last operation prior to the whole crew transferring to 617 Squadron. I remember him as a quiet man who always looked quite serious in photographs. Maybe that's understandable because Don was our navigator and, as I was later to discover, navigating is a serious business!

The daddy of the crew was wireless operator Len Eaton. We saw him as being far older than the rest of us, although he would still have been only about 28, and he was a quiet, calm character. Len had joined Joe's crew soon after Joe first started flying Lancasters in September 1942, with the final member of our crew, Ron Batson, having also first flown with Joe around that time. I actually shared a room with Ron and, with him being our mid-upper gunner and me having trained as a gunner, we immediately had something in common. We became firm friends during our time together on 97 and 617 Squadrons, which made it all the more frustrating for me that, despite making serious efforts, I was never able to get back in touch with Ron after the war.

We seven were the young men gathered around the crew ladder, chatting and smoking, getting ready to take our places aboard Chuck-Chuck. There comes a point when, with one last drag, it's time to go and the cigarettes are ground out beneath flying boots as we all turn towards the crew ladder. There's a moment for one last look around, taking in the vast expanse of the airfield in the watery, evening sunshine, other Lancs parked nearby with their crews also climbing aboard, and beyond the airfield the flatlands of Lincolnshire stretching off towards the North Sea. Here, in the midst of the seemingly endless farmland, is where I was born and, despite fate luring me away time after time, I somehow always seemed to end up back in bloody Lincolnshire …

The hamlet of Hameringham lies about 20 miles east of Lincoln and is unlikely to win many prizes in any 'prettiest village' tourist awards. It consists of little more than a collection of three farms and a church. Most of Lincolnshire is given over to agriculture, producing huge amounts of wheat and barley as well as most of the common vegetables, including potatoes, sugar beet and, nowadays, acre upon acre of oil seed rape. This is an uninspiring countryside. Flat, open fields, the odd copse of trees. It is dull. Nothing to inspire the soul or to lift the heart. In the winter it can be bitterly cold. I've heard it said that, if you stand on the top of Lincoln Cathedral, you can see the Ural Mountains in Russia. In my bomb aimer's position in the nose of a Lancaster, I have flown low enough over Lincoln Cathedral to steal the lead off the roof but I don't ever remember seeing any Russian mountains. The cathedral was a useful landmark for bomber crews returning from raids as it was tall enough to poke its towers up through fog or low cloud, and for a long time it housed the only real memorial to the men of Bomber Command.

Whether you could see Russia from Lincolnshire or not, you could certainly feel it. When the winter wind came in off the North Sea from the east it was like standing in a blast from a cold store – freezing air that felt like it came straight from Siberia. Colder than a witch's tit was how we used to describe it, and when it brought with it icy rain or snow, it was a thoroughly miserable environment. This is the place where I was born in November 1921, the sixth child of Ellen and Charles Johnson. I was described as 'a weakling baby' delivered to 'a somewhat worried mother'. I'll bet she was worried. My father was the foreman on an average-sized mixed arable farm. To say he was the foreman would be to give him a rather grand title. There was only one other worker on the farm. I've no doubt that he would have made his feelings known about my arrival – I was another mouth to feed, a burden, a liability. One of my earliest memories is of my father in a foul temper (his usual demeanour) telling someone that I had been 'a mistake'. I don't think that he knew I could hear him, but, had he known, I doubt he would have cared.

I had four brothers. Fred, the oldest, was already 19. Albert, Percy and Bill were 15, 11 and nine years old respectively, while Lena, the only girl, was seven. We lived in a dilapidated cottage close to some of the farm buildings and there was, of course, no electricity, hot water or any other modern conveniences, but, in that respect, we were really no different from thousands of other families who owed their living to farming. The work was hard and the pay was poor, although my father's meagre income was supplemented to some extent with food and firewood from the farm. Nevertheless, it would have been far from easy to provide for the family, yet my father would have seen this as entirely normal. This was the way that his father and, doubtless, generations before him would have lived. In the 1920s, we were living in a land of the 'haves' and the 'have-nots', with the Johnson family languishing very much in the 'have-nots' camp. My father expected nothing of his boys except that they would leave school, work on the land and bring in a wage to earn their keep. Poorly educated, with little or no knowledge of life outside the farm, except for the odd excursion to the local town on market day, he held no high expectations for any of his children. We were raised with the attitude that you just had to get on and do what had to be done, day by day.

At the age of 19, of course, Fred had been working for five years. An accident on a farm led him to develop epilepsy for which he received little or no medical treatment. He went to London to work as a lorry driver for a few years but eventually returned and buggered about on farms. He died aged 47 from a heart attack, probably brought on by the strain of an epileptic fit. Albert became a worker on local farms until he retired in 1964, aged 60. He died in 2000 aged 96. Percy worked as a waggoner, looking after horses on another farm, before training with the St John Ambulance Brigade and becoming the company medical orderly at the local ball bearing factory. He lived to be 94. Bill was a lorry driver for a local building company until he retired. He died sometime in the mid-seventies. The mere fact that I can't recall the exact year should give you an inkling that this was not a tightly woven, cohesive family unit. As I grew up and the brothers went their separate ways, it would not have been difficult for me to keep in touch with them or for them to keep in touch with each other, especially as they lived not too far apart, but

I chose to remain distant from them and, as far as I know, they from each other. With the exception of Fred, they all married and had children of their own and I hope, like me, they enjoyed a happiness with their new families that helped them to leave life with my father behind them.

The earth-shattering event that dragged the story of the Johnsons down from the level of mere hardship to a realm of tragedy bordering on the Dickensian was the death of my mother in 1924, shortly before my third birthday. She had been suffering from what was then known as Bright's disease, which was a catch-all term that covered a number of kidney problems. Nowadays, her condition would be treatable, but in the harsh world of 1925, the lack of any viable remedy meant that I lost my mother and was left with only the vaguest memories of her. Lena was to be my salvation. She was the one who looked after me – had she not been there I don't know what would have happened. My father may have persuaded relatives to take me. I certainly knew of no friends nearby who could have helped. My closest friend at the time was a pig that was kept in the field next to our cottage. He used to let me ride on his back. Not a bad friend for a young boy, I suppose …

Lena, only a child herself, took care of me as best she could and my father somehow managed to find the money to hire a housekeeper, Mrs Smith. Within a few months, however, there were more changes afoot when he found himself a new job on a farm near the village of Langford, just outside Newark in Nottinghamshire. Today the journey between Hameringham and Langford would take you about 30 minutes by car. That, of course, wasn't an option for us and it took a great deal longer travelling by horse and cart. The date was 25 March

1926 – Lady Day. Lady Day, also known as the Feast of the Annunciation of the Blessed Virgin, was the traditional day when farmworkers took up new jobs. Up until the middle of the eighteenth century, it had been seen as the start of the New Year because it generally marked the equinox, when the day and the night were roughly equal and the farming world was about to tumble into a new season. As such, it became the time when farmers entered into new contracts to take over new fields and take on new farmhands. Lady Day, therefore, was the day we moved to Langford.

Mrs Smith chose not to make the move with us and, with my older brothers all having left home, there was just me, my father and Lena. Lena was shortly to go into service with a Major Day and his wife in one of the local grand houses, leaving my father with his four-year-old 'burden'. Before long he had employed another housekeeper, Mrs Parker, who came with two young daughters in tow, Madge and Elsie, both a few years older than me. Quite what had happened to Mr Parker I have no idea, but Mrs Parker swiftly established herself rather too well for my liking. She and my father were married in early 1927. I suppose that meant he no longer had to pay her wages.

The accommodation in Langford was a few rooms at one end of a farmhouse. There was a kitchen and living room on the ground floor with two bedrooms upstairs. One bedroom was for the newly-weds and one was for the girls. I had a bed on the landing. It seems utterly primitive now, but these weren't unusual conditions for farmworkers in the 1920s. None of the things that we take so much for granted nowadays was available to us in Langford. We had no gas or electric power, with only the most basic sanitation and hygiene facilities. The lavatory, nothing more than a deep hole in the ground inside a wooden hut, was across a small pathway outside the back door. Water had to be brought in from the outside pump. We had no means of communicating with the rest of the world other than by written post. There was no television, no radio and no telephone, mobile or otherwise. What that meant was that people actually indulged in conversation to entertain one another, although my father wasn't really one for conversation. He spoke and you replied. A one-word answer would generally suffice. After a few short months, however, Mrs Parker began to rebel against the regime, showing her true colours. She was a vicious and hellish woman. In retrospect, I think she was everything that he deserved, but at the time, to a young boy like me, she was terrifying. Her arguments with my father regularly exploded into fights and on a number of occasions she threatened to knife him. I remember being very worried and sleeping in my father's bed, thinking that I could protect him, although I wouldn't have been any use whatsoever against a madwoman with a knife. Maybe old Mr Parker had thought the same thing and had scarpered years before.

That my father tolerated having me in his bed indicates not only that his wife and the girls were occupying the other three, but also that he was happy not to be left alone. Maybe he saw me as an early warning alarm in case the harridan sneaked in during the night. The situation in the house deteriorated until the summer of 1928, when I was sent to take a short holiday with an uncle who lived in a nearby village. When I got back, Mrs Parker and her girls were gone. The couple had separated.

When the wicked stepmother leaves, everyone is supposed

to live happily ever after, aren't they? Not in the Johnson fairy tale.

My father was now left with no one to look after him except me. It's not that he was a lazy man, but as a farmworker he had to be up at dawn and generally worked as long as the light lasted. During the lambing season or the harvest, he might only be home long enough to eat and sleep before going back out to work. This meant that the housework, and often the cooking as well, were jobs that I was expected to take on. I also had to help out with farm work too, and, by the time I was 11, I was herding and milking the cows, helping with the harvest and haymaking, feeding the pigs and doing all manner of other jobs. I can't say that I felt too resentful about all that at the time. It was tough, but other kids who lived on farms also had to muck in and help their families. In that respect, I don't think I was very much different from a lot of other young boys. We had no choice in the matter, so we just got on with it. Not having a mother in the house, of course, was what made the biggest difference. Helping out with chores is one thing, but running a home is completely different, especially if you have a man like my father to contend with.

I have no doubt that he had a lot of worries to deal with, especially as he was now having to pay a separation allowance to his ex-wife and some kind of maintenance support for the girls. We were scraping by with no spare cash whatsoever, living off vegetables, eggs, milk or whatever else my father could bring home from the farm. Breakfast was generally bread and lard. All of that helped to turn a man who could best be described as foul-tempered into an absolute ogre. No matter what I did, it seemed that nothing could please him, and, when he was unhappy with me, I got a thrashing. He shaved with a cut-throat razor and sharpened it with a long leather strop that he kept hanging on the back of the door. If ever he reached for it at anything other than shaving time, I knew I was in for it. Most of the time, I didn't even know what I had done to earn a beating but I do know that, to coin an old phrase, I had more beatings than hot dinners. Hot dinners were very few and far between.

That might make it sound like I was a poor, innocent angel suffering at the hands of a dreadful bully, which isn't entirely true. Like all young lads, I wasn't beyond getting into a bit of mischief. From the time I was seven I went to school in the nearby village of Winthorpe. It was a walk of about a mile and a half – a run if I was short of time. The school had just two classrooms: one for juniors aged seven to 11 and the other for seniors aged 12 to 14. Needless to say, I was expected to be home from school as quickly as my legs could carry me in order to get on with my chores. If I dawdled a little, maybe joining in a knockabout game of cricket in a field with some of the other boys, I would soon know that my father was home. He used to stand at the door and whistle, at which point I had better appear pretty damn quickly or I could expect him to be waiting with the razor strop in his hand. The one time that I may have deserved a whack was when I had managed to scrape together a few pennies – people might give me a penny for running an errand or suchlike – and went into the village shop to buy cigarettes. Naturally, I was too young to be smoking, and the lady behind the counter only gave me the fags because I said that George, one of the farmhands, had sent me to pick them up for him. It worked a treat and I left the shop the proud owner of five Woodbines. Unfortunately, later that day, George popped into the shop to buy five Woodbines and was surprised to hear that 'Young Len Johnson came by to pick them up for you earlier'. Found out. I'm pretty sure that George would have thought this was hilarious. My father's reaction, on the other hand, was entirely predictable …

Although I acquired a taste for tobacco at a young age, the same can't be said for alcohol. I tried my first sip of beer one morning when I found my father sleeping in his chair by the fire. It was the lambing season and he had been up all night. When he got in, he had had something to eat and a glass of beer. The glass, almost empty, was sitting on the table beside him. As it was my job to tidy things away and wash up, I took the glass and, on my way to the kitchen sink, drained the dregs of the beer. I doubt very much if this had been the finest of quality bottled ales in the first place, but going stale sitting in the bottom of the glass would not have enhanced the flavour at all. I was almost sick. It tasted absolutely foul. For many years afterwards, I couldn't bring myself to go near a pint of beer. Even the smell as I walked past a pub or sat in an RAF mess was enough to remind me of the beer in my father's glass. It was enough, in fact, to remind me of my father and memories of him were something I could definitely live without.

Things weren't all bad at home all of the time. There was always something that I had to look forward to – a visit from Lena. She came home whenever she had a day off and would immediately get her sleeves rolled up in the kitchen to embark on mammoth cooking and baking sessions, as often as not using ingredients that she had brought with her. Lena was the only one who ever asked me about school or took any interest in anything that I was doing. Kind and gentle, she gave me the attention and affection that every child needs. She looked after me as she always had done. Years before, when I was arguing with one of my older brothers, he shoved me over and went to give me a walloping. Lena stepped in front of him and started yelling at him, and his reaction to this was to draw back his arm to give her a slap. I remember being there, quick as a flash, and punching him right in the face. I was so small that it didn't have much effect – he barely flinched – but he must have got a bit of a shock because he thought better of what he was about to do, leaving us alone and storming off.

Imagine my delight when Lena came back to live with us permanently. That changed my young life entirely. Lena became my surrogate mother and, although I knew nothing of it at the time, she must have sacrificed her own independence to come home and make sure that I was properly looked after. Having Lena at home changed everything and was the first of a series of huge changes that were about to overtake me.

CHAPTER 2

# MERLIN MUSIC AND THE GREAT ESCAPE

Everybody hated it. It was a necessary evil – we all knew that – but that didn't mean that we had to like it. Well, what was there to like, really? A chemical toilet isn't exactly a thing of great beauty, is it? And the smell can be pretty awful. Yet the Elsan toilet was always there to greet us when we climbed the ladder and stuck our heads in through Chuck-Chuck's crew door, emitting its least offensive pong – just a faint aroma of disinfectant. Fortunately, the greeting was brief and with a bit of willpower you might not have to see the thing again for the rest of the trip. Once in the air we avoided using it if we possibly could. This part of the Lanc didn't benefit from any of the heat that was channelled in from the starboard inboard engine. That blasted out from a vent by the radio operator's station. Len Eaton could be sitting there in a comfortable heat of 15 degrees Celsius or thereabouts, but, back there, the temperature might be minus 20 degrees or below. When it's that cold, you don't want to be baring any flesh unless it's an absolute necessity. It didn't help that, if we were above 10,000 feet, you had to use a handheld oxygen bottle when you were moving about inside the aircraft, making fiddling around with gloves, zips and buttons even more tricky.

To avoid having to use the dreaded Elsan, and as part of their pre-flight routine, some aircrew liked to water the rear wheel of their Lanc before boarding. Some people came to rely on rituals like that – putting on their flight gear in the same order while sitting in the same spot by the lockers, or always being the third to board the aircraft. They believed that it brought them luck before setting off on an operation. I can't say that I was ever bothered by that sort of thing. For me, superstition counted a lot less than the faith that I had in the crew, and the unshakeable belief that Joe would always bring us back.

Directly ahead as you hauled yourself in through the crew door was the flare chute. When the bombs were dropped over the target, a flare would be released automatically to provide illumination for the camera to photograph our bombing effort. The photograph would be studied later to judge how close we got.

Prior to joining Joe's crew, I flew a few trips as a 'tail-end Charlie' rear gunner. That meant turning left at the crew door and climbing up onto the tail spar. I then had to clamber through a set of doors that separated the rear gunner's station from the rest of the aircraft, hang my parachute in its place on my left and slide forwards, feet first, into the turret. Even for someone as slim, fit and lithe as I then was, the rear turret was a cramped space. It didn't help that we had to wear so many layers of clothing. On my feet I had silk socks, woollen socks and my big sheepskin-lined flying boots. To keep the rest of me warm, I wore silk long johns, a shirt, my blue battledress uniform, a thick woollen jumper, an electrically heated overall suit and flying overalls that covered the whole lot. I also wore at least two pairs of gloves, one pair electrically heated like the suit, and the huge flying gauntlets that came up almost to my elbows. Then there was a Mae West life jacket, my parachute harness and flying helmet with oxygen mask and goggles attached.

Once I had squirmed into the hard seat, I closed the turret's two sliding doors behind me and settled in. That was me for the rest of the flight – up to nine hours or more. I didn't want to have to move wearing all that kit and I certainly didn't want to start fiddling around with it all just to visit the Elsan. Apart from any inconvenience to myself, the gunners were the aircraft's early warning system and you weren't much use as a lookout if you were sitting on the toilet. Night fighters liked to attack from behind, making the lonely rear gunner the most important lookout. I had four .303 calibre Browning machine guns at my disposal but my primary job was to spot enemy aircraft and warn the pilot, who would then take evasive action. Shouting the warning over the intercom was more important than trying to take aim, and once the pilot started throwing the aircraft around all over the sky you had practically no chance of getting a shot in. Nevertheless, the rear gunner packed the biggest punch when it came to defending the Lancaster, and German pilots knew that perfectly well. If a night fighter pilot could take out the rear gunner, his path was clear to attack the Lancaster from behind, and the cannon with which the German night fighters were armed had a far greater range than the Browning machine guns. This meant that the rear gunner was the most vulnerable of all of us aboard a Lanc, giving the tail-end Charlie the shortest life expectancy amongst Lancaster crews. On Joe's crew, of course, Dave Rodger was in the rear turret and, thankfully, he beat the odds.

Adding to the discomfort, although no rear gunner cared too much about that, was the fact that a large section of the turret's Perspex was removed – an alteration known as the Gransden Lodge modification – to give the gunner an unobstructed field of vision, free from frozen condensation or oil smears. Of course, this made the turret even colder, but it did mean that what you might have thought was a speck of dirt on the Perspex didn't suddenly turn out to be a Messerschmitt. The feeling was that it was better to be cold than to be cold and dead.

I didn't do many trips as a rear gunner so, for the most part, on boarding the aircraft I turned right, heading towards the nose, making my way up the sloping walkway inside the fuselage, the Lancaster sitting back on its tail wheel with its nose in the air when at rest. The Lanc was a big aircraft in its day. It would, of course, be dwarfed by a modern jumbo jet, the Boeing 747 having twice its wingspan with a fuselage three times the length of the Lanc, but, compared with four-engined bombers of the time, the Lanc was just a little smaller than the Stirling or the American B-17 Flying Fortress. Yet it could carry a greater payload than any other bomber until the B-29 Superfortress came along, and its huge bomb bay meant that there really wasn't a lot of spare room. Clambering through the fuselage, flanked by the ammunition channels on either side that swept down from a pair of hoppers near the mid-upper turret to feed a constant stream of .303 rounds all the way to the guns in the rear turret, it took just a couple of steps to reach the first major obstacle. This was the mid-upper turret, which I had to dodge round and duck under. My very first operational trip was made sitting in this turret.

The mid-upper gunner had a far easier time than the tail-end Charlie. To install myself in the turret, I stowed my parachute in its space on the left, flipped down a step attached to the fuselage and climbed up into the turret, where my head and shoulders were inside the Perspex dome. I then swung a little bench seat into position under my backside. The seat was suspended on clips attached to either side of the turret, a bit like a hammock or a garden swing but not nearly as comfortable. Ammunition for the twin Brownings in the mid-upper was supplied via a belt feed from two hoppers that were built into the lower section of the turret. Although not as cold as the rear turret, the mid-upper gunner still needed to wear an electrically heated suit. The suit could become unbearably hot when the aircraft was still on the ground, so we usually preferred to wait until we were airborne before plugging ourselves in. Making any sort of equipment check was, in any case, better done once the engines had started up.

The majority of my trips were made not as a gunner but as a bomb aimer. That meant that I had to skirt round and under Ron Batson in the mid-upper turret, then take a step up as the walkway ran along the top of the bomb bay. There was now a good deal less headroom, so I had my head bowed as I made my way forwards where ducts for wiring and hydraulics lines laced the walls. The small window in the escape hatch in the roof shed a little light into the gloom. Early Lancs had a series of small side windows about a foot wide and six inches high that helped bring more of the fading outside natural light into the fuselage, but in service these windows were often painted over on the outside with camouflage markings and on later aircraft they were missing altogether.

Next came the two wing spars. The smaller rear spar was easy enough to step over, and here there was a little space on the left taken up by the rest station. This wasn't a place for a quiet kip if you were feeling a bit weary, but was intended for wounded crew members. It wasn't a flat bed but a reclined bench where you could lie back but not lie down. I suppose it took up less room that way. I never had cause to try it out and I'm very glad to say that I never saw anyone else in need of it either.

Next came the main spar, requiring a bit of a scramble. The main wing spar on a Lancaster ran just behind the leading edge of each wing, supporting the four Merlins, and right through the fuselage, leaving an arched gap between the spar and the ceiling. Everyone had to bend double to climb through. It wasn't so difficult for a small fry like me, even with all of the kit I was wearing, but a bulkier bloke wasn't best suited to the Lancaster. How Joe managed, I've no idea.

By now, deep inside the fuselage, there were other smells taking over from the Elsan's disinfectant. The smell of the canvas and sheepskin of my flying kit was such a regular, commonplace thing that I didn't really notice it after a while. Even the whiff of the rubber and soft chamois leather of the oxygen mask dangling loose under my chin was such a routine sensation that it didn't make much of an impression, but the sweet aroma of engine oil, lubricating grease, aviation fuel and glycol (used as a coolant in the engine and also as a de-icer on the cockpit windows) was unmistakable. That was Chuck-Chuck's perfume. It was a heady scent.

On the left as you came over the main spar was the wireless operator's station. Here Len Eaton sat facing forwards with a small desk in front of him and his radio transmitter and receiver towering towards the ceiling. Len did not, of course, have the luxury of voice communications with base when we were over enemy-occupied Europe, instead receiving and tapping out messages in Morse code. Stowed below Len's desk was his pigeon. As I understand it, military aircraft leaving the UK were supposed to be equipped with two carrier pigeons in case the aircraft had to make a crash-landing and the radio was knocked out. The radio operator could then send a pigeon with a message tied to its leg, letting those back home know the aircraft's location. I only recall Len ever having one pigeon, not two, and I think that, later in the war, they gave up on carrying pigeons altogether.

Forward of the radio operator was where our navigator, Don MacLean, worked his magic. He sat at a table facing the port side with enough room to spread out his maps, check his timings and keep us on course. Don had the luxury of a little more space, but, if he was sitting in his seat by the time you got there, it didn't leave you much room to squeeze past. There was another small space in front of Don's chart table where a 'spare' pilot could sit. Before they went out for the first time on an operation, pilots would do two or three trips as a passenger to get a feel for what it was like flying in the thick of it. Ordinarily, this would be where the flight engineer sat, monitoring his instruments and gauges that were on a panel on the starboard fuselage. When the pilot needed him, especially for take-off, the flight engineer would sit on a chair that folded down and swung out from its mounting close to his bank of instruments. Bill Radcliffe would spend a lot of the trip on this swing-out seat, because from there he could scan the sky. Another pair of eyes looking out for fighters was always welcome.

Beneath the Perspex astrodome above Don's station and the whole 'greenhouse' canopy of the cockpit, there was plenty of light and I could clearly see the banks of gauges and dials that Joe and Bill used to monitor Chuck-Chuck's behaviour. Joe's seat was high up on the port side. There was a large section of armour plate behind the pilot's head in a Lanc – the only armour plating on the whole aircraft. The Lanc's skin was aluminium and just a couple of millimetres thick – not even as thick as the bodywork on your car. You could have stuck a screwdriver through it, so it was never going to stand up against large chunks of red-hot shrapnel, let alone the 20mm cannon rounds that a night fighter could send our way. Of course, all aeroplanes were the same, and still are. The skin has to be thin and light in order to keep the weight down. Cynics are prone to say that the armour plate behind Joe would never have stopped a cannon round but that's hardly the point. Any protection the pilot could be given was worth having because without him we'd all had it.

Once past the pilot's seat, I dropped down below the flight deck into my 'office'. I had to get to this point in the aircraft before Bill Radcliffe was settled into the swing-out seat, otherwise he blocked my way down into the nose. By rights, I should have been sitting in my crash position with my back to the main spar during take-off, but you couldn't see a thing from there and I much preferred to be down in my office. The entire nose section of the Lanc was forward of the bomb bay and down here I had more space to move around than most of the others but several jobs to do. Above me, but still below

Joe's line of sight and forward of the cockpit, was my own gun turret fitted with two .303 calibre Brownings. During most of the trip I was a gunner, but, because I had such a good view of the ground ahead through the Perspex bubble that formed the nose cone, I would also help out the navigator by picking up landmarks. Then, once we were approaching the target, I took up my position as bomb aimer. I had a padded bench to support me when I lay face down in the nose of the aircraft to use the bombsights during the bombing run.

From my office I could hear Bill upstairs helping Joe to strap himself in. I could watch the ground crew performing their final chores. One would remove the protective cover from the pitot head, the tube that pointed forwards and measured air pressure, which was transformed into the Lanc's speed on the pilot's air speed indicator. Another would be trundling forwards with the accumulator trolley to provide electric power to help with the engine start-up. And then the music would begin.

There is simply no other way to describe it. A Rolls-Royce Merlin engine on song is a beautiful sound. Four of them make music that takes your breath away – quite literally. Everyone knows that feeling when a big firework goes off at a display. You can feel the shock wave from the explosion hitting you, compressing your chest for an instant, making you gasp. Inside the cylinders of any combustion engine, like the engine in most cars, there is a controlled explosion when the fuel and air are ignited. That's where the power comes from. Most cars have four cylinders and the average car might have an engine capacity of 1.6 litres. A car engine can create a bit of a din when it's started up. The Merlin engine had 12 cylinders and a capacity of 27 litres, with an explosion firing in each cylinder several times a second. That is what created the breathtaking thunder when a Merlin started up. One Merlin on its own made an incredible sound. Four running in harmony was simply sublime. I was always in awe of the power that created that sound, and still am when I hear those engines today.

The music began when the starboard inner turned over with a splutter of smoke, a bark, and then the mighty roar as all 12 cylinders began firing. If we were off on an op, the engines would rarely be started from stone cold. Either the ground crew would have run them up or Joe would have had us all aboard for an air test earlier in the day. Next came the starboard outer, the propeller turning slowly anti-clockwise before the engine caught and the prop turned to a blur. The entire aircraft was now vibrating, trembling as though anxious to get off the ground. The port inner came next, then the port outer, settling and balancing the vibration to a constant, insistent buzz.

If you compare a Lanc with a modern aircraft, you might think that it looks a bit primitive, but to me, sitting in the nose in 1942, it was a technological wonder. You have to remember that, only a few short years earlier, most aircraft were biplanes built from canvas and wood with wires bracing the wings to keep them in shape. These aeroplanes were slow and very basic. The Gloster Gauntlet biplane fighter, which entered service with the RAF just seven years before the Lanc, had neither the speed nor the service ceiling of our heavy bomber – it would never have been able to catch us. The Gauntlet was being phased out around the time that the Lanc was coming into service and the bomber was a far more sophisticated aircraft. In my 'office' in the nose I had banks of switches to deal with and an elaborate bombsight that could calculate the trajectory of the payload, taking into account wind speed and the terminal velocity of the falling bombs. This was a £50,000 aircraft – a huge amount of money at a time when I was earning a reasonably good wage of just under £5 a week.

So there I was, smiling to myself in the nose of Chuck-Chuck with two Merlin engines howling either side, feeling the expectation build as the aircraft was prepared for take-off. Outside, far off across the runway and the various dispersal areas, were the fields and farms of Lincolnshire. How had a simple farm lad whose best friend was a pig come to be sitting at the sharp end of Britain's most technologically advanced war machine? Looking back, it's clear that Miss V. Boast had a lot to do with it.

I never knew her first name. After all, as a child, you're never actually on first-name terms with your teachers, are you? To me she was Miss Boast, the headmistress at Winthorpe Elementary School, not a friend or a relative whose first name I could be expected to know. It would seem, however, that Miss Boast knew me and my situation far better than I knew her. I was doing reasonably well at school, although I didn't have any academic ambitions at all. The clever kids went on from a school like ours to a grammar school, but there was no way that I was going to be allowed to sit the 'Eleven Plus' exam that you had to pass to get into a grammar school. Apart from anything else, even if I had passed, we would not have been able to afford the uniform. Miss Boast must have known this, just as she must have known all about my situation at home. I think that's why she came up with the idea that I should go to the Lord Wandsworth Agricultural College in Hampshire.

In 1932, aged 11, I had a chat with a man from the college.

I don't remember his name but, at our school, it was a red-letter day when a stranger came to visit, so I recall the interview well enough. It was a general chat rather than a test or an exam but I suppose that Miss Boast would have given the college access to my school reports to let them see what sort of a student I was. She had applied to the college on my behalf, having first learned all about the place and, I suspect, without having consulted my father at all. That got me as far as being accepted by the college without his being able to scotch the idea from the outset. I certainly don't recall telling him anything about it. There would never have been an opportunity, really. Any meals that we had together were eaten in silence and, in any case, he took no interest whatsoever in anything that I was doing at school. It was Miss Boast who officially informed him that I had been accepted into the Lord Wandsworth Agricultural College.

This was a boarding school that had been established for children of agricultural families – children who had been orphaned or had lost one parent. The school prospectus from the early 1930s states that: 'The Trustees undertake the entire responsibility for the maintenance and education up to the age of 21 years or such earlier age as the child may be judged to be in a position to earn its own living.' You might think that the phrase 'entire responsibility' would have been of interest to my father, especially as he now had Lena back as a domestic slave, but he didn't care enough about me, or care enough about anything to do with my education, even to read the prospectus. When he was told about the college plan, his reaction was typically blunt, forthright and entirely negative. 'No – you will leave school when you're 14, get a job and start bringing some money into the house!'

Far from admitting defeat, Miss Boast very astutely launched a tactical counterattack by calling in reinforcements in the shape of the local squire's wife, Mrs Curtis. This lady took a keen interest in the welfare of the village children and treated my father to a stern lecture about how he was denying me the chance of a better education and considerably improved prospects for a better life. My father's response to anyone talking to him like that would normally have been short and far from sweet, but he was smart enough to know that, if he sent the squire's wife packing, the squire would get to hear about it and that could have serious implications for his future employment. Without even a hint of appreciation for those who had devoted their time and effort to my future welfare, my father washed his hands of me with the words, 'I suppose he'd better go then.'

In September 1932 I left Langford, Lena travelling with me on the bus to Newark and waving me off as I boarded the train bound for London. It was a daunting journey – exciting, but a little nerve-racking as well for a youngster who had never travelled more than about 20 miles on a bus before. The tickets, of course, had all been paid for by the college and I was met at King's Cross Station by a man from Lord Wandsworth's, Mr Brown, who took me on the London Underground to Waterloo Station. It's tempting to think that, as an 11-year-old country bumpkin, I was totally overawed by the great metropolis and the railway that ran under the streets, but my whole upbringing up to that time had made me a very pragmatic youngster. I didn't feel that I had been transported to another world, just that this was how the rest of the world lived. I think I was probably too concerned about what was happening to me to enjoy my first trip to London.

At Waterloo, we met up with a group of boys who were also bound for the college and together we boarded another train for the journey out to Winchfield. School transport then ferried us all to the college at Long Sutton.

Lord Wandsworth College is a remarkable institution. It still exists today, albeit now as a thoroughly modern school for boarders and day pupils, boys and girls. The school takes its name from Baron Stern, 1st Lord Wandsworth, who provided the funds used to establish it. Sydney James Stern was born in 1844, the son of Viscount de Stern, senior partner of bankers Stern Brothers. Educated at Cambridge, he spent some time working in his father's firm but was more interested in embarking on a political career. Having failed to be elected as an MP on four previous occasions, he eventually won the seat for Stowmarket in Suffolk in 1891. Representing a rural constituency, it's not surprising that he took a considerable interest in rural poverty and the well-being of working-class people in agriculture. During his time as an MP he was the author of a Bill for better housing for the less fortunate in rural districts. On the death of his father, he inherited not only considerable wealth but also the title of Viscount de Stern. In 1895 he was granted a peerage, largely as the result of a generous donation to Liberal Party funds. 'Cash for peerages' was clearly not of major concern at the end of the nineteenth century and he took the title Lord Wandsworth from the area of London where his family had significant property interests. He never married and when he died in 1912 he left a large fortune to charitable causes, including over £1 million (approximately £80 million at today's value) towards the establishment of a residential foundation for orphan children.

Lord Wandsworth had appointed four close friends as

trustees and his instructions for setting up the orphanage had been quite specific. He wanted to establish an orphanage for the upbringing of children, preferably from the families of agricultural labourers and with preference given to those born 'in the north-west parliamentary district of Suffolk for which I was a member of Parliament'. The trustees, however, chose to expand his lordship's proposed scheme into a far more ambitious project. A number of sites were considered and in 1914 they purchased an estate, comprising 950 acres and two farms, in the rather isolated village of Long Sutton in Hampshire. All the existing farm equipment was sold, and the intentions of the trustees were made clear in a notice that the auctioneers of the machinery posted, stating that: 'The Trustees intend to stock the farm with entirely new implements. The Long Sutton Estate has been acquired by the Lord Wandsworth Trustees for the institution of a fully equipped and endowed agricultural college where a scientific and practical training will be given in every branch connected with agriculture.' So much for the simple orphanage.

While development of the estate continued at pace, with 25 workers including labourers, shepherds, pigmen, cowmen, tractor drivers and a management team in place by 1921, people became concerned that there were very few actual 'orphans' around. Some 10 years after the death of the benefactor, there were only 17 children under care and little educational work was being undertaken. Lord Wandsworth's will had created considerable public interest and questions were raised in the House of Commons about what progress was being made. In 1922 the Trustees responded with a stroke of brilliance, or perhaps a little good fortune, by appointing Colonel W. L. Julyan. From the outset he saw the future of the establishment as primarily educational, although this was to be no ordinary school. It would be an agricultural college, teaching a general education syllabus along with agricultural science and practical work. True to Lord Wandsworth's wishes it would be exclusively for orphan or one-parent children from needy agricultural families.

The prospectus stated that:

*The general scheme of instruction is to provide a boy with a normal course of education until he reaches the age of about 14 years. He learns to read and write and to lay the necessary foundations of his mental development ... The boy who shows the intellectual capacity is picked out for special instruction that will fit him to pass the necessary examinations and to proceed to some place of higher or technical education such as an Agricultural College or a University. If the boy is not of the type to make use of higher education as he grows older and develops an inclination to one side or another, his training becomes specialised so that he may eventually become qualified to take charge of a herd, a poultry establishment, the tractor equipment of a farm, farm accounts etc. ...*

By the early 1930s the school was being run by the Principal, Colonel Little; the Warden, Colonel Julyan; the Secretary (Bursar), Captain Radcliffe; six masters and two farm managers. They took 'entire responsibility' for around 150 disadvantaged boys, providing them with whatever opportunities they could in order to create a better life. 'Everyone is good at something' was their credo. Their aim was to find that something and to build on it. This was not like the schools that we hear so much of today, schools that appear to care more for their ranking in government league tables, protecting their status by rejecting those who do not achieve at the highest level. The college came to mean a great deal to me. It was my home for six years, but it took a little getting used to.

When I first arrived, like all newcomers, I went to the Junior House, across the fields from the main school buildings. We slept in dormitories of 12, making this a new, embarrassing and somewhat frightening experience. The boys had an initiation ceremony, which involved the large laundry basket that was put out at the end of the dormitory at the end of each week for the collection of dirty linen. At the earliest opportunity, a new boy was stripped, dumped in the basket, and taken on a high-speed ride down the dormitory, being pushed and shoved this way and that. You were then thrown into a cold bath. Horseplay like that was hardly a threatening experience, considering how I had been brought up, but it did nothing to calm my apprehension. With the initiation over, however, I did start to settle in to school life, and it wasn't at all bad.

We were equipped with school clothes, day suits, Sunday suits, shirts, underclothes, socks, boots and new pyjamas. I had never worn a pair of pyjamas before, or underwear for that matter. At home I would go to sleep in my day shirt. Food was basic but good and plentiful. We had breakfast, lunch, high tea and something to drink before bedtime. This was luxurious compared with what I had been used to. If any of us juniors stepped out of line, however, one of the punishments meted out by the prefects was the 'bread and water tea'. On one occasion, for whatever reason, the whole junior school was subjected to this. The punishment backfired when the kitchen staff took pity on us and produced masses of freshly baked bread. It tasted delicious and we all enjoyed our meal just as much as we would normally have done.

Of course, this new kind of school life was thoroughly alien to me and I felt out of sorts for a good while. The daily routine helped but I struggled in getting to grips with being taught different subjects by different masters. Then there was organised sport – something else that was completely new to me. We had football (soccer), cricket and cross-country running. Those who were interested and had some musical knowledge, or aptitude, were encouraged to learn to play the piano. There was a lot going on and I don't think I was really comfortable with it all until I went up to the senior school. Perhaps I couldn't quite believe that this new life was happening to me. It was, after all, a far better lifestyle than I had ever known before, but it was all very strange. I was surrounded by boys from all parts of the country. They, naturally, all spoke with different accents, but before long we were all adopting the kind of 'neutral' accent that so many children of service families seem to acquire. It was something that we all did in an effort to feel like we were fitting in, although I admit that my broad Lincolnshire dialect took some getting rid of.

Going home on holidays (of which there were few – Christmas and a summer break) meant being escorted to King's Cross the first time that I made the trip. Once home, I made a point of going back to my old elementary school and showing off my new clothes and new posh accent, making a beeline for the senior girls who were still there and were, of course, very impressed. That, of course, was as far as it went. I had no idea what to do with a girl, whether I managed to impress her or not. I met up with my old friends from the village but we didn't seem to have that much in common any more. I had most definitely moved on, my life had changed, and, through no fault of their own, they were still stuck in the same old rut. I should think that they even resented me swanning around and showing off. At home, Lena was the only one who wanted to know how I was getting on. My father showed his customary degree of interest – none whatsoever. With him it was back to the old 'speak when you are spoken to' routine. Naturally, I was also required to do my share of work on the farm.

When I was 13, I moved up to senior school, where things were very different. Classes were geared to preparation for the School Certificate exams, which meant eight different subjects – English, maths, history, geography, biology, chemistry, physics and woodwork. We also had to gain some practical experience working on the farm and in the school gardens. Sport became a serious interest and I played house football and cricket as well as becoming a pretty good cross-country and middle-distance runner. The years spent trotting a mile and a half to Winthorpe School had obviously paid off. In my final two years I played for the school first XI at both football and cricket. I thought I was pretty good at both, although an entry in the 1939 school magazine – *The Sower* – gives an entirely different impression.

*Unquestionably the defence was not the rock-like structure we should have wished to see. The full-backs, Johnson, Searle and Davies (when he recovered from his accident) were not certain to clear the ball in an emergency and positional defence sometimes made dangerous gaps.*

*In the circumstances, our goalkeepers were sometimes overworked and likely to produce a jumpy state of nerves.*

I think that may be a little harsh, but the same issue of the magazine records me being second in the batting averages (23.2) and 'an outstanding fielder at point'.

The same year I won the inter-house 880 yards and One Mile events. From time to time girls from another local school would come to Lord Wandsworth College to watch our sports days and attend a dance afterwards. When I won both my races, my friend Bill Tacchi, who had beaten me in the same races the year before, said, 'You only did that to impress your girlfriend!' Girlfriend? That was news to me. I didn't know I had a girlfriend. I was painfully shy and had no confidence with girls. Bill, miffed at being beaten into second place, was just pulling my leg. At the dance, most of us boys, having been taught some dance steps at school, shuffled around the hall with some unfortunate girl, finding the enforced socialising incredibly awkward. Playing cricket or running was far easier!

Academically, I managed to keep my head above water, although I wasn't the most gifted of students. Our headmaster was called Mr Johnson, which didn't do me many favours. If you got caught doing something you shouldn't, he was the one who administered the caning. He used to boast that he could lay six of the best on the width of a sixpence. I only had one occasion to discover how right that was. I've no idea what my crime was, but I'm fairly sure I must have deserved it. Fortunately, you didn't get a caning for bad handwriting, otherwise I'd have been seeing a lot more of Mr Johnson. Our English master Mr James – inevitably known as 'Jimmy'

– once said to me, 'You know, Johnson, they say you can tell a person's character from his handwriting. Yours must be pretty awful.'

For maths we had Mr Bowden, who loved telling what he considered to be jokes. One of these went: 'Why is a mouse when it spins? Because the higher the fewer.' I still don't get it, even after 70 years. Biology was Mr Goodliffe. In one of the lessons on reproduction, he recited a limerick:

*There once was a young fellow called Sarkey*
*Who had an affair with a darky.*
*The result of his sins was triplets, not twins,*
*One white, one black and one khaki.*

Of course, this is totally unacceptable nowadays, and I'm not even sure that it did any good in helping us to appreciate the importance of chromosomes.

My School Certificate results were adequate but no better. To pass your School Cert you had to pass at least seven out of the eight papers with at least one distinction. This I managed to achieve. When we met shortly after the results were known, the headmaster said to me, 'Congratulations, Johnson. How did you manage it?' I had thought of becoming a vet but I was never going to be able to pass all the required exams, so I decided to make a career in horticulture. This meant working full time in the gardens, which I thoroughly enjoyed. The head gardener also tutored us on the Royal Horticultural Society Junior Certificate, which I eventually passed. When it was time for me to leave school, I applied for and got a job as an assistant park keeper in Basingstoke. It was December 1939 when I left Lord Wandsworth Agricultural College. War had been declared three months previously and none of us knew what lay in store, so in such uncertain times it was a huge comfort for me to have the college there in the background, always looking out for my best interests.

The college had not only helped me to find the job in Basingstoke but had also arranged my digs. In mid-December, Colonel Little wrote to the borough surveyor:

> *We are pleased for the above (G. L. Johnson) to accept the post in your Parks and Gardens on the terms stated:-*
> *Weekly wage, first year 27/6d per week [£1.35]*
> *Weekly wage, second year 30/- per week [£1.50]*
> *Minimum Term of engagement – two years*
> *… We trust that this lad will give you every satisfaction.*

On 28 December, Captain Radcliffe confirmed with a Mrs Martin that she would provide:

> *… board and lodging for one of our students, George Leonard Johnson, who is starting work at the Basingstoke Memorial Park on 1st January.*
> *Please confirm that you are willing to provide full board and washing for the sum of 25/- [£1.25] per week.*
> *You will find Johnson a very steady and well behaved boy. He was Head Prefect in this school and a Patrol Scout Leader and I am sure he will not give you any trouble.*

I remember Mrs Martin and her family very well. They were good to me at a time when I was going through another great upheaval. I wrote to Captain Radcliffe on 8 January 1940, saying:

*I arrived here last Sunday and by now I have settled into my new home. The lodgings are very good and although, as you know, I have to share a room, my roommate is a very nice fellow. He is the middle son of three living with their mother. The food is good and there is plenty of it. Everyone seems to almost go out of their way to make me feel at home and be one of the family.*

My roommate was Fred. I doubt that he was best pleased at his new sleeping arrangements but he probably wasn't given much choice. Money was tight for so many people in those days and his mother must have been pleased to have a guaranteed regular rent coming in. I had very little cash to spare but did have the college reaching out to make sure that I coped. On 10 January, Captain Radcliffe wrote to me saying:

*Your financial position seems to be as follows:-*
*Wages £1 7s 6d*
*Lodging Fees £1 5s 0d*
*Insurance 1s 0d*
*Hospital 2d*
*Pocket Money 2s 6d*
*Total £1 8s 8d*
*Leaving a balance of 1s 2d a week to be contributed by the College (in addition to the 5/- per week which we are saving for you here)*

The college was basically making sure that I could make ends meet, even including an allowance for pocket money. Captain Radcliffe also recommended an insurance company with which I should take out a policy, with the college paying the weekly premium of 1/3d (1 shilling and 3 old pence) 'until you are earning sufficient to do this out of your own pocket'. They carried on paying it until 1945, never questioning whether I could meet the cost myself, more than fulfilling their obligation to take 'entire responsibility' for me until I was 21. Whenever I needed anything, such as a few shillings from my savings after I had been forced to take unpaid time off work when I had the flu, the college was there for me. Even when I decided to join a local cricket club in May 1940, they did their best:

*I am hoping to join a cricket club in the near future. I was over at Long Sutton the other day and Mr Warner very generously offered to help with trousers and shirts and if necessary the subscription. I would also like a pair of cricket boots and also a cricket bat if possible. There are, of course, club bats but it would be so much better to have one so as to be sure of using the same one every time. The subscription is only 4/6d per season ... I am going on holiday on June 8th and would you please forward me four pounds to cover the travelling and holiday expenses.*

For the first time Captain Radcliffe seemed to be a little peevish in his response:

*I will send you the £4 you ask for but you are running your balance perilously low. I will remind Mr Warner about your flannels and shirts. We will provide you with some cricket boots if you will let me know what they cost. You ought to be able to get them for about 12/6d but I am afraid the College cannot give you a bat.*

They couldn't give me a bat, but they had, in fact, given me so much more. I know that I didn't truly appreciate what the college did for me at the time, perhaps because the only lifestyle with which I could compare college life was so far removed from it – the grim place that was my home. Perhaps I also took the efforts that they made on my behalf a little for granted. Certainly, it wasn't until I was older and wiser that I realised just how much Lord Wandsworth College had done for me and how good they had been to me. The military men who ran the school gave me a glimpse of life in an institution that certainly stood me in good stead when it came to serving in the RAF. Yet 'institution' seems too cold and harsh a word to describe Lord Wandsworth College and its ethos. True to their word, they cared for me and cared about me, which is something that, aside from my lovely sister Lena, I had not experienced before. They had taken a shy and nervous little boy and helped him take the first steps towards becoming an increasingly confident young man. For that I will be forever grateful.

In 2008, I returned to Lord Wandsworth College for the first time since 1940. I spent a fine day out being treated like royalty by the alumni association and being shown round the fabulous modern school. They have had to move with the times and only around 10 per cent of the pupils now have their fees paid by the foundation. Their academic record these days is truly excellent and their recreational and sports facilities are marvellous. The school has produced a clutch of England rugby internationals, including 2003 Rugby World Cup hero Jonny Wilkinson.

While I was visiting the college, I asked if anyone knew what had happened to another former student – my old best pal

Charlie Cole. School records show that Charlie had trained as a fighter pilot and been stationed in India. In January 1944 he disappeared on a mission and his body was never found. His name appears on the Singapore Memorial within Kranji Cemetery which bears the names of 24,000 casualties of the Commonwealth land and air forces who have no known grave, including airmen who died during operations over the whole of southern and eastern Asia.

Such is the way of things. Poor old Charlie's luck ran out a long way from home on the other side of the world. I, too, was to travel far afield over the coming months, but my luck was to hold good.

# CHAPTER 3

# JOURNEY INTO DARKNESS AND THE BABBACOMBE BOMBSHELL

This was it. This was the most exciting bit, the bit that I most looked forward to. Nothing else could really compare. Joe and Bill had finished running through their pre-flight checks. Len had switched on the intercom and we had all plugged in our radio leads so that we could check in and confirm that we could hear and speak to each other. The banter and chatter had now been left behind. We identified ourselves as 'rear gunner', 'navigator' or 'bomb aimer' so that it was clear which station was checking in. We all had jobs to do and relied on each other to do those jobs properly, so there was no more clowning around. This was when it all started to get serious, yet I still had a growing feeling of child-like excitement, not about the operation ahead, but anticipating the thrill of take-off.

We plugged in our oxygen feeds and took a whiff to make sure that we'd be able to breathe once we were up amongst the angels, and Dave, Ron and I had tried out the hand controls that rotated our turrets. The hydraulic power was provided by the engines, so the turrets couldn't be tested until the Merlins were up and running. Then, down on the ground behind me, one of the ground crew scuttled in under the wing and dragged away the chocks that were wedged under the main wheels. Another of our ground crew was out in front, signalling Joe to move forwards, and then we were rolling.

We trundled round the taxiways, heading for the main runway with Bill checking his instruments and Joe steering Chuck-Chuck by balancing the brakes, rudders and engines. There were no little tug tractors to push or pull us out of our dispersal parking place. Chuck-Chuck was moving under her own steam from the word go. The inner engines had work to do powering the hydraulics for the brakes and powering electrical generators, but the outers were running slower, with Joe revving them up when he needed them to pull Chuck-Chuck round to port or to starboard. In the fading light, as the rest of the squadron's aircraft lumbered towards the end of the runway to await their turn to take off, they formed a fantastic Lancaster parade, and I had a Perspex-enclosed ringside seat. I was loving every second of it.

At the end of the runway, Joe lined us up and we waited for the signal to go. Near the control truck, there was always a small knot of people, always some of our ground crew, there to wave us off. No one ever gives the ground crews the credit that they deserve for the work that they did in making sure that our aircraft were in the best possible condition. They worked outdoors all year round in all weathers at the dispersal points, not only repairing damage, maintaining the engines, fixing aerials or replacing guns, but also undertaking all but the most extensive repairs. The handful of ground crew who dealt with these tasks were backed up by a small army of engineers, technicians and armourers. Together, they could work miracles. Changing an engine on an aircraft like a Lanc might take a few days under normal circumstances. These guys could do it in five hours if they had to. That sort of attention required the aircraft to be towed into a hangar, but that didn't happen very often. A Lanc might never need a major overhaul because Lancasters didn't wear out – they didn't get the chance. At one point during the bombing campaign, the operational life expectancy of a Lanc was just 40 hours' flying time, somewhere between five and 10 trips. And when an aircraft failed to return from an op, it hit the ground crew pretty hard. Each aircraft had its own aircrew and its own ground crew – we were all part of a team. If we had any problems with the aircraft, we would talk to the ground crew and they would sort it out. Reports had to be made about faults, of course, but the ground crew was always anxious to put things right for us, and having a word could get things done a lot quicker than making a report. They were very proud of their aircraft and they did a superb job.

We would see the ground crew for a bit of a chat when we took the aircraft up for an air test and some of them were always there when we climbed aboard before an op, just as some of them were always there when we were taking off – and some were waiting when we came back. At take-off they would be there at the edge of the runway, near the control truck, watching for any stray fluid leak and listening for any minor hiccup from the engines. The signal light on the control truck shone red, then green. There was time to acknowledge a wave from the ground crew as Joe pushed the throttles open, with Bill holding them hard against the stops, and Chuck-Chuck rumbled forwards, quickly picking up speed.

The acceleration was immense, and sitting in the nose, watching the ground flashing past, I revelled in the sheer exhilaration of it. On a grass runway, there were a few undulations, the big wheels rolling over slight dips and rises. On concrete it was different, smoother but with more of a rumble from the hard surface. Either way, we certainly ate up the ground. On a take-off run without a bomb load aboard, I could feel the aircraft levelling out slightly as the tail wheel lifted after less than 15 seconds. Ten seconds later came the calm, floating sensation as the main undercarriage left the ground and we were airborne. With a full bomb load, it would take a few seconds longer to get off the ground and we would be moving a bit faster – 110 miles per hour (mph) or thereabouts. You might think that's not such an impressive rate of acceleration. From rest to 110mph in 25 seconds – a modern production car with a reasonable performance could outstrip a Lanc in a drag race down the runway. But we didn't have cars capable of that sort of thing back then. Even if we had done, I would have known bugger all about anything like that. Many of us youngsters flying off on night bombing missions over Germany, including some of the pilots, had yet to learn to drive.

As soon as the aircraft started to climb, still flying straight ahead with the end of the runway disappearing below us, the wheels were raised. Reducing the drag caused by the undercarriage made us more streamlined, giving the engines less work to do. Now we were really starting to gain height, banking in a gentle turn into the circuit until we reached the right altitude to set out over the North Sea. I could see other

Lancs above, and then below, doing the same thing, their navigation lights making them easy to spot as the darkness of night closed in. I have often been asked how we managed to avoid crashing into each other when hundreds of bombers were assembling for a major raid, all circling to gain height. There are stories, of course, of mid-air collisions, but I certainly never saw that happen. Despite the fact that there were scores of bases all over England – around 30 Bomber Command bases in Lincolnshire alone – it was all very organised. Aircraft from neighbouring bases would circle either clockwise or anti-clockwise in their own climbing pattern in their own allocated airspace. It could take half an hour or so to reach our operational altitude, depending on what the altitude was and the load we were carrying. Navigation lights helped you to see other Lancs, but those were switched off as soon as we formed into waves and headed out towards the coast. We were all told what altitude we should be at and each wave had its own timing schedule. Depending on how many aircraft were involved, the entire bomber stream might stretch out for 70 miles or more. Then, in the black of night, it became more difficult to spot other aircraft. And if it was difficult to spot a Lanc, a Messerschmitt 110 or Junkers 88 night fighter could be practically invisible.

Those of us gunners with heated suits would now have them plugged in to keep us warm, and above 10,000 feet we were on oxygen. As bomb aimer, I now had a few preparations to make. The instrument board on the right of the bomb aimer's position included a series of switches. At the briefing earlier that afternoon, the Armaments Officer would have given us details of what sort of payload we were to be carrying and the bombs would be arranged on the racks accordingly. Obviously, if we were carrying one big 4,000-pound (lb) 'cookie' and eight Small Bomb Containers (SBCs), they would be loaded in the bomb bay differently to a straightforward payload of 14 high-explosive bombs of 1,000lb each. The cookie was a blast bomb designed to destroy or damage buildings, blowing the roofs off any that it didn't flatten, and the SBCs each held 24 30lb incendiary bomblets (or as many as 236 4lb incendiaries), which were designed to set fire to the damaged buildings. The high explosives might be used to destroy dockyards or railway facilities. So, depending on how our ordnance was loaded, I now had to flick the selector switches, fuse the bombs and set the distributor. This ensured that the bombs were released in the right order, helping to keep the aircraft stable, and that they left the bomb bay 'live'.

From my office I could see into the bomb bay by shining an Aldis lamp through an inspection window but I had no real need to see the bombs. In fact, often as not I would never see them at all. There's a notion that bomb aimers would inspect the bombs in the racks while the aircraft was still on the ground, walking under the open bomb bay doors to give the bombs a little pat for luck or to chalk silly messages on them, addressing the bombs to Hitler with compliments. I don't recall ever having the chance or the desire to inspect the bombs in the bomb bay. If we ever met the armourers when they were dealing with the bombs, we might write a message to Hitler, although it was far from complimentary. The armourers spent much more time with the payload than I, or any other bomb aimer, ever did. These were the blokes who collected the bombs from the bomb dumps and transported them on low trolleys hauled by tractors to the fusing shed, where the fuses would be inserted. My fusing switches simply sent an electrical charge that made the fuses 'live'. The armourers were the ones who had to deal with a trolley train loaded with thousands of pounds of explosives at the dispersal area, making sure that the correct train was delivered to the correct Lanc. They then used winches in the Lanc's bomb bay to hoist the bombs up off the trolleys and into position on the racks. Guiding the bombs into position, pushing them this way or that to make sure that they didn't clatter into the bomb doors or damage the sides of the bomb bay required a good deal of muscle power. As you might expect, it could also be quite dangerous. Electrical gremlins and other technical faults with the bombs were not unknown.

Just a week or so before 617 Squadron began assembling at Scampton in 1943, a 4,000lb cookie went off while a Lanc was being bombed up. It caused a series of massive explosions that destroyed six other aircraft and damaged five more. Several of the ground crew lost their lives and many more were injured.

Then there was the story of Gus Walker. In December 1942, just as I was about to join Joe's crew at Woodhall Spa in Lincolnshire, Gp Cpt George Augustus Walker was Station Commander at Syerston, a few miles to the east in Nottinghamshire. He was watching his bomber crews taxiing towards the runway one evening, about to head off for Turin, when he spotted a fire beneath the reserve aircraft, which was parked at its dispersal point. Incendiaries had fallen from the bomb bay and ignited. Jumping aboard a fire truck, he sped off towards the aircraft to try to stop the fire spreading. Abandoning the truck, Gus, who had played rugby for England, sprinted towards the reserve Lanc carrying a rake to drag the incendiaries clear. Just then, the Lanc's cookie detonated in the bomb bay. Gus was hurled through the air, the force of the explosion ripping off his right arm. Apparently, in the ambulance on his way to hospital, he asked one of his officers to find out if the RAF would accept a one-armed Station Commander back into his old job in a few weeks. They did, and two months later he returned to Syerston. He went on to have a distinguished career in the RAF, becoming Sir Augustus Walker, an RAF Air Chief Marshal and NATO's European Deputy Commander-in-Chief. He was also rather a good one-armed golfer.

The point is that the armourers who had to deal with the Lanc's deadly payload had my utmost respect and I wasn't at all disappointed that, by the time I showed up with the rest of the crew ready to set off on an op, the loading had long since been completed and the bomb doors were firmly shut. Loading the bombs wasn't my responsibility – I just dropped the bloody things.

Back over the North Sea, once I had set the switches and the distributor, I became a gunner again until we were closer to the target. This was when the tension really started to mount. When your job was to scan the darkness, straining to spot anything out of the ordinary – the momentary flare of engine exhaust as an aircraft banked, or even just a shadow in the sky, lighter or darker than its surroundings – you had to concentrate hard. There was no chit-chat or joking over the intercom, just information being relayed as and when it was necessary.

Moonlight made it easier to see, but dangerously easy to be seen, so most ops were staged when there was no moon to give us away. Of course, any trace of an aircraft that you spotted out over the sea was more likely to be one of ours than one of theirs. Night fighters were known to roam on patrol along likely routes for incoming bombers, but they had limited range and were really more of a danger closer to their home territory. However, other Lancs, or a Stirling or Halifax, were as much of a hazard. You really didn't want to meet one unexpectedly in the dark and have him accidentally shave off your tail.

There is another notion that, once the aircraft was high in the sky en route to its target, the gunners would let fly a few rounds to 'test their guns'. We never did this. Flying at night, you would be firing blind into the darkness. Apart from the obvious risk that you might actually hit something, making you very unpopular if it was another Lanc, there would be a muzzle flash in the darkness as the guns fired. That could easily give away your position, and, if that didn't do it, then you have to consider that one in five rounds loaded in our guns' ammunition belts were tracer rounds. These burned as they flew through the air, allowing you to see where your bullet stream was heading and adjust your aim onto the target. Any fighter pilot out there, however, could just as easily use the tracer rounds to follow the bullet stream right back to your guns, again telling him exactly where you were. Testing the guns, therefore, was a bad idea. Aside from all that, we trusted the armourers on our ground crew implicitly. One look at the guns when we climbed into our turrets was enough to tell us that their work was up to scratch, as usual. The armourers made sure that our guns would fire if and when we needed them, so what was the point in wasting ammunition, blasting away at the darkness?

After an hour and a half, or thereabouts, of scanning the night sky, as we thundered towards Germany at around 200mph, the call would come through from Don – 'Enemy coast ahead' – and the tension would be cranked up another notch. We knew that we were expected. We knew they'd have spotted us because they had radar that worked every bit as well as our own. They would be directing their fighters towards us and only the cloak of darkness could hide us.

Down below, stomping his feet to keep them warm, some poor sod on sentry duty manning coastal defences would be able to hear us flying over, even if he couldn't see us. He'd be glad we were passing him by, off to deliver our payload elsewhere. He'd be feeling the chill of the damp night air – no electrically heated suit for him – and looking forward to his next fag break. I knew that feeling well enough. I'd done enough sentry duty when I first joined up to last me a lifetime ...

In late June 1940, I decided that it was time for me to do something about the war. I suppose that it shows how far I had progressed during the years that I spent at Lord Wandsworth College. They had taken me from being a shy, introverted country boy, so lacking in confidence and social skills that I could only really describe myself as a bit of a loner, and helped me to become almost a fully functioning human being. I was still very uncomfortable meeting new people or in situations where I was expected to fit in, but I was now able to make friends more easily and I was certainly starting to know my own mind. I had come to realise that my father was not the 'be all and end all' and that there were other opinions that mattered more than his – my own included.

Things had changed at my digs at Mrs Martin's house. Sadly, Mrs Martin had died and her daughter, who had been living next door, had taken over the running of the house. I was still sharing a room with Fred, and we had become friends. Fred had an Alsatian dog and my sister, Lena, had taken to breeding Alsatians, so once, when I had a few days off, I took Fred home with me to Langford for a visit. He and Lena got on very well. In fact, they got on so well that they kept in touch and were later talking of getting married. At that point, my father told Lena in no uncertain terms that he would not be able to manage if she left him on his own and said: 'If you get married, I will kill myself.' Bullied into submission, she acquiesced. That was pretty much the last straw for me as far as he was concerned. He had now completely ruined Lena's life and I would never forgive him for that.

Although I was 18 years old, the minimum age for enlisting as an adult, I still wrote to Lord Wandsworth College asking for their permission. They had looked after me for so long that it seemed unthinkable to take such a drastic step without at least letting them know what I was doing. They had no problem with me joining up, so I volunteered for the RAF.

Why the RAF? Well, I had spent years up to my knees in mud and I had heard some bloody awful stories about trench warfare in the last war, so I didn't fancy the Army. I had barely ever even seen the sea and couldn't swim, so the Navy was out. The real truth is, I wanted to fly as aircrew and that was that.

'Why volunteer?' is also a good question. With my nineteenth birthday approaching, I would eventually have been conscripted anyway and as a conscript I might not have had much choice over which branch of the military I served in, but there was more to it than that. By the end of June 1940, remember, France had fallen and the Nazis were knocking on the door. Our boys had been evacuated from Dunkirk at the beginning of the month and there was a lot of talk about an imminent invasion. Church bells were silenced and would only ring again to signal either the end of the war or a German invasion. Churchill had made his speech where he had said that '... the battle of France is over. I expect that the battle of Britain is about to begin.' He had no way of knowing then that what we now call the Battle of Britain was to be an air war. I wasn't trying to set myself up to fight in the Battle of Britain, but joining the RAF did seem like the quickest way for me to start hitting back at the Nazis. That was what I most wanted to do. I was anxious to fight. My motivation was anti-Hitler. He was the bastard who had started all this and he needed sorting out. We were under threat. Everything that we stood for – our country, our families, our way of life – was being attacked by this little maniac. He could not be allowed to win. So for me and many, many others like me, there was no alternative. We were in a pickle and something had to be done. There was also the subconscious fear that Germany might win and what would happen to us then?

It was obvious to me that I wasn't the only one thinking this way, not least because Fred decided to join the RAF around the same time. When our papers came through we were both ordered to report to RAF Cardington in Bedfordshire. I had applied for navigator training because I didn't believe that I had either the aptitude or the co-ordination to be a pilot. The selection committee disagreed and I was accepted for pilot training. This should have been the first hint that, although I had chosen what I thought was a route into the war on a fast track, the RAF was about to put me on a very slow train. Even if I had spotted the clue, there wasn't much I could do about it now.

On arrival at Cardington, there was a short induction and then the group that I was with all took their oath of allegiance to the King, signed on and were sent for a medical. And that's pretty much as far as I got. The Medical Officer told me that I had a hernia. That came as a total surprise. Goodness knows how long I had been living and working with a hernia, but it hadn't been hindering me much at all. Nevertheless, I was told to go home, get it fixed and come back in six months' time. I went back to my digs in Basingstoke and was soon summoned to the local hospital where I had my operation in August. Like a good patient, I did what I was told in order to get better quickly. They told me that I mustn't move about, so I stayed in bed. One afternoon a few of us were wheeled outside in our beds to enjoy the sunshine from a balcony where we could look out over the town. When we heard the air raid sirens sounding, the others hopped out of bed and fled indoors. I had no idea whether I was allowed out of bed, whether I would be able to stand or whether I could walk, so I stayed put. I watched the German bombers creeping over the town, too far away for me to tell what type they were, and the sinister black shapes tumbling out of their bellies. It was the first time that I had ever seen bombs being dropped.

I've no idea what the Luftwaffe was after in Basingstoke. There were some engineering works in the town, but they were most likely trying to hit the railway line from London to the south coast. It wasn't a huge raid, but they did quite a bit of damage and several people lost their lives. I later read that one woman was killed by machine-gun fire from one of the bombers. The whole business made me really angry. Now I wanted to get into the war more than ever. Right then, however, I didn't have to worry about the Germans so much as the nursing sister on our ward who came out and gave me a proper telling-off for not having taken cover! After that, knowing that I was able to get out of bed, I got better pretty quickly and went back to work for the parks department. The RAF clearly heard that I was on the mend as well because I received a letter telling me to present myself at Cardington again on 6 November, less than three weeks before my nineteenth birthday.

RAF Cardington started out as a construction works for building airships and had two massive hangars, each over 800 feet long. During the war the place was used for making barrage balloons, along with the hydrogen gas to go in them, and also served as No. 2 Recruits Centre – the first stop for many of those about to serve in the RAF. We were issued with our kit at Cardington, including a battledress tunic, a dress tunic, two pairs of trousers, two shirts, four collars, a pair of boots, a pair of shoes (in the Army it would have been two pairs of boots) and a whole long list of other bits and pieces. Once again I was being clothed by an institution far better than I ever had been at home! The difference with the RAF was that you were warned that anything you lost, broke, destroyed or had stolen would be replaced, with the cost stopped from your wages.

It would seem that the base was also well known for its entertainment. The gym was regularly turned into a dance hall and there was a concert party that staged shows. In 1940, a young Aircraftman 2nd Class, Walter Bygraves, did a turn at one of the shows, impersonating Max Wall. It is said that he went down so well that he decided to keep part of Max Wall's name and became Max Bygraves. Most of what I remember about the place is washing in cold water and seemingly endless hours of square bashing. How did I manage to miss all of the fun? Probably because I wasn't actually there for very long at all – just a couple of weeks before I was shipped out to another recruit centre at Morecambe. There things continued along pretty much the same lines – physical training, marching, anti-gas training, marching, aircraft handling, marching, rifle practice, marching, and then a bit more marching, just to make sure we knew our left from our right. Not all of us did. At Morecambe there was one poor lad who simply couldn't get it right. There's always one, isn't there? Marching is just exaggerated walking, swinging your arms, but some people get flustered about it and end up swinging their right arm forwards with their right leg. Try it. It's not actually an easy thing to do. It's much easier to march as you would walk, right arm and left leg forwards, then left arm and right leg forwards. That's what comes naturally to most of us. The corporal who was drilling us – loud and angry as all drill instructors always are – eventually yelled at me to 'Take that idiot away and show him how to march!' My introduction to being an instructor!

A week or so before Christmas 1940, I was posted to No. 12 Flying Training School at Grantham – back to bloody Lincolnshire again. This station had been a training facility for the Royal Flying Corps during the Great War and had become an RAF training base in 1918. Although they flew Hawker Hind and Hawker Hart biplanes at the base as well as Andovers and various other types, there was very little training of absolute novice pilots going on and I certainly wasn't ever given the impression that I would be put in an aircraft here. Instead, I was regularly put in a truck and sent as part of a squad to do guard duty at nearby Harlaxton airfield, a satellite station to Grantham, where the Officers' Mess was the fabulous Harlaxton Manor. There was nothing fabulous about those night-time stints on guard duty. Our basic training and drills had given us enough of an idea about how to handle our Lee-Enfield rifles so that we didn't shoot our own feet off, but the two hours on and two hours off was incredibly tedious.

I was given other work to do at Grantham, but it was scarcely less boring. I had to take hourly weather reports and phone them through to headquarters. I was being paid five shillings a day, which was more than I had been earning with the parks department in Basingstoke, but the repetitive, soul-destroying work was not what I had joined up for. I wanted to be doing my bit to smash the Nazis, and this didn't feel like it. There was one brief moment of combat while on guard duty when I spotted a large rat that had somehow sneaked into the guard hut. I drove it into a corner and despatched it with a single thrust of my bayonet. After more than four months of service, I had finally managed to kill something.

The frustration that I felt at not being able to strike back at Hitler was heightened by the news that we were hearing about German attacks. By the spring of 1941, the Battle of Britain was long finished and the very real fear held by ordinary people that we might be invaded had subsided. But London was being hammered in the Blitz, Coventry had been devastated, and Birmingham, Southampton and most other major cities had been visited by the Luftwaffe bombers. I had seen first-hand what they could do. At Grantham, a German pilot had followed an Anson to the airfield as it returned after a training flight. On 3 March 1941, I described in a letter to Captain Radcliffe, with whom I had kept in touch, what happened when the German bombed the married quarters buildings at the base.

*Just over a week ago when night flying was in progress from here, a Gerry followed one of our Ansons in and dropped about four bombs across the married quarters. One fell on, and another just outside, No. 30, which is the last house in our block. Another fell on No. 53, which is in the row behind, and directly behind us, and another on No. 64, which is behind that again. This happened about one o'clock in the morning so we had a most severe shaking, all the glass out of our windows was blown in and the blackout was ripped to tatters. We had a beautiful fire burning but we had to pour water on it to put it out, so you can imagine the mess that made. Half the ceiling was down the wall, which in one corner was cracked from top to bottom. I went downstairs to see if the fellows were alright down there and the first thing I trod on was the front door lying in the hall.*

*The worst damage was done to No. 53, the bomb landed just outside and blasted a hole right through the house. One fellow was killed outright, two have died since and there were about twenty other casualties.*

*Two nights later, when night flying had been transferred to the auxiliary landing field at Harlaxton, one of our planes was machine gunned as he came in to land. The pupil pilot was injured in the shoulder but he managed to land the plane quite safely.*

I think that the tone of the letter is quite dispassionate. I simply seem to be describing what happened without saying how it made me feel. I suppose I was still rather unsure about how to express my emotions, or even how to deal with feelings other than the rage and hatred that I felt towards the Nazis. That's something that was going to change dramatically over the next few months. My life was to be turned around, all due to one quite remarkable young lady – Gwyneth Morgan.

In April, I was sent to the Aircrew Receiving Centre at Babbacombe in Torbay. I suppose I had heard of Devon but had never been anywhere near it. We were billeted in the Downs Hotel on Babbacombe Downs Road, arriving late on Saturday evening when the blackout curtains were closed. I remember getting up the next morning, opening the curtains and seeing brilliant sunshine, blue sea and red cliffs contrasting with the lush green grass. I was absolutely mesmerised. It was just so beautiful, unlike anything I had ever seen before. A few evenings later, I went for a walk along the cliff road with my roommate. I don't actually recall his name. There were so many short postings, so many of us who met, spent a few days in each other's company and then never saw each other again that it is difficult to keep track of all of the names. Anyway, two young ladies were coming towards us and I don't know why but for some reason I said, 'Are you going our way?' My son has since described that as the corniest chat-up line in history, but it got a response. 'That depends on which way your way is.' Those were the first words that Gwyn ever spoke to me.

My immediate reaction – inside my own head – was something along the lines of: Bloody hell! What do we do now? Lord Wandsworth College may have brought me out of my shell, but neither they nor the RAF had given any instruction on what to do next. I was still quite a shy young man, still a bit of a loner and still very insecure in the company of girls. Back at Lord Wandsworth's, Charlie Cole had said to me one evening, 'I've got a date for us with two of the farmworkers' daughters.' I had no choice but to tag along. He hitched up with one and hitched me up with the other. I was so shy I didn't know what to do. We were walking through the woods and this other girl came up from behind us, took my arm and put it around my partner. 'Go on, kiss her,' she said. I couldn't and I didn't. I was afraid. Shyness, not wanting to take the risk for fear of rejection, call it what you will but I couldn't make the move. It will come as no surprise that I never saw her again.

But, on that evening in Babbacombe, fate was far kinder to me. The girls began chatting to us and we chatted back. We eventually split into two couples. Gwyn and I strolled off one way, and the others took their own direction. We walked and talked until eventually it came time to go home. I walked with her along the coast road until we got close to her home. Then it suddenly dawned on me that I didn't know how to get back. I was lost. Admitting to being so clueless on a first date was a bit awkward, but Gwyn came to my rescue. She went back with me until I reached familiar territory and then I walked her back again. I didn't think that I could have made much of an impression, but Gwyn was clearly interested enough to agree to another meeting. From then on we met fairly regularly – in fact, most evenings for the remainder of the three weeks that I had in Torbay. We had got to the kissing and cuddling stage but no real relationship had developed. It would be silly to say that this was love at first sight, but when I was posted to Newquay we agreed to write, to stay in touch. I could hardly believe that I had a real live girlfriend.

It's worth me explaining what a massive influence Gwyn was to have over the whole of the rest of my life, even if we do get a little ahead of ourselves at this point. Throughout everything else that happened to me, everything else that I ever did, Gwyn was there for me, although things didn't always all go entirely smoothly, especially at the beginning. It was, perhaps, a classic wartime romance. Over the next 10 months, because of my postings, we were not able to meet regularly, but we wrote to each other. Well, actually, I wrote many letters and she occasionally replied. While I was with the Initial Training Wing in Newquay, Gwyn joined the Women's Auxiliary Air Force (WAAF), having lied about her age – she was only 17 at the time – and was sent to Innsworth in Gloucestershire for recruit training. Three months later, I was in Cheshire awaiting shipment to America for pilot training and travelled down to spend the afternoon with her. We were not to meet again for a further seven months.

We had little communication while I was in the States because the postal service was not as good as it might have been, but we did try to keep in some sort of contact. Perhaps this was not, as yet, a love affair in full bloom but there was enough mutual interest to keep the relationship alive. A proper, powerful bond began to develop when I came back to the UK and was posted to the Personnel Receiving Centre in Bournemouth. By now Gwyn was at Middle Wallop, a fighter station near Andover. The two places aren't very far apart, so we arranged to meet in Bournemouth. There were two railway stations: Bournemouth Central and Bournemouth West. I suggested that she went to Central but when I arrived to meet her there was no one there. I immediately thought that she had gone to the other station and rushed over to

Bournemouth West. But she wasn't there either. So I shuttled between the two stations until I eventually asked a porter at Bournemouth Central if he had seen a young WAAF roaming around on her own. 'Yes,' he said, 'and the last time I saw her she said that she would be back here at four o'clock, and if you're not here, she says don't bother any more!'

That was a close call, but when we eventually did meet that day, we went for a short stay at my old digs in Basingstoke. From then on we met up whenever we could and kept in touch by telephone and in letters. While she was at Middle Wallop, Gwyn was persuaded to take a trip in a Beaufighter aircraft. The observer who flew with night fighter ace John Cunningham, who became known as 'Cat's Eyes' Cunningham, got her to the steps of the aircraft, all kitted out, including a parachute, and there she stopped. That was to be the closest she ever got to flying in her life. Despite the fact that she had been a WAAF working around flyers and aircraft, and that I was to have a career in the RAF, Gwyn never, ever went up in any kind of aeroplane, military or civilian.

By the time I had completed training as an air gunner and was on active service with 97 Squadron at Woodhall Spa, Gwyn was at No. 8 Initial Training Wing in Newquay and our romance was in full swing, or at least as full a swing as the war would let us have. We could only meet when I was on leave, but bomber squadron aircrew were granted one week's leave for every six weeks of operational duty. This was to give us time to rest and recuperate away from the tensions of the air war. Whenever I got a chance, I travelled down to the South-West to see Gwyn either in Newquay or with her family in Torquay. We spent many evenings sitting or lying on the headland, talking about life and our future together. I don't remember any one specific proposal of marriage and there was certainly no 'down on one knee' moment. Everything just seemed to develop and we both understood that we would be married as soon as we could.

It was during this summer of 1942 that I met Gwyn's family for the first time, and for me it was a cultural shock of almost seismic proportions. The Morgan family came from the Rhondda Valley in South Wales. Gwyn's father, Bill, was a coal miner until the early 1930s when he was forced to leave the pits through ill health. With no welfare state to look after him, he walked from South Wales to Devon looking for work, eventually being taken on as a labourer for the Gas Board in Torquay. He moved his wife and family down and they set up home in a small council house in Hele village. He was a big man and as strong as an ox. Whilst working down the mines, he earned additional income by bare-knuckle boxing. On Sunday mornings, after chapel, two men would square up against each other toe to toe on the bridge over the valley stream. The object was to beat your opponent back to his bank and thus be declared the winner. Locals would gamble on the outcome and the winner would receive a small amount of prize money. If you lost, you got nothing except a battering. Bill was the archetypal Welsh miner – fiercely loyal to his country, rugby and the Labour Party. He enjoyed his pint 'down the club' and a small flutter on the horses, but he was totally under the control of the five-foot-high human dynamo that was Nell, his wife. She was firmly in control of the whole family and yet I can never remember seeing or hearing her lose her temper. Nell always made me feel welcome, the kettle was always boiling and a cup of tea was essential for every visitor. She could create the most tasty meals from nothing and provide for however many people seemed to crowd into that tiny house. I felt an instant attraction to Nell, perhaps because I had never really had a mother.

In the middle of 1942, Bill was in North Africa with the 8th Army and the family consisted of Nell, Gwyn, Gwyn's younger sister, Eunice, and her two brothers, John and David. I walked into an environment the likes of which I had never seen or experienced before. I found some of the conversations in the family so different. They talked to each other about anything. They talked to each other non-stop. My family didn't. We didn't bother to talk to each other. In this family there was a sense of cohesion that there had never been in mine. In my family, everyone lived their own lives and they were completely independent. This family was tightly knit and they were all much closer together. They discussed as a family what they were going to do, looking for others to make comments or a contribution. And they laughed. Of course, life was difficult but there was a place for fun and for enjoying each other's company. In terms of family life, I had moved from a grey cell of silence into this noisy, garrulous Welsh world. When other relatives were present, the noise and the laughter were just cranked up a further notch. My first reaction was: 'What the hell have I let myself in for?'

Gwyn was very supportive. She could see how alien the whole situation was to me and basically said, 'This is us. This is who we are and I hope you will come to appreciate it, even though it may seem strange to you at the moment.' All I could think was: My God, I could get used to this; I could get accustomed to this way of life. When we talked about why I had such a basic fear of meeting people, I had to put it down to my own upbringing. Gwyn's response to that was: 'Well, you are not with them anymore, you are with me.'

We drifted into engagement in October 1942 and then disaster struck. In November I received the classic 'Dear John' letter. Gwyn was breaking off the engagement – she had found someone else. He was an ex-journalist on the *Daily Express* who was a cadet under training in Newquay. Somehow, no wartime romance is complete without a chapter of this kind. I was staggered, completely taken aback, but determined not to lose Gwyn. I fired off a long letter asking Gwyn to reconsider, and, with a stroke of genius, I also wrote to Nell explaining what had happened. She in turn spoke to Gwyn in the strongest possible terms, telling her not to be so bloody stupid, and in a few short weeks we were back together. I wasn't about to let anything like that happen again. No more indecisive 'drifting'. I sat Gwyn down and set the wedding date. My tour of duty on 97 Squadron was due to finish at the end of March 1943, at which time I would have a week's leave and then go on to ground duties for six months. The date we agreed was 3 April, although fate had yet another card to play closer to the time.

I can't stress strongly enough what an incredible impact Gwyn had on me. She changed my whole life. She became my life. I adored her and I know that, in her own way, she loved me too. She was not given to any great show of affection in public and to outsiders could sometimes seem demanding, always wanting to be the centre of attention. In later years, when Margaret Thatcher came to power, Gwyn found her absolute role model. Mrs T was everything that she admired. 'The lady's not for turning' became her favourite expression when her argument was going badly. Don't let any of that make you think that Gwyn was some kind of ogre. Nothing could be further from the truth. She had a great sense of fun and was wonderful to be with. To me, she was a tower of strength. I could always discuss problems with her and we would always come to some form of solution. She was my wife and I couldn't have lived my life without her. She gave me self-confidence and a self-belief that helped me to go forwards and make something of my life. In a relatively short space of time I found that I could go into a crowded room and introduce myself. Perhaps I had lost my fear of rejection, but without Gwyn and her family that would not have been possible.

Above all, Gwyn gave me something that I had never had. Lord Wandsworth College and perhaps even the RAF had stood in as commendable substitutes but it was Gwyn who gave me a real family. I had lived without knowing love for so long and with her I was able to find it.

If all of that sounds like a 'happy ever after' ending, then remember that there was still a war on and, at that time, Bomber Command provided the only effective means of striking back at the Nazis in Europe. We still had a job to do.

CHAPTER 4

# NIGHT FIGHTERS AND A FIASCO IN FLORIDA

'Eat carrots.' That's what they told us. 'Eat carrots to improve your night vision.' Sitting in the nose of a Lanc sailing through the night sky over Germany, I'd have given anything to have improved night vision, to be able to see in the dark, to be able to spot a German night fighter before he spotted us. If I'd thought it would work, I'd have eaten enough carrots to turn me bright orange. The Ministry of Information mounted a huge propaganda campaign during the war based around the fact that carrots are packed with vitamin A, which is good for your eyes. Everyone, especially civilians, was led to believe that eating carrots would help you to see better on darkened streets during the blackout and that RAF night fighter pilots had been eating carrots for years to give them superhuman night vision. This was why, so the stories went, night fighter pilots such as 'Cat's Eyes' Cunningham were so good at shooting down German bombers in the dark. Of course, it was all a load of nonsense. Vitamin A may well help to keep your eyes healthy, but it doesn't give you enhanced eyesight or improve your night vision.

The fact is that, since the early part of the war, Cunningham and many of his fellow RAF night fighter pilots had been using the new and top secret airborne interception (AI) radar to track down German bombers over Britain. The carrot propaganda was partly to try to disguise the fact that we had this kind of radar by fooling the Germans into believing that our lads could see in the dark, and partly to get people to eat more carrots, simply because they could be grown quite easily in a garden or on an allotment. Bolstering the diet of the general public with food that could be home-grown saved on food imports, which all had to come into the UK on the Atlantic convoys.

Naturally, the Germans had their own version of the AI radar, so they weren't taken in for a second by all the bull about carrots. These early AI radars were, however, useful only up to a point. They could lead a fighter towards a bomber, but the fighter pilot and his radar operator still had to use the 'Mark 1 eyeball' once they were close. The AI sets couldn't aim and fire their guns – they had to be able to see the bomber to do that. Being in the same general vicinity as a bomber didn't mean that the fighter would actually get the chance to take a shot at it. The fighter pilot had to be able to point his aircraft, with its fixed guns, directly at the target, allowing for deflection, of course, so that his rounds would arrive at a point in space at the same time as his target. We never flew straight and level on exactly the same course for very long. Joe made regular little changes, weaving about in the air to throw fighters off the scent and make us a more difficult target. It was all part of the deadly cat-and-mouse game where, for the fighter pilot, coming close wasn't always good enough. With us cruising at 200mph and a fighter closing on us even faster, we could pass by in the darkness without seeing each other and be more than two miles apart, heading in different directions, in less than 20 seconds.

If a fighter was actually seen closing in on us, then all hell would break loose. If a gunner, or anyone else, spotted one coming in, he immediately got on the intercom and reported, 'Fighter to starboard ... Stand by ... Corkscrew starboard ... Go!' That wasn't always the way it went, of course. If you waited long enough to get that lot out, you'd probably have cannon rounds zipping past your ears, so it would simply be shortened to 'Corkscrew starboard!' or even 'Corkscrew right!', most of us being less likely to get our right and left mixed up than we would our port and starboard. The pilot would then put the aircraft into a steep, banking, power dive. The aircraft would complain a bit, creaking and groaning, anything that wasn't tied down would fly off whatever surface it was sitting on, and the noise of the wind rush outside would set up a low moaning that rose in pitch, combining with the rising engine tone to create a deafening howl as the airspeed shot up to 270mph or more. The pilot would scoop the aircraft out of the dive and set it straight into a steep climb to port until we were back at more or less our original altitude, whereupon he would immediately roll us to starboard and into a dive again, the whole sequence of manoeuvres roughly tracing the shape of a corkscrew. In the first dive we might lose 1,000 feet, in the second perhaps half that, but, if the fighter was still with us, the whole gut-churning roller-coaster ride would be repeated.

In the dark, given the very limited range of the AI radar,

the corkscrew was considered to be the most effective way of losing a fighter. Being thrown around the sky like a stunt plane put a huge strain on the aircraft but, even with a full bomb bay, the Lanc could take it. The strain that it put on the pilot was immense. He had no power controls or electronic 'fly-by-wire' gizmos, remember. He was using the strength in his arms and legs to operate flaps, ailerons and rudders. For the pilot, handling the corkscrew has been compared to competing in a top-class rowing race. We were put through the wringer in the corkscrew on training flights but, thankfully, we were never forced to use it on an op.

Not that that meant our trips were stress-free. Once we were over blacked-out Europe, we were all feeling the tension, suffering the apprehension of not knowing who or what might be tracking us out there in the darkness. Focusing on my job, concentrating on scanning the sky methodically, quadrant by quadrant, was what helped me to stay in control. I think that I was more worried about not doing my job properly and letting the others down than I was about the Germans.

At the briefing back at Woodhall Spa that afternoon, all of the crews had crowded into the briefing room, having earlier seen the notices posted in the flight offices letting us know who was on the 'battle order' for that night. By the time we filed into the briefing room, speculation was rife about where the target would be. Pilots and navigators might already have been briefed, but it was at the full crew briefing when most of us found out where we were headed. There was a lot of chat going on in the room as we filed into the rows of seats facing a small stage. Through drifting wisps of cigarette smoke we could see a curtain on the wall at the back of the stage, and behind the curtain was hidden a huge map of Europe. When the base's senior officers entered the room, all conversation stopped and we stood to attention with a great cacophony of chair legs scraping the floor. Once the officers were settled, we could take our seats again and the curtain was at last drawn back to show us the target. All eyes were now on the red tapes that stretched out from our base on the east coast of England. These showed our route to the target, and our route home again. If the tapes were short, then we might be raiding a port in northern France – Saint-Nazaire is one I recall. More often than not, however, the tapes stretched all the way into the heart of Germany. The sight of the target would bring a few groans and sighs, and not just because of where we were going. There would be a few nods and winks, too. Bets had been placed. Later, money would change hands.

We would then be treated to a series of short lectures. The Station Commander would tell us about the importance of the target – munitions works, railway yards, aircraft factories – and why we were out to obliterate it. The Armaments Officer would let us know the type of payload that we would be carrying and, as bomb aimer, I would have to take note of exactly what would be loaded into the bomb bay of our Lanc – not every aircraft was loaded with the same selection of bombs. The Met Officer would tell us what sort of weather we could expect on the way out, over the target and on our return. Without the kind of weather radar and satellites that we have today, his was not an exact science and we would often arrive over a target that was supposed to be under clear skies to find that it was totally obscured by cloud. The Met Officer would also give us estimates of wind speeds, essential for navigation and for accurate bombing. These would be updated during the course of the flight but they were often wildly inaccurate.

The Intelligence Officer would give us the latest update on the territory that we would be flying over. His information came from reconnaissance flights and from agents on the ground, letting us know where new anti-aircraft defences had been set up or new fighter bases established and reminding us where the long-established ones were. These defences were put in place by the Germans to protect obvious targets – the targets that we were going for – and our planners mapped out our routes to and from the target to keep us clear of heavily defended areas that were not our chosen target on that trip. Drifting off course over a heavy concentration of flak batteries could be fatal, but, with good navigation, these hotspots could be avoided. The night fighters were a constant threat. If they approached from the right angle, they could spot us by the glow of the engine exhausts. We could spot other aircraft that way, too. It was even possible to tell a Halifax or a Stirling from a Lanc by the colour and position of the exhausts. And if we could do it, the Germans most certainly could too.

Night fighters, therefore, were the main focus of our concentration – and maintaining that concentration was essential. You couldn't afford to start feeling drowsy. Sometimes the heated suits that we wore actually made you feel too warm and, sitting in the dark, at night, nice and cosy in your all-over electric blanket, tired from dealing with all of the stress, it was possible to start dozing off. We were issued with 'wakey-wakey' pills, caffeine tablets or Benzedrine, if we wanted them. The thought of waking up to the sound of cannon rounds slamming into the aircraft was enough to stop me from nodding off, so I didn't take the pills, but there were plenty of other things that some aircrew say they were issued with that I might have liked. I've read about crews picking up sandwiches and flasks of coffee to see them through their trips, the goodies prepared for them by WAAFs before the airmen went off to get kitted up. That would have been nice, but I don't remember ever being offered coffee and sandwiches. I've even heard of someone who was offered a revolver when he was being issued with his kit but refused it because he didn't have anywhere to put it. That's a different RAF from the one that I was in. I was never offered a personal weapon and, as far as I know, neither were any of the others on our crew. If you were forced to bail out over enemy territory, with heavily armed German troops hunting you down, a service revolver wouldn't really have been much good for self-defence anyway. Seems like poppycock to me.

The most effective defence against capture was to try to make sure that you didn't get shot down in the first place – easier said than done. Most of those who caught a packet did so through no fault of their own, but, if spotting the danger coming could stop us from being blasted out of the sky, I wasn't going to be caught napping. And I didn't need carrots to help me. Having grown up on a farm, I had seen enough vegetables, including carrots, to last me a lifetime. There was one vegetable, though, that I had neither tasted nor even seen until the RAF sent me on a jaunt that, under any other circumstances, would have counted as the trip of a lifetime …

Having been sent from Grantham down to Torquay (not the trip of a lifetime), spending a lovely three weeks at Babbacombe, getting to know Gwyn, not having too much work to do and generally enjoying the countryside or lazing around on the beaches, in the last week of June 1941 I was packed off by coach, along with the others, to No. 7 Initial Training Wing in Newquay. Here, we had a lot of work to get through, including classroom sessions. I was billeted at the Beachcroft Hotel, but the 'holiday' atmosphere that we had enjoyed in Torquay was now well and truly over. We were up at 6.30 am and the first working parade was at 7.45 am. There was an hour's break for lunch at 12.30 pm, then we were back working until 6.00 pm. In the evening, your time was supposed to be your own, but you would still have a day's notes to copy up and make sense of, or even another lecture.

The 12-week course covered aircraft recognition, anti-gas procedures, armaments, airframes and aero engines, meteorology, navigation, parachute procedures and signalling systems – both Morse and light. This was naturally accompanied by the usual rounds of square bashing and physical fitness exercises. There were also stints on guard duty when we might be taken by truck as far afield as Plymouth. I was on guard duty one night at the Barbican, Plymouth's historic dockyard area, from where I could see the town and the modern naval docks being bombed, fires and explosions lighting up the sky. Once again, I felt the frustration of not being able to hit back, but at least I was now well on my way to being able to do something more positive than pacing back and forth in the dark.

At Newquay we were assessed throughout the programme and there was a written examination at the end of the course with a pass mark of 70 per cent required for future continuation as aircrew. They actually decided to shorten the course by about a week, which meant us having to work on Saturday afternoons. None of us enjoyed Newquay the way that we had

Torquay, but, even though I was anxious to try to get to see Gwyn whenever I could, we were left in no doubt that there was a war on and we were being prepared to do our bit.

I got through the course with marks that confirmed me for pilot training, but I was still very unsure about it. I wasn't convinced that I was pilot material, not at all confident that I had the right sort of co-ordination, but if that's what the RAF wanted to do with me, then who was I to say no? Everything in my life now seemed to be changing so fast. I had never been so far from home, I had a girl who seemed genuinely interested in me – even my name had changed. Len Johnson had become 'Johnny' Johnson in the way that everyone in the services acquired those classic nicknames. If you were called Carpenter, you became 'Chips' Carpenter; if your name was White, you became 'Chalky'; if you were tall, you were called 'Lofty'; if you were short, you were called 'Shorty'. In fact, as more of a joke, if you were short, you might be called 'Lofty'. I got off quite lightly with 'Johnny'. My only previous nickname had been at Lord Wandsworth's and it was much worse. I had developed dry skin on my face and Matron's solution was to apply lard. Yes, you read that correctly. The moisturiser she rubbed into my face was lard. It can't have been as bad as it sounds because the condition cleared up, but the nickname stuck for far longer. I became known as 'Lard Face', or just 'Lardy' for short.

By June 1941, we had learned that we were probably to be sent abroad, possibly to America, for pilot training. Had the circumstances been different, this would most definitely have qualified as the trip of a lifetime. I wrote to Captain Radcliffe at Lord Wandsworth's, letting him know how I was getting on.

*We have been given reason to believe that the majority of us are going abroad, probably the USA. So at the moment there is a great deal of keenness and excitement. We have also been given to understand that we will be lucky to get any leave at the end of this course, which isn't so exciting.*

*What do you think of the war situation at the moment, sir? It seems to be pretty grim to me. The loss of the* Hood *with so few survivors was a great shock although it was somewhat compensated by the sinking of the* Bismarck. *In Crete our fellows seem to be having a terrific struggle. Still I suppose something will turn up in our favour before very long, at least I hope so.*

There was some other chat about Basingstoke and my usual request for money from my savings, this time so that I would have a bit extra in my pocket for going abroad, but the letter shows something of my thoughts at the time. The war was not going well and I was anxious to get into it. Captain Radcliffe responded with perhaps the most affectionate letter he had ever sent to me.

*Dear Johnson*
*Many thanks for your letter of 1st June. I was very glad to hear from you and feel very guilty at not having answered your previous letter.*

*I am glad that you have at last got into a training unit and that you feel that you are really on the job. It will be a great experience for you if you go overseas as you expect. You will find the country and the people full of interest if looked at from the right angle. Many people get bored in foreign countries because the inhabitants are so different from what they are accustomed to at home. That, in my opinion (and I have visited a good many foreign countries), is what makes travel so absorbingly interesting. We come up against different ideas, different customs and different modes of life and that should go a long way to broadening our minds.*

*The war situation is pretty grim at present. The loss of Crete was a bad blow but by all events the defence of the Island for those twelve days was a magnificent performance and must have given Hitler a nasty shock. I have always resolutely refused to be a pessimist and <u>know</u> that we shall come out on top in the end. But the way will be long and hard. Crete has taught us what we may expect if and when this country is invaded. But the Germans will find it a very different proposition on the sea, in the air and on the land and the slaughter (of the enemy) will be simply ghastly.*

*Yes, Basingstoke did extremely well in the War Weapons Week, raising over a million after starting out to get £200,000.*

*You have a balance of £5-0-3 in your account which I will send on Friday.*

*We are getting on here quite well but it is becoming increasingly difficult to supply food and clothing. However, so far the boys haven't gone hungry or in rags, though they may do the latter before the war is over!*

*All good wishes,*

The military men of Lord Wandsworth College knew what I was going through and Captain Radcliffe was able to write to me offering guidance, encouragement and even a touch of humour, all of which meant a great deal to me. It was the sort of letter that I could never expect my own father to send – and that my father, always running true to form, never did.

The rumours about America turned out to be true. Training pilots in the UK was a huge problem because there was so much air activity and so many aircraft in the sky, not all of them friendly. Nobody wanted trainee pilots getting caught up in any kind of potential combat situation. We also had blackout conditions at night, which made life difficult when it came to learning about night flying and, naturally, the British weather didn't help. Flying days were fair weather days and those could be few and far between during a British winter. Under the Empire Air Training Scheme, pilots from Britain and the Commonwealth were sent to countries such as South Africa, Rhodesia or Canada for pilot training, and another plan, known as the Arnold Scheme, allowed for training in the United States. Named after General Henry Harley 'Hap' (short for 'Happy') Arnold, who was head of the United States Army Air Corps, the scheme was intended to train RAF pilots alongside Army Air Corps cadets at a number of facilities spread across the south-eastern United States in Alabama, Georgia, South Carolina and Florida. RAF personnel were present on the bases to supervise the flying instruction and oversee the courses, but the bases were run by the Army Air Corps. To cross the Atlantic nowadays, you need only pop along to your nearest international airport with direct flights to America in the morning and you can be there shortly after you leave, allowing for the time difference. My journey to the United States was to take almost three weeks and started with a trip to Wilmslow in Cheshire, where we had to hang around waiting for places on a ship in a westward-bound convoy out of Liverpool. There were very few aircraft that could make the whole hop across the Atlantic at that time, and those that could were not capable of carrying very many passengers. We had to travel on a troop ship. While we were waiting, I managed a brief visit with Gwyn, and was also issued with a civilian suit. It wasn't a very good suit, but it was a suit, nonetheless. Why were we given civilian clothes?

The answer is that we were to travel from Liverpool to Canada, then from Trenton, Ontario, by rail into the United States. Our rail journey would take us all the way down the east coast of America to Florida. America was not actually in the war yet. The United States didn't wade in until December 1941, following the Japanese attack on Pearl Harbor, and, although there were many Americans pushing for the US to get involved, there were just as many who felt that America should remain neutral. German and Italian immigrant families didn't want their sons to be sent off to Europe to fight against other Germans and Italians, while there was a whole raft of Americans who simply wanted to leave the 'old world' in Europe behind. Everyone, of course, remembered the carnage on the battlefields of Europe less than 25 years before. If British airmen were seen travelling in uniform in the United States, clearly on their way to train at American bases, it would have upset a lot of Americans and put the country's neutral status at stake. The suits were for us to wear while in transit in America, although first we had to survive the crossing of the Atlantic.

Having only recently been introduced to the sea, and still not being able to swim, boarding a ship (also a first) to cross an ocean that was infested with U-boats wasn't a prospect that filled me with joy, but everyone else was having to do it, so I had to knuckle down and get on with it, too. Sleeping in a hammock was a novel experience at first. Getting used to climbing into it was the tricky bit. Once you were in, it was quite comfortable. There were hundreds of us strung up in our hammock cocoons at night below decks and it could get quite rowdy. One Flight Sergeant helped to pass the time by teaching us rugby songs, which gave us all a bit of a laugh. We were also expected to parade on deck for medical inspection stark naked. There we were, lined up in rows in our birthday suits in the sunshine as the Medical Officer gave us the once-over to pass us FFI – Free From Infection. This wasn't so bad in the middle of the summer in the Atlantic, but I wouldn't have fancied it in the winter at all!

Once we disembarked in Canada, the rest of the journey was by train. We had, as I recall, one change of trains in America before we were southbound, in our suits, headed for Florida. It involved an overnight journey but there were no sleeper cars for us. We slept as best we could, sitting up or slumping down to get comfortable. We weren't alone in our carriages or separated from the general public. I do remember sitting beside a young lady for a while who took quite a shine to me but she definitely wasn't 'going my way' – Florida – so I was able to resist temptation! What a journey – a real eye-opener for a Lincolnshire lad – and at the end of it was a country that was totally alien to me. We had come from a warm summer in England but the heat and humidity in Florida were something that I had never experienced before. They took some getting used to, as did everything else about Florida.

We were headed for Carlstrom Field, just outside the town of Arcadia. Carlstrom had been established in 1917 as a training base for American pilots during the First War but had been mothballed in the 1920s, much to the dismay of the locals in Arcadia, who had loved having the airmen around to boost local trade. When WWII broke out, it was suggested that training facilities might be needed once more and a campaign was soon underway to reinstate Carlstrom. The whole place was rebuilt in just a few months, creating a strange air base with the brand-new accommodation buildings and recreation facilities – including a swimming pool flanked by palm trees like a mini oasis (I never went near it) – surrounded by a perfectly circular road. At one point on the circle was the main gate and, at the opposite side, outside the circle were the hangars and the runway. It was all new and as if it were on another planet compared with the bleak RAF bases of Lincolnshire.

The base and the tropical weather weren't the only strange things. We were issued with tropical kit for the first time – lightweight khaki long trousers and shorts as well as khaki shirts. We were fed better than we had ever been. Good food and plenty of it. Back home, people were struggling to feed their families and most types of food were rationed, but here there were no shortages. I developed a taste for iced coffee, which was served up in jugs on the table in the mess hall at every meal. The local people were really friendly and welcoming, although I didn't go into town much. There wasn't really much there except a bar and a few restaurants, and, as I wasn't a drinker, Arcadia wasn't a huge attraction for me. I remember being surprised at how many of the buildings were made of wood, a bit like an old 'Wild West' town. I suppose I was used to seeing everything built from bricks and mortar, which made me think of wooden buildings as temporary structures – sheds, garages, outhouses and barracks huts. The huts that we were billeted in on the base were wooden as well, and it was in the huts that the petty discipline of the Army Air Corps first hit home.

To make it look, I suppose, like we were not being given instruction by the US military, the flying instructors that we had were all civilians, but the camp was most definitely run by the Army Air Corps. They had drill instructors of the worst kind and inspections that we couldn't believe. It wasn't simply that these petty-minded Air Corps idiots didn't realise that we had already been through basic training; they just seemed determined to show us how things were done in their neck of the woods. There was also a system of 'hazing', in which their more senior cadets were allowed to lord it over us newcomers, keeping a tally of reprimands that they called 'gigs'. You had a gig chalked up against you if you were spotted walking on the grass or were talking out of turn. There was no talking at breakfast, for example. Bed making had to be done absolutely precisely. The bedclothes had to be tucked in with hospital corners at an angle of exactly 45 degrees – one officer even brought a protractor to measure the angle and make sure you were spot on. If you weren't, the whole bed was tipped over and you had to start again, with a gig marked against you. Three gigs and you were given a senseless punishment such as marching up and down a concrete path in full kit in the full heat of the Florida sun. They were stupid little men, all too fond of the sound of their own voices. They weren't even very good at being smart, not by our standards. They had us slopping along, marching to a lazy 'hup, two, three, four', when we were used to a sharp, crisp 116 paces to the minute. None of us could understand what all of that nonsense was about. It certainly had nothing to do with teaching us to fly.

The flying instructors, on the other hand, were wonderful. The aircraft we were using for initial training was the Stearman PT-17 biplane. It was a bit like a British Tiger Moth, although it was painted like something out of a circus. The fuselage was sky blue, the wings were bright yellow with huge American 'star' roundels on them, and the tail was red and white stripes. There was no drab camouflage required in Florida! The PT-17 was well powered and highly manoeuvrable, making it excellent as a trainer and also very popular as an aerobatics machine or for crop dusting. If you watch any American movie where a biplane is featured, it's more than likely to be a Stearman. It had one small vice in that it had a tendency towards 'ground looping', turning sharply to the left or right on the ground when it was supposed to be taxiing straight ahead.

The initial primary flying course took 9 to 10 weeks, with 60 hours of instruction. Pass the primary course and you were moved on to basic flying training in Georgia or Alabama, after which you would progress to the Maxwell Field airbase in Alabama for advanced instruction. I made it to Maxwell Field, although not because I was on the advanced course.

Unlike some of the cadets, the first time that I climbed into the PT-17 for a flying lesson wasn't the first time that I had been in an aircraft. I had hitched a lift in an Anson when I was stationed at Grantham and they were doing a short hop between bases and home again. I had loved it and couldn't wait to get back in the sky again, but I wasn't at all sure that I should be doing so as a pilot. I did manage to go solo once in Florida, but my landing was a bit too heavy. Fortunately there was no damage to the aircraft but that was more by luck than judgement. My instructor, having tried valiantly to get me through the course, eventually had to admit defeat. 'Sorry, son,' he said. 'I don't think that you're going to make it as a pilot.' I just smiled and said, 'Don't worry, neither do I.'

In a way, I think that I was relieved to be able to put the idea of becoming a pilot behind me. I certainly wasn't alone in failing the course. There were quite a few of us who were described in American parlance as having 'washed out' as pilots and we became part of the statistics that showed how 2,687 of the 7,885 cadets who undertook training on the Arnold Scheme between 1941 and 1943 failed the first part of the course. That's around a 35 per cent fail rate, although I understand that it was sometimes as high as 50 per cent. The programme was clearly of huge value in providing the RAF with new pilots and the fail rate shows that high standards were maintained, but, having specially selected the trainee pilots, the RAF must have wondered how they could be getting it so wrong. I understand that it was later thought that taking young men out of their home environment and shipping them off to somewhere as unusual as Florida, where the climate, the food, the scenery and even the everyday language used by the locals were strange to them, did nothing to help put them in the right frame of mind to produce their best effort on the training course. Improvements came when more RAF instructors were used, but I doubt that would have helped me much. I didn't see it as a disgrace to have failed, and I don't think that any of the others who 'washed out' at the same time as me saw it that way either.

The Army Air Corps weren't so kind. Their petty disciplinarians didn't use the term 'washed-out' pilots but 'f***ed-up' pilots. None of us was sorry to be leaving them behind. When we left their mess hall for the last time, one of the lads who had been on the course said, 'Let's show them how to march properly, the way we march in the RAF!' We formed two ranks, dressed off, and marched smartly past the mess hall, breaking out into a raucous rendition of 'Colonel Bogey' as we did so. I've no idea what they thought of that, but it made us smile.

Sadly, Britain was rather more than a quick march away. We arrived at Maxwell Field, Montgomery, Alabama in September and were stuck there for about six weeks until our passage back to Canada was arranged. We were still subject to the mind-numbing discipline of the Army Air Corps, with more square bashing and fitness training but not much else to fill the time. There were occasional pleasant diversions. I remember that two of us were invited into the home of a family called Debardlens. They were most hospitable. I particularly recall a private swimming pool and two very nubile daughters, but we were guests, on our best behaviour. When chatting with the lady of the house about food, the rationing situation back home and so forth, she mentioned corn on the cob. Corn on the what? She couldn't believe that we had never heard of it. 'Mamma,' she called to the maid, 'these boys never had corn on the cob!' The maid couldn't believe it either, and quickly rustled some up for us. It was delicious – far better than carrots, whether they make you see in the dark or not.

When we finally left Alabama, we had a long trek to Moncton, New Brunswick, where we then had to wait another six or seven weeks for a ship home. Here we had absolutely nothing to do but sit around trying to be patient. The Canadian winter was bloody cold with deep snow everywhere. We spent Christmas in Moncton, where there was a large store called Eaton's – part of the country's biggest department store chain at the time – where we could buy all sorts of goods that were not available at home. It was the perfect place to do our Christmas shopping. I made a huge error in not buying nylon stockings and Gwyn was not slow to show her disappointment on my return. The other gifts were, of course, gratefully received, but how could I not have realised that stockings were what was really required?

We came home in January on a troop ship that took a southern route across the Atlantic to avoid the U-boat packs' hunting grounds. During the voyage we ran into what is known as an Azores High, which meant stormy winds and rough seas. Everyone was as sick as a dog for two days. The sight of a wet and wintry Liverpool was most welcome. By the middle of January 1942, I was in Bournemouth at the RAF's Personnel Receiving Centre and was billeted at the Cecil Hotel, along with some other returned airmen, while the powers that be decided what to do with us. We had a bit of drill now and again but were basically just sitting around. One of the few things that made this bearable was that the NCO (non-commissioned officer) in charge was Sam Bartram. Sam had been the Charlton Athletic goalkeeper before the war and was a legend even then. Everyone agreed that he was the best goalkeeper never to be awarded a full England cap. Sam was a strict disciplinarian, but he was a great guy to be around. He played 22 consecutive years for Charlton until his retirement in 1956 at the age of 42.

The only advantage of being in Bournemouth was that it allowed me to start seeing Gwyn again for a couple of months prior to me being posted to the Aircrew Training Centre at Hastings. This was where they were supposed to sort people out and by now I had had enough of doing nothing. I decided to apply for the gunnery course because I thought that would be the quickest way to get into the war, the gunnery course being the shortest aircrew course. I thought that this would at last let me start fighting Hitler. That's what I had joined the RAF to do, but after 16 months the only thing that I had killed was a rat in a guard house. The president of the selection board said to me, 'I think you will be too afraid to be a gunner, Johnson.' To which I replied, 'If I was going to be afraid, sir, I wouldn't be here.' That seemed to do the trick and I was despatched to 14 Initial Training Wing (ITW) at Bridlington. This was a rehash of the ITW at Newquay where I had been a year before, although it was more specifically designed for gunners. There was more Morse code, service discipline and medical lectures.

Everywhere we went there always seemed to be lectures on the medical risks of fraternising with the local ladies. We were shown gruesome films about the horrifying things that would happen to your private parts if you caught various diseases, and there were always posters around warning us about sexually transmitted diseases, often using cheery little rhymes. 'They said squeeze, and he squose and a bubble arose,' was one, and, towards the end of the war, 'A blob on the knob slows demob.' One of the more serious posters said: 'The easy girlfriend spreads Syphilis and Gonorrhoea, which unless properly treated may result in blindness, insanity, paralysis, premature death.' There was a time when a rumour had been circulating that a few of us might be posted to Greece. We were warned that Greek girls were quite 'willing' and we should beware the possible consequences of close encounters. That gave rise to a little unofficial ditty, the lyrics of which are unprintable but that finished, 'Don't care if I do go blind – post me to Athens!'

From Bridlington I was sent to the Air Gunnery School in Morpeth. The six-week course covered the care and maintenance of equipment and air-to-air firing against drogue targets that were towed behind other aircraft. I learned how to harmonise the guns so that the four (or two) guns in the turret were aiming slightly inwards, forming a cone of fire with the rounds all coming together at the same point in space; I learned about 'deflection' and how to aim my shots so that the moving target flew into that point in space just as my rounds arrived there; I learned about 'bullet drop' as gravity pulled the rounds downwards; I learned how to strip and reassemble the guns, and pretty much everything about the .303 calibre Browning machine gun.

The aircraft that was used for training us in how to operate a gun turret and bring the guns to bear while we were in the air was the Blackburn Botha. The Botha had a pretty poor reputation. It had been introduced in 1939 as a reconnaissance aircraft and torpedo bomber, but it was woefully underpowered and disturbingly unstable. If one of its engines went, the Botha was going nowhere except into the sea. There were several accidents and the aircraft was swiftly withdrawn from front-line service, but not retired completely. Instead, it was passed on to the training squadrons. From a gunner's point of view, it was a nightmare. The dorsal turret was very cramped, even for someone as slim as me. It was difficult to get into and even more difficult to get out of. If anything had gone wrong on one of our training flights, I doubt I would have been able to get out of that turret before we were in the drink. There were a number of accidents and casualties – they should have scrapped all of those bloody awful Bothas.

On the plus side, it was good to be doing some proper training at last. The feel of the cold gunmetal, the smell of the gun oil and the whiff of cordite as the Brownings ate up the ammunition belt were fantastic. We fired at drogues towed behind Ansons or other Bothas and you could see your rounds hammering into the target. Very satisfying. I wouldn't say that I was the best shot on the course, but I put in a pretty good performance. On the drogues, a hit rate of around 50 per cent was regarded as a good score and I managed that without any trouble. I passed the course and was promoted to Sergeant with a pay increase to 7/6d (37 pence) per day, paid fortnightly. After a couple of weeks training on Manchesters and Lancasters, I was posted to 97 Squadron at Woodhall Spa in July 1942, ready to get into the war at last.

CHAPTER 5

# BOMBS GONE AND MY WAR BEGINS

Now I was beginning to feel frightened. All of the tension, all of the stress of the previous few hours was now being distilled down into one base emotion – fear. From my Perspex vantage point in the nose of Chuck-Chuck, I could see what was coming, see what we were about to fly into. In the distance, with a raid underway, I could see searchlights stretching their white fingers up into the sky, seeking out aircraft to light up, pinpointing them for the flak gunners. The pyrotechnics were incredible, with flak bursts and tracer cutting through the darkness and creating a storm of fire that looked impossible to fly through. Yes, I was scared and I don't mind admitting it. One look at what we were flying towards was enough to send a real shiver down your spine. We all felt it. We all felt the fear. I didn't know anyone then, and I don't know anyone now, who would deny it. I think that anyone who wasn't at least a bit apprehensive was either lacking in emotion or a stranger to the truth. Frankly put, they would be lying.

But you had to block it out. You had to fight it. You had to keep the fear under control, and the best way for me to do that was to focus completely on what I had to do. If I concentrated on doing my job, I didn't have time to feel scared. I could block out the outside world if I just kept my mind on the job in hand, and my chance to do that came when we heard Don on the intercom: 'Navigator to Skipper. Estimate 10 minutes to target. Watch out for TIs.' That was my cue to drop down from my turret into the bomb aimer's position. The TIs were target indicators – flares dropped by the Pathfinder Force (PFF) that could be seen from many miles away. Don would also give us any course correction required and the wind speed. The wind speed was important to me because I had to check the setting on my bombsight and adjust it if necessary. I hear a lot of talk about the bomb aimer's 'computer' on the Lanc, a device that worked out all sorts of things for you. It's another one of those things that makes me think that I must have been in a different RAF to so many other people. I never had a computer. The settings that I had to adjust on my bombsight were quite straightforward – knobs to turn. There were no computers involved.

Nevertheless, the wind speed was vitally important. The Lanc could bomb from as high as 22,000 feet – that's just over four miles high – although on most of our trips we bombed from far lower, maybe three miles up. At that sort of altitude, the bombs can easily be blown off course by cross-winds, so I had to set up the bombsight to take that into consideration. The wind speed could be calculated by Don using landmarks on the ground to see how far the aircraft had drifted off course, but a far better way of doing it, especially at night, was to use the Gee system. Gee relied on radio signal pulses transmitted from base stations in the UK and picked up by a receiver on board the aircraft. The receiver used the difference between the timed pulses from the different base stations to work out how far it was from each transmitter and, therefore, the aircraft's precise position – precise to within a mile, which wasn't bad accuracy for the 1940s. Using regular location fixes, Don could work out how the wind was affecting Chuck-Chuck and calculate the wind speed and direction. In fact, the squadron's navigation leader would be doing that and transmitting the information by Morse back to Woodhall Spa. From there, it would be re-broadcast, again using Morse, to be picked up by the wireless operator in each Lanc. Len Eaton would decipher the coded message and pass the wind speed on to Don. He needed to know in order to check his navigation but would pass the details on to me because I needed them to set my bombsight. Other settings – our altitude, the target altitude, our speed and so forth – could pretty much be done by the Instrument Officer back at base. Once I had checked the settings, I had to look out for the TIs.

The TIs were brightly burning flares dropped by PFF Mosquitoes or Lancs flying ahead of the main bomber stream. They dropped white flares to mark the attack run and to illuminate the blacked-out target for the following PFF aircraft to drop red, green or yellow target markers. At the operation briefing, we were told what colours were to be used, so we knew what to aim for. The Germans, of course, used to light their own flares and start fires to throw us off the scent, but their flares were never quite the right colour of red or green, and, once a raid was underway, the real fires from burning buildings were much bigger than anything the enemy would dare set up. Even with fires blazing, though, I knew not to aim for the flames if there were still TIs visible. Bomb aimers had been warned about 'creep back'; this was where successive aircraft, or waves of aircraft, aiming at fires burning on the ground in order to offload their bombs and get away from the target area as quickly as possible ended up dropping their bombs progressively short of the actual target, always aiming for the closest fire. I had to aim for the TIs. I reached across to the instrument panel on my right and unclipped the bomb release switch, holding it in my right hand with my thumb covering the button on top, the switch's cable trailing back to the panel.

'Two minutes to target,' came Don's voice over the intercom. Joe reached down to his left to pull a lever, then flipped a switch in the cockpit.

'Bomb doors open,' he reported. 'Master switch on.' With the master switch on, the bomb release button in my hand was now 'live'. On later Lancs, opening the bomb doors would automatically enable the master switch.

Looking into the bombsight, I had a view of the ground way ahead of us. As we were travelling at more than 200mph, our payload would leave the bomb bay still moving forwards at that speed. Because we had four Merlins to power us forwards and the bombs didn't, air resistance would immediately start to slow the bombs' forward speed while the force of gravity made them accelerate downwards. Therefore, the bombs would travel in a steepening arc towards the ground, not fall straight down. This meant that, depending on the altitude, our speed, the bombs' terminal velocity and their air resistance or 'drag', we might be dropping them a mile or more before we were actually flying over the target. That's what the bombsight was there to help with. Through the sight I could see a set of illuminated cross hairs moving towards the target. If I set it up correctly, and pressed the bomb release button when the cross hairs were bang on the TIs, I would have done my best to place the bombs where they were meant to go.

Watching the cross hairs creeping towards the TIs, I had to give a running commentary to Joe so that he could keep Chuck-Chuck flying straight and level towards the target. 'Left, left … right … steady …' Meanwhile, the closer we came, the more stuff came flying up at us. It didn't matter that we were at an altitude of 15,000 or 20,000 feet – the German 88mm anti-aircraft gun was accurate to 25,000 or 30,000 feet. They had 50,000 guns positioned from the North Sea coast all the way into the heart of Germany, with 15,000 of them capable of reaching us at any altitude. Sometimes it seemed like every one of them was firing at us! There were different colours of tracer, some rounds rocketing past us to burst higher up, some exploding far below, and some coming perilously close. It was quite a display – not pretty, but something that would have been impressive to watch had they not been trying to kill us.

Now and again, by the light of the explosions or silhouetted against the fires down below, I would spot another Lanc or a Halifax. There was talk about a special kind of flak shell called 'Scarecrow' that the Germans used to try to demoralise bomber crews. It would explode in a massive fireball and a shower of burning debris – some said that they had even seen little parachutes drifting away from these air bursts, the intention being to make it look like an exploding aircraft. Scarecrow was supposed to make the bomber crews so terrified that we would want to turn tail and head for home, but the fact is that it didn't exist. What people who saw these explosions were witnessing was a real bomber being destroyed.

In all the raids that I went on, I never saw another aircraft going down in flames. I know that others did, and Don had to take careful note of the time and position of such sightings, but I never saw it happen. I think that is probably because, as we approached the target area, I was doing my utmost to ignore everything else that was going on, to focus solely on those cross hairs and to keep giving Joe his instructions – 'Right, right ... Steady ...'

Lying on my stomach to look into the bombsight, I could now feel every slight movement of the aircraft. Closing on the target was never a smooth, effortless flying carpet ride. I had a bit of padding on the bench where I lay, but all of the usual noise and vibration that you grew accustomed to when you had been airborne in Chuck-Chuck for a few hours was now joined by jolting and buffeting that made it feel like you were driving down a rutted track, lying in the back of a truck. Exploding flak shells, even those going off too far away to do us any damage, would still send out shock waves that could give Chuck-Chuck a real jolt. Sometimes these would be accompanied by a rasping noise that sounded like hail stones or loose road chippings rattling off your car. Shrapnel from a flak burst. It had travelled too far, making it too weak to do any damage, but that sinister sound did nothing to calm your nerves.

Thermals created by fires far below, the hot air rising and swirling, as well as, sometimes, the concussion from other crews' bombs bursting on the ground also helped to keep the run into the target pretty bumpy, with me calling out a constant stream of instructions to Joe in order to keep us on the right line. For me, that kept the fear at bay. I saw nothing but those cross hairs and thought about nothing but staying on track. That may be why I never saw the night fighter.

On 21 December 1942, nine Lancs from 97 Squadron participated in a raid on Munich. This was my first trip with Joe's crew, and the official record of the encounter with the night fighter reads as follows:

*On the night of 21/22nd December, 1942, at 21.10 hours when flying at a height of 15,000 feet with an I.A.S.* [indicated air speed] *of 180 and a course of 300 in weather conditions of good visibility and bright moonlight, and just about to make a bombing run over Munich, Lancaster M/97 sighted an enemy aircraft at a range of 1,000 yards, this aircraft was identified as a Ju 88.*

*The enemy aircraft was first seen flying parallel with our aircraft and it immediately turned in to the Lancasters starboard, our aircraft then turned in on top of the enemy, who went underneath our aircraft's stern, the Lancaster once again turned in to it. The enemy aircraft then turned into the port side of our Lancaster which turned on top of the enemy who again made a starboard approach and tracer from its guns was seen to pass under the nose of the Lancaster. The enemy aircraft then disappeared from view and was not seen again.*

*The enemy aircraft carried no lights, no action was taken with I.F.F.* [Identification Friend or Foe]. *There was no flak reported at the time but two or three searchlights were probing the sky but the Lancaster was not held.*

*There were no casualties to the members of the Lancasters crew, and they did not open fire.*

I don't remember a thing about it. You would think that, lying in the nose with bright moonlight, I would have been able to see everything that was going on, but, for me, there are two key points in the report. The first is 'just about to make a bombing run', which means that I would have been doing my best to block out anything that distracted me from my bombsight. The second is the evasive action that Joe appears to have taken. There is no violent corkscrew. He was obviously keen to keep us on target and I may well have been cursing him for not sticking to my 'Left, left … Steady' instructions. Of course, the other option is that the report could be complete bull. It's not unknown for official reports to be totally wrong or to be allocated to the wrong crews.

The only time that I do remember spotting a couple of fighters was on a daylight trip to Milan with Flt Sgt Colin Smith's crew. We had bombed the railway marshalling yard from 8,000 feet and were on our way home when I saw two fighters, either Fiats or Macchis – too far away to tell. I reported the sighting and was then bombarded with requests for constant updates on their movements, but there was nothing I could say. The fighters simply buggered off. There was no way that they didn't see us, but they made no move to attack. Maybe they were low on fuel or out of ammo and decided to go home, or maybe they simply thought better of having a go at a Lancaster when it was clear that we must have spotted them. Fighter pilots like to be able to surprise you, and, if they lost the element of surprise, they were quite likely to leave you well alone and go looking for easier prey.

That's probably what happened with the mysterious Ju 88 as well – he went looking for an easy target rather than wasting fuel dancing around the sky with us … if he ever existed. Suffice to say that I never saw that night fighter, or any other night fighter, on any of our ops.

Nevertheless, it serves as a good illustration of how I could focus in order to keep calm and do my job. The others, after all, had risked their lives to get us to this point in space above this city and, if I didn't do my job properly, all of their efforts would have been for nothing. I was always determined not to have anyone think that I had let the team down. With the cross hairs on the TIs and the switch in my hand, I pushed the button, giving the call, 'Bombs gone!' The aircraft bucked as the massive load departed, but Joe had to hold her on course, flying straight and level for a few agonising seconds longer until the camera took its photo of the bombs dropping towards the target.

Now we could go home …

From the late summer of 1942 until spring 1943, home for me was Woodhall Spa in Lincolnshire. After more than 18 months of training, travelling and buggering about, I was at last to see active duty, flying off to take the war to the Germans from a base that was only half an hour by car from where I had been born. The name Woodhall Spa comes from a failed coal-mining project in the nineteenth century, the mine shaft turning up nothing but spongy rock and spring water. The water, however, was found to be rich in minerals, allowing one local landowner to cash in on the Victorian health fad that had made drinking and bathing in mineral water the fashionable thing to do. Hotels sprang up to accommodate the well-to-do holidaymakers visiting the new spa.

The RAF base, just over a mile south of the village, was

opened in early 1942 as a satellite station to RAF Coningsby and 97 Squadron moved in in March 1942. Originally formed in 1917 as part of the Royal Flying Corps, 97 Squadron had a somewhat chequered and even exotic history. They first saw action in the summer of 1918, when they took their Handley Page 0/400s on night bombing operations over Europe from their base in France. These fragile-looking biplanes were the largest aeroplanes ever built in Britain at the time, with a wingspan very nearly as big as a Lanc's but with only two engines and a payload capacity of just 2,000lb. Such were the technological advances in aviation that 25 years later the Lanc would be carrying 10 times that weight of bombs.

Following the Armistice, in 1919 the squadron was sent to the North-West Frontier of India in support of the British Indian Army conflict with the Wazir tribes. Flying DH10 biplanes, they bombed local strongholds and villages as well as supporting infantry operations. It was during just such operations that a young RAF officer, Arthur Travers Harris, came to realise the importance of strategic bombing. When he later became head of Bomber Command, 'Bomber' Harris's tactics were to have a profound effect on all of us.

Detachments from 97 Squadron also established India's first airmail service between Bombay and Karachi before the unit was disbanded in March 1920. Reformed in 1935, 97 was to experience a number of stops and starts, taking on a number of different roles until February 1941 when it was reformed once more as 97 (Straits Settlements) Squadron at RAF Waddington. The 'Straits Settlements' title refers to a large donation that had been given to Britain by the Malay States for the purchase of Manchester heavy bombers. The squadron moved to RAF Coningsby with their Manchesters in late February/early March 1941 and by 8 April they had begun operations, with six Manchesters scheduled to take part in a night attack on Kiel. In the end, only four of the 97 Squadron aircraft were fit to fly. The Avro Manchester was the forerunner of the Lanc but proved to be a real disappointment. Its Rolls-Royce Vulture engines were neither powerful nor reliable enough, the aircraft had problems with its hydraulics, and it simply wasn't up to the job as a heavy bomber. The designer, Roy Chadwick, listened to the complaints about the Manchester and redesigned it, addressing many of the problems and giving it a longer wingspan to accommodate four Merlin engines. As was typical of so much of the strategic planning during the war, bickering and differences of opinion amongst senior RAF staff resulted in a good deal of to-ing and fro-ing but Chadwick's perseverance and dogged determination ultimately led to the Lancaster's first test flight in January 1941. After the inevitable initial teething problems had been resolved, Avro was given the go-ahead to put the new aircraft into production, with outstanding Manchester orders scrapped in favour of the Lancaster. Only around 200 Manchesters were ever built and they were retired from front-line service in 1942 as soon as the new Lancaster started to roll off the production lines. More than 7,300 Lancasters were built and the aircraft stayed in service (with the Canadians) until 1963.

There is no doubting the quality of the Lancaster as the outstanding bomber of WWII. It was streets ahead of anything else that the Allies or the enemy had and Bomber Harris was to describe it as 'our shining sword'. In 1940, with the Spitfire and Hurricane pilots of the RAF refusing to allow the Germans to achieve the air superiority that they needed for the proposed invasion of Britain to stand any chance of success, Churchill said that: 'The fighters are our salvation but the bombers alone provide the means of victory.' The Lancaster would prove to be the key weapon in the bomber offensive and would pass into history as one of the iconic aircraft of WWII. It was noisy, smelly and very uncomfortable, but it was a wonderful aeroplane. In the hands of a good pilot it could do anything. It was strong and would take a considerable beating without mishap.

The first of the new aircraft were delivered in early 1942 to 44 Squadron, who flew their initial operational sorties with their Lancasters in March, the unit having previously operated Hampdens, which had a maximum bomb load of 4,000lb. The Lanc would normally carry at least 14,000lb and was later modified to take the 22,000lb Grand Slam bomb – a very considerable increase in strike power. In January 1942, 97 Squadron began converting to Lancasters and was relocated to Woodhall Spa in March. By the time I joined them, they were an experienced, battle-hardened outfit. It might have been a bit daunting for a compete newcomer, but this was what I had been waiting for for so long – at last I was to see some action with a unit that was in the thick of it.

The men of 97 Squadron had particularly distinguished themselves on 17 April 1942 when a complement of six aircraft, together with six from 44 Squadron, attacked the MAN diesel engine works at Augsburg in daylight. Two aircraft, including the 97 leader, Sqn Ldr Sherwood, were shot down by heavy defensive flak. He had a miraculous escape by being thrown from the Lancaster as it crashed. The Lancs of 44 Squadron, led by Sqn Ldr John Nettleton, lost five of their six bombers to Messerschmitts on the outward run, but Nettleton pressed on alone. The attack was an outstanding propaganda success, with Air Marshal Harris sending a signal:

*The resounding blow which has been struck at the enemy's submarine and tank building programme will echo around the world. The full effect on his submarine campaigns cannot be immediately apparent, but nevertheless they will be enormous. The gallant adventure penetrating deep into the heart of Germany in daylight and pressed home with outstanding determination in the face of bitter and unforeseen opposition takes its place amongst the most courageous operations of the war. The officers and men who took part, those who returned, and those who fell, have indeed served their country well.*

Churchill congratulated everyone with the message:

*We must plainly regard the attack of the Lancasters on the U-boat engine factory at Augsburg as an outstanding achievement of the Royal Air Force. Undeterred by heavy losses at the outset, 44 and 97 Squadrons pierced and struck a vital point with deadly precision in broad daylight. Pray convey the thanks of His Majesty's Government to the officers and men who accomplished this memorial feat of arms in which no life was lost in vain.*

Nettleton was awarded the VC. His post-operation observations for newsreels and in the press were pretty flowery, particularly in regard to the low-level flying on the outward leg. The bravery and skill of all of those involved are to be admired, but I always felt that Nettleton was rather full of himself. Guy Gibson was already building a reputation as the outstanding pilot in Bomber Command and it did seem like Nettleton was trying to out-Gibson Gibson.

The Augsburg raid was a fantastic success in terms of striking back at the Germans, and, to let everyone know that such a blow had been delivered, some of those who returned had to do their bit for the media, but there was another side to the operation. Twelve aircraft had left the UK and only five had returned. In terms of aircraft, that's a 58 per cent loss rate. Early bombing raids using Wellingtons, Hampdens and Whitleys had demonstrated that daylight operations produced unsustainable losses and the arrival of the Lancaster had done nothing to change that. Night raids were to become the norm.

On the nights of 27/28 and 28/29 April, 97 Squadron was involved in the unsuccessful attacks on the battleship *Tirpitz* at Trondheim in Norway (a job that 617 Squadron would finish in 1944) and in May/June they played a full role in the first 1,000 bomber attacks on Cologne, Essen and Bremen. These massive raids on German cities have been heavily criticised in some quarters over recent years.

Much has been written about Harris's carpet-bombing strategy and many arguments have been raised. Some people seem to want to make Bomber Harris out to be some kind of monster. I have nothing but contempt for such 'revisionist historians'. They weren't there. They have no comprehension of the mood of the country at that time. Our towns and cities were being bombed and the people in Britain wanted to fight back. Bomber Harris (actually, we always referred to him as 'Butch') knew exactly how people felt. He said:

*The Nazis entered this war under the rather childish delusion that they were going to bomb everyone else and nobody was going to bomb them. At Rotterdam, London, Warsaw and half a hundred other places, they put that rather naive theory into operation. They have sowed the wind, and now they are going to reap the whirlwind.*

The 'whirlwind' idea is a reference to the Bible (Hosea 8:7), Harris's intention being to rain fire of biblical proportions on German cities. And we were right behind him. The aircrews thought he was a great leader. I can't really say exactly why, but the majority of us had complete confidence in him. He was a hard man, but he had a soft side that was obvious when he visited the squadrons and talked to the men. He was looked upon as our boss and he was doing the best job that he could. We believed in him, he believed in us, and we fought for him. I know that there were appalling German casualties – I had first-hand experience from Grantham, remember, of the lethal power of just a few bombs – but when people ask if I felt any regret about the havoc we were creating below us, I have to say that, at the time, I never gave it a thought. It is, perhaps, not a particularly nice thing to say, but in truth I never did think about the consequences for the civilians – the non-combatants who hadn't asked for this, but were getting it anyway. Terrible things were happening to people in Britain too, so I suppose it was a question of 'tit for tat'. Certainly, in the back of my mind, there was always the thought: Serves you buggers right. You shouldn't have started it. What we were doing was fighting fire with fire. And if we were more successful than they were, so much the better.

Of course, we didn't always operate like a well-oiled

precision instrument. Things could, and did, go badly wrong. I had a taste of that on my very first trip. During my first few months with 97 Squadron, I wasn't part of a regular crew and didn't fly as many ops as most of the others. I was a spare gunner and was left sitting around, waiting to be told if I was needed. If a gunner was wounded, ill or on leave, I was drafted in to fly with that crew. When the Order of Battle was posted on the morning of a raid, anyone who was short of a gunner took me along with them. I went on about 10 ops over those first few months – Augsburg, Nuremberg, Munich, Karlsruhe, Bremen, Wismar, Milan, Hamburg and Genoa. My own log book was stolen from the back of my car in Singapore in 1958, but I can piece together what happened from memory and from squadron records. My memory is usually pretty good and the squadron records are notoriously inaccurate – but, where memory and the records coincide, I can be sure we're on the right track.

My first op was as mid-upper gunner with Sqn Ldr Coton's crew. He was one of the flight commanders for a raid on the port of Gdynia in Poland, where the Germans were building their only aircraft carrier, the *Graf Zeppelin*. No one wanted the German navy to get their hands on an aircraft carrier, so bombing the unfinished carrier was a good plan. We set off as planned, carrying an 8,000lb cookie for the first time, as I recall. We were just over an hour from base, toddling out across the North Sea, when I looked out and saw fuel pouring out of one of the port engines. I knew that wasn't good, but this was my very first op. I didn't want to be the one to have to call it off and was a bit nervous when I clicked onto the intercom: 'Mid-upper to Skipper. Looks like a port engine fuel leak.'

'Oh dear,' was his response. 'We'll have to go back.'

The flight engineer switched off the fuel supply to that engine, diverting it to another tank, and we went home. And we landed with the 8,000 pounder still on board. One other aircraft also had to turn back due to an engine failure. Some of them managed to drop their bombs somewhere near the *Graf Zeppelin* but I don't think anyone actually hit the ship. It was the Germans who denied themselves the use of their aircraft carrier by never allocating enough resources to complete it. They scuppered it towards the end of the war.

The very next night with the same bomb load, Wg Cdr Collier decided he would take the crew. The target was Nuremberg. As we approached the target there was this great conflagration going on in the distance. Clearly it was a raid and, thinking that our main force had been hoodwinked by the Germans, Collier said, 'The silly buggers are bombing the decoy.' We had the squadron nav leader as our navigator and, as was customary at that time, he was also the bomb aimer. He, too, was convinced that we had the right target, but we were experiencing no opposition at all. The bomb was dropped and then all hell broke loose from the ground defences. We got out of there sharpish and, when we landed back at Woodhall Spa, the Wing Commander was fuming at the debriefing.

'The silly sods were all bombing the wrong target,' he said.

'Well, sir,' said the Intelligence Officer, 'we shall just have to wait for the photographs to be developed to see what actually happened, won't we?'

When the photographs did come out, it was clear that we had not been to Nuremberg but had, instead, bombed Augsburg, some 75 miles to the south. The navigator said that there must have been a tremendous change of wind about which no one had told him. No more was said about the incident. Augsburg, after all, was still a perfectly good target!

The fact is that dropping bombs on Germany was not an exact science. By 1942, the Nuremberg/Augsburg mix-up should have been avoidable, but, earlier in the war, the RAF's bombing success rate was really quite dreadful. By 1942, we were made well aware that previous bombing attempts had been poor and that we were expected to do better, but none of us knew until much later about the 'Butt Report'. In 1941, responding to criticisms of RAF bombing and the accuracy claims of bomber crews, a civil servant called David Bensusan-Butt made a study of bombing camera images and dropped his own bombshell:

> *An examination of photographs taken during night bombing in June and July points to the following conclusions:*
>
> *Of those aircraft recorded as attacking their target, only one in three got within five miles.*
>
> *Over the French ports, the proportion was two in three; over Germany as a whole, the proportion was one in four; over the Ruhr, it was only one in ten.*
>
> *In the full moon the proportion was two in five; in the new moon it was only one in fifteen.*

The report was a real shocker for Churchill and the War Cabinet, but its contents weren't for our consumption. We were told that we had to do better and we were well aware that previous efforts had not been good. Crews would claim to have hit the target but, in reality, this was frequently only a calculated guess. There were a few individuals who, having seen the opposition that they had to go into, would say, 'Sod this!' They would get as close in as they dared and then swing the aircraft off to port or starboard with the bomb doors open in order to fling the payload in the general direction of the target.

We knew we could do better. By 1942, we had the Mark 14 bombsight, which replaced the old CSBS (Course Setting Bomb Sight) that had been in use since the First World War. The Mark 14 wasn't absolutely reliable, depending on the Instrument Officer and bomb aimer to set it up correctly but also relying on accurate target marking. That was pretty ropey in the early days until the PFF got their act together. If it was cloudy we had to use aerial marking, flares floating down on parachutes, hopefully above the target and not drifting too much in the wind. Gee and then another radio navigation system called Oboe and later the H2S ground-mapping radar all helped to produce increasingly accurate bombing results. By the time we had the Stabilised Automatic Bomb Sight (SABS) on 617 Squadron towards the end of 1943, we could drop from 15,000 feet and regularly hit within 100 yards of the target – a real improvement on five miles!

Of course, on my first few ops, I was flying as a gunner, not a bomb aimer, and, although I never actually had any notions about not coming back from a raid, there was one occasion when I really thought I'd had it. I was flying with Colin Smith's crew, and the squadron records document that there was:

*Extremely bad weather conditions on return, thunder and active static conditions. Route as detailed.*

It wasn't quite as routine as that makes it sound. We had been on a raid to Wismar in north Germany. It was a long trip and this was the second time we had been there. On each occasion it was clouded over and we had to bomb on aerial markers. This time, when we completed the bombing run, we dropped down to 10,000 feet to head for home, so we had our oxygen masks off. Suddenly there was this godawful flash. I was temporarily blinded. My night vision was gone – I couldn't see a thing. The pilot was struggling to control the aircraft. We were going down at a fair rate of knots. He hadn't got his mike set on and people were calling, 'Colin, are you all right – are you all right?' He couldn't answer but we could feel he was struggling like hell. He actually got it under control at 2,000 feet. During the whole process the flight engineer, blinded just as I and the pilot had been, couldn't see the instruments. I was sitting in the front turret and, as my sight started to come back, it looked like all the Perspex had been burned out. There were just metal strips left. I remember thinking – so this is what it's like to be dead. I don't know why I thought that – silly, really – but that was the thought that went through my mind. Then, as the night vision returned, I could see that the turret was actually still intact. Then the mid-upper gunner said that he saw this St Elmo's fire creeping towards his turret along the aerial and then – wham! – struck by lightning. We went from 10,000 feet to 2,000 in the blink of an eye.

Modern airliners are regularly struck by lightning, flying as they do in all weathers, but they are designed to cope with it and suffer no ill effects. Back in the 1940s, a lightning strike could easily bring down a Lanc. That was probably the hairiest experience of my entire operational career.

To drive forward the improvements in bombing accuracy,

it was decided that the Lancaster had to have a specialist bomb aimer. It was no longer to be another job handled by the navigator. Ideally, what they wanted were gunners who could double up as front gunners for the flight out and home but take the bomb-aiming position on approach to the target. They were training bomb aimers locally to fill these vacancies, so there would be no protracted journey to Canada or the United States, and, since the difference in pay was from 7/6d (37½p) per day to 12/6d (62½p), I thought I would have a go. The course was at Fulbeck and didn't take very long at all. In late November I was back with the squadron, this time as a spare bomb aimer rather than a spare gunner.

From now on, I would spend my time on ops in my Perspex office, which was a great place to be during a trip but not without its hazards. Bob Hay, who was the 617 Squadron bomb leader and flew in Mickey Martin's crew, was in his office during a raid on the Anthéor railway viaduct in the South of France when the aircraft came under gunfire from the bridge. A single round came straight through the fuselage and hit him in the head, killing him instantly. I shared a room at one time with another bomb aimer, Bernie May. He was in the nose of his Lanc when it overshot the runway at Blida in North Africa, where we used to stop over after bombing targets in Italy. The aircraft crashed and the nose cone was smashed in. Bernie was killed, although the rest of the crew walked away from the wreck. By the time we got back to base a couple of days later, all of his personal effects had gone from our room. It was as though he had never existed.

Not long after I came back from the bomb aimers' course, there came another one of those strange, lucky instances that had a huge impact on my life. Plt Off Joe McCarthy was looking for a new bomb aimer. His old bomb aimer must have finished his tour – notched up enough operations to be able to step down from combat missions – and I was the front runner for his job. That seemed fine to me, until I heard that McCarthy was an American. My first reaction to that was: 'Oh, God, no ... not a Yank!' My experiences in Florida had left me with an inbuilt dislike of American flyers en masse. Our treatment at the hands of the US Army Air Corps had made it impossible for me to like them, or so I thought. As soon as I met Joe, however, we just seemed to gel. We talked about this and that and we got on very well together, right from the beginning. He talked about the other crew members and then introduced me to them. Even though I was still something of a loner and ill at ease when it came to meeting new people, I instinctively felt that this was a good crew. I didn't know them that well at first – obviously we got to know each other gradually – but from the word go I think the thing that united us was an inbuilt confidence in Joe. Well over 6 feet and solid with it, he was a big bloke in more ways than one. Big in stature, big in personality and, thank God, he was big in ability as a pilot. I soon came to believe, and I know the others felt the same, that he was the best pilot on the squadron.

Joe inspired confidence and had an easy, relaxed manner, although he didn't tolerate any nonsense when we were in the air. Born on Long Island in 1919, he was just a couple of years older than me but his size and strength of character meant that I came to regard him as an older, wiser brother. I suppose, given that he was the boss, we all really looked on him as a kind of father figure. He was certainly there to listen and advise when we went to him with any gripes or worries – and we discussed personal matters with him.

Joe's best friend, whom he had known since they worked together as lifeguards at Coney Island, was Don Curtin. The two of them headed to Canada by bus in 1941 to join the RCAF because they wanted to get into the war. They were at first rejected by the Canadians and told to return at a later date. A smart recruitment officer changed his mind, however, when the boys explained that they would not be coming back because they didn't have enough money to get home, let alone make another trip!

When Joe flew his first operational flight in the summer of 1942, Don was flying on the same trip. Joe made it to Dusseldorf and back without any problems, but Don was dogged by night fighters and flak, nursing home a badly damaged aircraft with three wounded crew on board, one of whom died from his injuries once they were back in England. Don was awarded the Distinguished Flying Cross (DFC) for what had been a harrowing baptism of fire over Germany. Both Joe and Don qualified to fly Lancs and were posted to 106 Squadron, although Joe was immediately reassigned to 97 Squadron, which was short of pilots.

I joined Joe's crew in December 1942 and our tenth mission together was to Nuremberg in February 1943. Along with our Lancs in 97 Squadron, 106 Squadron was also involved in the raid and Don was flying that night. We returned unscathed but, sadly, Don and his crew were shot down over Nuremberg. None of them survived. At the time, we heard nothing about Don's death. This was not news that it was felt could be passed on to Joe, for fear that it might have an adverse effect on his performance and future plans, so the Commanding Officer (CO) of 106 Squadron decided to delay telling Joe. That CO was Guy Gibson.

My first trip with Joe's crew came on the night of 21/22 December 1942 with Munich as the target. This, of course, is the op where we supposedly tangled with the Ju 88. Why is it that first-timers are always a problem? Visibility over Munich was 10/10ths cloud. We bombed using marker flares with some success, or at least some estimated success, but all was not well with Chuck-Chuck. In Joe's log book, he states that:

*Starboard outer engine u/s. Port inner also gave trouble.*
*Forced to land at Bottesford. Terrible weather.*

One engine out of action and another giving trouble? Terrible weather? That doesn't really sit comfortably alongside the night fighter report, does it? Such is the reliability of wartime records.

This seems like a fairly typical night for 97 Squadron – for most squadrons, in fact. Of the eight other bombers on this raid, three reported good results, four reported 'no results seen' and one aborted the mission. One had elevator trouble on the way home and was forced to land at an alternative airfield and one had three members of crew injured by flak and fighter attack. But at least there were no fatalities.

And so it began. Three months of intensive action.

8 January: Duisburg
16 January: Berlin
17 January: Berlin
30 January: Hamburg
2 February: Cologne
4 February: Turin

11 February: Wilhelmshaven

21 February: Bremen

25 February: Nuremberg

26 February: Cologne

28 February: Saint-Nazaire

1 March: Berlin

3 March: Hamburg

8 March: Nuremberg

9 March: Munich

11 March: Stuttgart

12 March: Essen

22 March: Saint-Nazaire

Nineteen nights over enemy territory. Nineteen times in three months flying into danger and potential disaster. There were routines that we had to follow, but no trip was ever routine in itself. On each one of these 19 occasions brave people would die, suffer wounds or finish up as prisoners of war (POWs). But not our crew. We had no problem with night fighters and very few technical problems. On 17 January, we were struggling to gain altitude, bombing Berlin from 14,000 feet when we should have been at 18,000. We came back with one engine out of action. The only major problems we had were with oxygen and Hamburg. On 30 January, we were headed for Hamburg when we had to abort the mission owing to oxygen failure. It was Hamburg again on 3 March, and again the oxygen packed up. We were out over the Elbe estuary and we dropped the 4,000lb cookie on the town of Friedrichskoog before heading for home. There seemed little point in bringing it back.

At the end of March, Joe had completed his first tour with

97 Squadron – 30 trips. He was promoted to Flight Lieutenant and awarded the DFC. Part of the citation reads:

*Throughout his whole career, his conduct has set an example of high courage and efficiency to other members of the squadron.*

We would all stand testament to that. I suffered not so much as a scratch while flying with Joe, while others were being shot up and brought down on a regular basis. Some would put that down to luck, and I think that I had more than my fair share of that, but our survival was by no means all down to chance. The skill of our pilot had an awful lot to do with it. However, Lady Luck was certainly on our side. You could be a supreme pilot but run out of luck … Gibson was a good example of that.

Joe had tremendous skill. He had a clear way of thinking about whatever it was that we were going to do and how we were going to cope with anything that happened to the aircraft. We all went along with whatever he decided because we knew that he was thinking about it all the time. All of that forethought and planning was one of the reasons why he was so very good. In a way, he made his own luck.

Not everyone was so enamoured of their pilot. I remember flying with one fairly senior officer who used to call to his flight engineer, 'Engineer, fetch me my bottle, if you please.' On a Lanc, the pilot never left his seat to answer a call of nature. They had a funnel, tube and canister system that meant they could relieve themselves while still at the controls. This particular officer, however, preferred to use his own bottle. Once he had filled it, he would hold it out and call,

'Engineer, dispose of this for me, there's a good chap.' I'm not sure whether the long-suffering engineer chucked it in the Elsan or simply jettisoned it. I know what I would have done, although it seems a bit of a shame that, having suffered high explosives and incendiaries being dropped on them, just when he thought it was all over, some poor German would be hit by a bottle of wee.

Having finished his tour, Joe was informed that Don Curtin had been killed. We knew nothing about it. Don had been based at Syerston and Joe had been to visit him but there was otherwise very little contact between our squadron and 106. Joe had also been introduced to Wg Cdr Guy Gibson there, and having met Joe may have been what persuaded Gibson not to let him know about Don. Not surprisingly, Joe was very upset. After completing one tour of operations, crews would be given a well-earned leave and then be offered options about the next stage of their careers. These included staying on operations or taking a training role. Joe became a lifelong friend to me and my family and, although he never spoke to me about it, his son, Joe Jnr, told me that Joe and Don had planned to return to the United States together. We will never know if they simply wanted to visit their families before returning to Britain, or if they were thinking about joining the American military.

Without Don Curtin around, maybe it was easier for Joe to listen to what Guy Gibson now had to say.

# CHAPTER 6

# HEADING HOME AND TOASTING THE BRIDESMAIDS

We weren't out of the woods yet. We had delivered our payload but we were still a long way from home, still deep in enemy territory and still, in actual fact, over the target area. Persistent flak continued to burst too close for comfort and the searchlights carried on probing the darkness, seeking us out. All that we now wanted was to get the hell out of there. I checked my switches to make sure that we had no bombs 'hung up' in the bomb bay and let Joe know that he could close the doors. Heaving myself up from my prone position on the floor of the nose cone, I climbed back up into my gun turret. Those searchlights were always a problem. Some of them were directed by radar – if one of those latched onto you, you were in serious trouble because one would immediately be followed by four or five others. The beams of light, angled towards you from different stations on the ground, formed a cone and, if you were 'coned' by the lights, the flak gunners could then have a field day.

Not only did being coned make you a beautifully illuminated sitting duck, but also the beams suddenly lit up the cockpit brighter than daylight and your night vision was gone. The pilot and the engineer couldn't see their instruments but the way to lose the searchlights was to fling the Lanc into a corkscrew, with the pilot flying pretty much blind. Only he was properly strapped in, so everyone else had to brace themselves as best they could when the aircraft was thundering through its roller-coaster ride, otherwise you could find yourself bouncing off the ceiling. Thankfully, we were never coned. Joe watched the searchlights, watched them carving a route across the sky, and kept us clear by weaving his way through them. It took only a few seconds to clear the target area, but it always seemed like an eternity.

In the movies, you sometimes see bombers dropping their payload and then being thrown into a diving turn to pick up speed and go screaming home as fast as the engines can drag them through the air. In reality, that could easily end in disaster. With scores of bombers over a city, our route to the target, our altitude, the timing of our bombing run and our exit route were all carefully planned to try to avoid accidents. Inevitably, accidents happened. Timings could never be quite as spot on as everyone would like and a wave of bombers would end up strung out over the target, but the best way to avoid flying into another Lanc or a shower of incendiaries dropped by a bomber above us was to stick to the plan. Don gave Joe a course and Joe turned to head back to base, banking the mighty wings to wheel Chuck-Chuck round in a graceful, swooping curve. Now we really were on our way home.

That brought some sense of relief. The fear that I had fought off over the target now retreated a little, but I knew that I couldn't afford to relax. We were still being hunted. On our outward journey, we would fly dog-legs, making course changes to avoid flak hotspots, to avoid known fighter bases and to try to keep the Germans guessing about what our target was that night. That way we stood some chance of avoiding being ambushed by night fighters loitering along our projected route. When a big job was on, the planners would often organise diversionary raids to try to draw the fighter cover away from the main bomber stream. By the time we were heading home, however, the enemy knew where we had been and they knew where we were going, so it was easier for them to work out an interception.

Joe would coax as much speed as he could out of Chuck-Chuck, but Bill would always be keeping an eye on his fuel gauges. The four Merlins guzzled fuel at a rate of between 270 and 280 gallons per hour at normal cruising speed – more when climbing or manoeuvring. To try to put that into some sort of perspective, if you drove a modern, average family car for an hour you might use two gallons of fuel, probably a lot less. Bill wanted to get home quickly as much as any of us, but he wasn't about to send us all to the bottom of the North Sea by letting us run out of gas within sight of the finishing line. He knew that we relied on him to do his job just as he relied on us to do ours, and right now my job was once again to help make sure that we weren't 'jumped' by the Luftwaffe's finest.

I don't believe that I ever let myself think about anything except what I was supposed to be doing when we were out over enemy territory. It didn't do to let your mind wander. I never thought about what would happen if we were hit and the aircraft was going down. I knew where my parachute was, but I never even contemplated using it. We had all been through the drills and I knew how to clip the thing onto my harness. If the worst came to the worst, and Joe ordered us to abandon ship, I would be the one to open the hatch in the floor of my office and the first one to jump. I had to be first, otherwise I would be blocking the way for the others. Bill, Don and Len would follow me out through the forward hatch. Ron would use one of the rear hatches (he'd have to make sure that he didn't end up draped over the tail if he used the crew door) and Dave would open his turret doors to reach through and grab his parachute before clipping it on, rotating his turret fully to the left or right, and then tipping himself out backwards into the night.

Joe would be the last to go. The pilot had to hold the aircraft on a steady, straight, level course to give everyone else the best chance of getting out safely. There was an autopilot system on the Lanc that could fly straight and level under ideal circumstances, but if the aircraft was so badly damaged that we had to bail out, then you can assume that it wouldn't be able to cope. Many fine pilots lost their lives by staying at the controls to give their crews the chance to jump. My parachute, like those of the rest of the crew, was a chest parachute, fastening onto the harness in front of me – the sort of thing that a skydiver might have as a spare nowadays. Joe had a pilot's parachute, which would open behind him and on which he sat during the flight. If that sounds like he had a comfy silk cushion, think again. The parachute bags were packed so tightly that they were as hard as concrete.

So we knew what we would have to do in an emergency, if we got the chance – out through the hatches, wait a couple of seconds to clear the aircraft, and then pull the ripcord handle. The ripcord was something not to be touched until you really needed to use it in earnest. We were all told during training that the parachute pack had to be carried by the carrying handle. Try to pick it up by the ripcord handle and you would find yourself knee-deep in parachute silk and rigging lines before you could say Hermann Goering. Accidentally releasing the parachute meant that it had to be repacked, which not only made you very unpopular with the parachute packers, but also cost you 2/6d (12½p) – half a day's wages when you were in training. We were all extremely careful not to touch that ripcord handle.

It took a Lancaster crew well under a minute to exit the aircraft in training – you just had to hope that would be long enough when the chips were down. Our training, of course, didn't extend to making an actual parachute jump. The first time you would do that was when your Lanc was heading towards the ground. I never did a parachute jump then and I haven't to this day. Les Munro, a 617 Squadron pilot and a lifelong friend, told me at a squadron reunion some years ago that he and his wife had both done parachute jumps, just for fun, at a time when they must have been OAPs. Jumping from a doomed Lanc is one thing, but jumping out of a perfectly good aeroplane just for the hell of it sounds a bit crazy to me – and just the sort of thing that Les would love!

If you got your 2/6d worth and the parachute deployed correctly, you then had only to survive the landing unscathed to be able to congratulate yourself on being lost in the dark in a country whose people you had just bombed, so they would love to get their hands on you. We were trained on what we should try to do next – escape and evasion. Before we went off on an op, when we were being issued with our kit, we would be given a survival pack that contained, amongst other things, silk maps, a compass and Horlicks tablets. We were also given boiled sweets. I used to save them for Gwyn. Sweets were one of the first things that were rationed at the beginning of the war.

One night when there were no ops on, a group of us were taken out into the countryside by truck, having been told that we were taking part in an escape and evasion exercise. The idea of this particular exercise was to give us some idea of what we should do if we crash-landed in enemy territory and were being hunted by the Germans. Our survival would depend on which country we were in, what reaction we might get from the local populace (some might want to help you, some might want to lynch you), how close we were to German troops when we landed … and our own ingenuity. The fact that we would be wearing battledress and flying overalls didn't seem to matter. We actually had flying boots that were designed so that the legs could be cut off with a penknife (also issued to us), making them look like shoes – as if that would really have made much difference! Anyway, we were taken from Woodhall Spa, dropped off in the middle of nowhere in the middle of the night and told to find our own way back. I have to admit that we didn't take it very seriously, but the local Home Guard, police and security people were very keen. It really was like something out of *Dad's Army*.

Having been set down on my own, I found a railway line almost straight away and started walking along it. This was apparently completely against the rules. I don't really know why. Maybe it was because, in a real escape situation, the German railway lines would be guarded and I would be likely to be caught immediately. My railway line, however, wasn't being patrolled at all and I soon came across a signal box with a signalman inside. I walked in and asked him where I was. He was very friendly, didn't threaten to lynch me or anything like that, and warned me that, 'They're crawling all over the place looking for you lot.' He told me exactly where we were in relation to the airfield. All I had to do was skip across a few fields back to Woodhall village. There I met up with a kindly WAAF driver who was enjoying herself by circling around looking for our blokes and taking them back to their billets. We fugitive aircrew were soon tucked up all warm and cosy while the 'defence team' spent the entire night charging around the countryside looking for us.

Things would be very different if we were ever to find ourselves being hunted in the countryside for real. We carried no weapons and were basically told to put up no resistance if we were caught. Then it would simply be a case of name, rank and number … and hope for the best. Some crew members who were forced to bail out of their Lanc did manage to contact resistance groups and were smuggled home, but most of those who survived the jump were captured and ended up as POWs.

You can understand why, then, I would never allow myself to think about Chuck-Chuck being shot down, even if such a thought should try to surface. The truth is, the idea of not making it back home never really entered my head. We were not going to be shot down. That was something that happened to other crews, not to us. Not with Joe in charge. So we hammered on through the dark, heading for the coast, Joe calmly receiving course corrections from Don as he worked on his charts at his desk behind his blackout curtain. Because he had to see what he was doing at his map desk, Don's station could be curtained off so that he was able to switch on a light. Without the curtain, the light would affect Joe's and Bill's night vision, but would also shine out into the night through the cockpit greenhouse, giving away our position.

While Don kept an eye on our course, Len listened out for messages from home warning of any pitfalls we might encounter on the return leg, and the rest of us watched the sky. In the summer months, especially if it had been a long trip, the sky in the east would now be tinged with the soft silver of the coming dawn. We didn't want to be caught over Europe or crossing the coast when it was getting light. The darkness was our friend. We had to press on as fast as we could.

Joe gained a little altitude as we neared the coast, squeezing more power out of the engines, their constant thrum rising a tone or two. The coastal batteries knew that returning bombers were on their way and were always prepared to lay on a spectacular send-off. With plenty of height to spare, Joe could put Chuck-Chuck into a dive when we approached the coast, picking up speed in order to leave the flash of the guns and the thunder of the exploding shells far behind as quickly as possible. 'Coming up on the coast now, Skipper,' came Don's voice, and there in the distance I might just be able to pick out the phosphorescent glow of waves breaking on a cold, deserted beach.

Joe tilted Chuck-Chuck's nose towards the sea, and the rush of the outside air whipping over the aircraft's metal skin became a moaning wail as we accelerated in a shallow dive. It was likely that there would be a twinkling of flashes from the shore batteries far below, sending us a few parting gifts, but it was too little, too late. We were out over the sea.

This was the last leg of the journey. We were almost there ...

Little did we know at the time, but the entire nature of our bombing trips was about to change dramatically. In March 1943, Wg Cdr Guy Gibson, unarguably one of the best of the best in Bomber Command, was asked to form a special squadron, Squadron X, for one trip. This was to be a vitally important raid that would have a major impact on the Germans' ability to wage war and that could help bring the whole conflict to a swift conclusion. The popular story is that Gibson was given free rein to choose his own crews. This is not entirely true, but he certainly handpicked several of the crews and one of the pilots he approached was Joe McCarthy. Gibson knew Joe, of course, and between them they had at one time tried every ruse they could think of to have Joe transferred to 106 Squadron. Joe obviously had wanted to be with Don Curtin, and Gibson would have been very keen to have a pilot of Joe's ability. They never managed to make the transfer happen, but now Joe, along with a handful of 106 Squadron crews, was top of Gibson's list for Squadron X.

The way Joe put it was that he listened to what little Gibson could tell him about the new squadron and said he was in favour but that he would have to discuss it with us – his crew. Gibson had been given the task of forming the new squadron on 18 March, and, knowing the way that he never liked to let the grass grow under his feet, he would have got on with it straight away. It was, after all, a rush job and he had 22 crews to pull together. Gibson's chat with Joe, therefore, would have come when we had just one operation left to fly before our tours were up – the thirtieth mission. We couldn't simply be transferred into the new squadron; we would have to volunteer. RAF aircrew were all volunteers, but asking a volunteer who has survived the stress and trauma of a full operational tour to volunteer yet again isn't something anyone would do lightly. Joe got us all together and explained that he had no idea what the mission was but that he was clear that it was one trip only. That was all. We agreed to go with him.

I, however, had one significant problem. As I was coming to the end of the tour, I had told Gwyn that I could take a week's leave and that I would then perhaps go on to six months of ground duty, all of which was pretty much standard procedure. Accordingly, we had decided that 3 April would be our wedding day. We were to be married in Torquay. Gwyn, still serving as a WAAF, had arranged her leave and was working out all of the wedding arrangements with her family. I wrote to her and said, 'We are joining this new squadron, but it's only for one trip. Don't worry, I will be there on the third.' The only response I got was: 'Well, if you are not there on the third, don't bother to contact me again.' At least I knew where I stood, and I wasn't at all worried about missing my own wedding day ... yet.

Since the beginning of 1943, we had been to Germany many times, flying deep into the heart of the country to bomb Berlin, Munich, Nuremberg and Stuttgart, as well as a handful of other targets. We had been to Turin in Italy and had bombed the French port of Saint-Nazaire. The city of Saint-Nazaire had been firebombed and levelled early in the year, with leaflets having been dropped prior to the three-day bombing campaign, advising the population to evacuate as their town was to be destroyed. Saint-Nazaire was important because it was a major port and home to one of the largest of the Kriegsmarine's U-boat bases. The docks and the U-boat pens were our main targets as the submarines operating from this base, on the Bay of Biscay, had direct access to the North

Atlantic shipping lanes. Unfortunately, the roof of the U-boat pens consisted of between 25 and 30 feet of steel, granite and reinforced concrete and the numerous raids that were launched against them failed. They are still there today. The city had to be completely rebuilt after the war. Our final op with 97 Squadron was to attack the docks at Saint-Nazaire on the night of 22/23 March.

We left Woodhall Spa at 10 minutes past seven in the evening and bombed the docks through scattered cloud from 11,500 feet. We had bright moonlight that night – not our favourite thing for a bombing raid – but were back in the UK before midnight after what the records describe as an 'Uneventful trip'. We landed, probably due to fog, away from home but flew back to base the following morning. During the course of the next week, we received our postings and were packed onto a transport flight for the short hop north to Scampton, on the other side of Lincoln, officially joining the ranks of 617 Squadron. No sooner had we arrived than I heard the news that made my heart sink.

I was in seriously big trouble. This was close to 'panic stations'. Orders had been issued at Scampton stating that all leave was cancelled. My first thought was: Oh, my God! I've had it! Gwyn will never speak to me again! I couldn't help but think of the 'don't bother to contact me again' message, and the only person I could now turn to was Joe. But he was way ahead of me. He got the crew together and marched us all up to Gibson's office. He saw us straight away, no doubt realising that a pilot with his entire crew knocking on his door meant that something pretty serious was up. Joe laid it on the line.

'The thing is, sir,' he said, very forcibly, 'we've all just finished our tour and we are all entitled to a week's leave. My bomb aimer is due to be married on the third of April and let me tell you he *is* going to get married on the third of April!'

There was a short pause while the others, no doubt, wished that they were anywhere else except standing in the office of Wg Cdr Guy Gibson DSO, DFC and Bar, who had a fearsome reputation as a strict disciplinarian and had been known by the crews of 106 Squadron as 'The Arch-Bastard'.

He looked us up and down and said, 'Very well. You can have four days. Dismissed.'

Thank you, Joe! I left for Torquay immediately, before our new CO could change his mind.

Why was it that everything in this relationship was so difficult? There are always a few hiccups that crop up in the run-up to a wedding, and if you mix in the fact that both the bride and the groom are serving in different military units when there's a war going on, then you can expect a few more. Nothing, however, could have prepared us for the bombshell dropped by the choirboy. The day before the wedding, a local choirboy arrived at Gwyn's family home in Torquay with a letter from the vicar that basically said: 'The bishop has decreed that unless you can produce evidence that the bride's father is agreeable to this wedding we cannot go ahead.' Gwyn was only 18. In those days, if the bride was under 21 she needed not merely her parents' permission to marry, but specifically her father's permission. It wasn't just a polite custom, 'asking the bride's father', as it is nowadays; it was a legal requirement. We all knew that Bill Morgan was very happy about his daughter having got together with me. We all knew that he was happy about us having become engaged. But at that precise moment, he was somewhere in the deserts of North Africa, serving with the 8th Army and helping Monty put an end to Rommel's capers in Tunisia. There was no way that we could contact him, not within 24 hours.

That really took the wind out of our sails, but not Nell's. Gwyn's mother was not about to let anything spoil her daughter's wedding. It was bad enough that there was a war on and Bill couldn't be there, but there was no way she was going to tolerate a simple administrative slip-up. She racked her brains for a solution, then scurried around collecting together all of Bill's letters from North Africa, poring over them for anything that might help and, lo and behold, there it was. In one letter, while discussing family matters, Bill told Nell that, should Gwyn's relationship with me continue, he would be pleased to see us getting married one day. It was a shame that, in the event, he was to miss Gwyn's 'big day', but those few words were all the evidence that Nell needed to prove that he agreed to the wedding. The letter was taken to the vicar, the contents conveyed to the bishop, and we were back on course!

The wedding itself was fantastic. Gwyn looked gorgeous. She wore a wedding dress borrowed from one of her friends. Rationing meant that, even if we could have afforded a wedding dress, the clothing coupons needed for one would have been very difficult to come by, but the dress was altered to fit perfectly. The only thing that she had to buy was a veil. The reception was back at the house. The only representative from my family was my sister, Lena. I don't remember any cards or presents from any of my family, except for a very large ham that my father had sent down (presumably with Lena). It was so big that it couldn't be cooked in any normal pot. Nell boiled it in the copper boiler that they used for washing clothes.

The reception was mayhem. For me, the shy lad from Lincolnshire, to be (almost) the centre of attention at a loud and happy party in a small house would at one time have been unbearable, but this was Gwyn's family – my new family – and with Gwyn on my arm I felt like I could do anything. Women were bustling about 'doing things' and men were enjoying a drink, something that was still a bit of an issue for me. That was all to change in the very near future as I came to love being part of the Morgan family more and more and also began to join in the 'mess culture' with my RAF friends. On my wedding day, however, I was still very much a non-drinker, although I did take a small sip from a glass of port to toast the bridesmaids. We had a real wedding cake – again something that was difficult to come by with wartime rationing. The cake was created by a friend who worked for a bakery and had been secreting ingredients during the build-up to the big day. She made a terrific fruit cake, properly iced. This was a great example of how people would muck in and help each other in those difficult times.

We had no time for a honeymoon, of course, and just spent a day floating around Torquay. Our first day as a married couple. On the Monday morning, we had to head back. We were going to different RAF stations and we had £1 between us. We took ten shillings each – we had travel warrants but just the ten bob each. It doesn't sound like much, but we weren't worried about money then. Payday would come round pretty soon. It was a very strange way to start married life. One of the rules at the time was that married couples, if they were both in the service, were not allowed to be posted to the same station. Maybe they thought that could cause discipline problems or that, in the event of an attack, a husband and wife could both be killed and their children orphaned. Whatever the reason, we managed to get round it to an extent by wangling a compassionate posting for Gwyn to a satellite station called Ingham, which was right next door to Scampton.

We saw each other when we could but by then 617 Squadron was in training for the special operation and security was very tight. You had to be very careful with telephone calls, which were monitored, and letters were censored. Having Gwyn next door didn't last long, though. A signals officer from Hemswell was working with her one day and simply said, 'You are too good for this small base. We need you at Hemswell.' She was transferred straight away and, while it is nice to be appreciated for being good at your job, Hemswell was eight miles from Scampton. I have no idea how many times I made that trip, either on foot or on a 'borrowed' RAF bicycle. I vividly remember on one occasion cycling back at night when the chain broke. It was pouring with rain, so I spent the night in a telephone box before walking back to camp at first light.

The Hemswell jaunts happened whenever I could get away from Scampton, although we were certainly being put through our paces there. The training was intense once it started, but to begin with we didn't have enough of anything, not even chairs for the briefing room. We definitely didn't have enough aircraft, which is probably why Gibson gave us the four days off – he didn't have a Lancaster to put us in. The Lancs that we did have often weren't up to much. Other squadrons had been ordered to donate aircraft with which we could train and, naturally, they didn't send us their newest and best machines.

The aircrew, however, were something else. I remember that

we were all seriously impressed with the number of hugely experienced crews we met as 617's personnel began to assemble at Scampton. Plenty of them had finished at least one tour and some were well into their second. Many of them seemed to be decorated – there were a lot of serious medal ribbons on show. We regarded ourselves as a well-proven crew, of course, but we were more than a little curious about why they needed quite so much experience in the squadron. We knew it was a special outfit for just one trip, but, just judging by the quality of the crews that were around us, this was obviously going to be something really out of the ordinary.

All of us knew a bit about Guy Gibson and his reputation. His operational record was truly impressive with over 40 missions flying Hampdens, 99 as a Beaufighter pilot and a full tour on Manchesters and Lancs – and the rumour was that he hadn't bothered recording absolutely every trip he'd been on. He was clearly an outstanding pilot but he was also a stickler for discipline and the etiquette of the service. He demanded discipline in the air as well as on the base, where he expected to see saluting and to hear superior officers being addressed as 'sir' or by rank. His attitude hadn't gone down too well with the aircrews at 106. I think that when he came to 617 he knew that he had to achieve a great deal in a short time and, like the rest of us, he believed that we would be together for just one trip, so he calmed down a bit.

He was very demanding when it came to something that he needed for the squadron. He would ring Group or Bomber Command as necessary and, if they said, 'We are sorry, we can't do that,' he would say, 'Well, if that's the case I shall need to stay in my office until you change your mind.' There could be no special op without Gibson – there wasn't time to replace him – so he usually got his own way. They came through with whatever he wanted.

He wasn't a big man – only about 5 feet 6 inches – but he was bombastic and arrogant. Those are not qualities that I admire, but, in the spring of 1943, Guy Gibson was one of the best and most experienced pilots in the RAF. And he was still only 24 years old. I think that anyone who had achieved what he had, anyone with that record, had earned the right to be arrogant. He was also very brave and a leader by example, as he later showed over the Mohne when drawing the enemy's flak while other crews were making their attacks.

He certainly believed in remaining somewhat distant from his men. He worked through his officers, and they dwelt on his every word. He had little time for NCOs and no time at all for other ranks. I found that strange because three of his pilots were Flight Sergeants and these were the men he had to mould into a highly co-ordinated, effective team. The ground crews were part of that team – a vital part – and they certainly deserved far more respect than Gibson afforded them. These men were transferred in from all over 5 Group and the man in charge of them was Flt Sgt G. E. Powell, known to us all as 'Chiefy' Powell. Chiefy quickly weeded out the ne'er-do-wells that he felt other squadrons, having been asked to supply personnel, had offloaded on 617. He made sure that the ground crews we had were the best available, not something that I should think Guy Gibson fully appreciated.

Typical of Gibson's behaviour was when he called in Dave Shannon's bomb aimer, Len Sumpter, a Flight Sergeant, and tore into him for dropping a practice bomb some way short of the target. That was the only time he ever talked to Sumpter. He certainly never spoke directly to me. Gibson was a long way from the charming, sensitive Richard Todd portrayal in *The Dam Busters* film. At the opening ceremony for the Bomber Command Memorial in 2012, I was seated next to one of Gibson's distant family relatives. If Gibson was not the most popular of commanding officers, she was quite clear that he was not much liked within the family either. Despite that, he was an absolute inspiration for 617 and is rightly credited for the enormous part he played in making the raid such a success. That, after all, is what he was there for – not to win any kind of popularity contest.

I am often asked about the 'squadron spirit' at 617. For all his qualities as a leader, I don't think that Gibson managed to instil in us any kind of 'squadron spirit' in the beginning. The squadron certainly has that now, with many years of distinguished service behind it, but we were brand new then, and we were going to be together for only a short time. We were a scratch team. Normally there was always the squadron element. You identified yourself as being part of a squadron, but in the sense of a 'squadron spirit', a pride in the squadron such as you would have as a player in a football or cricket team, that was really only manifest in the pilots. There was an element of that with the captains and Gibson, but it didn't really go lower than that. We were not particularly close to the other crews at first, and during training, even during operations, we were focused on our own crew. We didn't have much time to spend socialising in the mess. I didn't drink in those days so the only times I would go to the Sergeants' Mess were to eat and to pick up my cigarette ration. Basically, it was all about us, as a crew. It may sound a bit isolationist but that's the way it was. We wanted to get through the special op and then expected to move on.

At Scampton I was billeted in married quarters, the houses that would have been occupied by a couple or a family having been given over to aircrew, who shared rooms. I shared with Ron Batson. I had shared with Ron before, at Woodhall Spa, where we were in barracks huts that were sectioned off into small rooms, and I felt that we had become firm friends. He was a little like me, not really a big conversationalist, but we chatted about this and that. Obviously we had a few things in common with us both having trained as gunners, and we both had sweethearts to think about (although by this time I had married mine) – Ron had taken up with the daughter of a local butcher. Ron wasn't a great socialiser but we did spend quite a bit of time together. I remember he always had his own toilet paper – not a bad thing as it could often be in short supply – so you always knew where he was going when he wandered off carrying a newspaper and a bog roll! Apart from Joe, Ron was the crewmate I was closest to.

People have asked me, 'What makes a crew work well together?' My best response is, of course, competence in doing what you were asked to do, and the determination to do it well. But there was more to it than that. I think three words sum it up: loyalty, respect and discipline. Loyalty and respect not just in relation to your country but to each other. We needed each other and we needed to be a strong team in order to survive, each trusting the others to do their bit as well as they could. Respect in the sense of acknowledging what others could bring to the party and being grateful for it. Discipline in that you had accepted personal responsibility for doing a particular job, and doing that job to the very best of your ability, which took concentration and total commitment. There was no room for complacency or shortcuts. It was all about mutual trust. If that went wrong, and in some crews it did, only trouble lay ahead. Our crew, with the exception of Don, had been together on 20 raids by now and we knew what we were doing.

That doesn't mean to say that we were all goody two-shoes. I may not have been a drinker, but some of the others were certainly very good at letting their hair down. I don't think that any of our crew were wild party animals, though. Joe liked a drink and he was a big lad, so he could put away quite a bit. One of the gunners when we were at Woodhall Spa decided to take him on in a drinking contest. It was a day when we had no ops and no flying. They started with a quick bout at lunchtime and then had a kip in the afternoon. When the bar opened again at 6.30 pm, they were back at it. Joe carried the gunner off to bed at about 9.00 pm. If he'd had a few the night before, Joe liked to take Chuck-Chuck up for an air test the following morning to blow the cobwebs away and make sure that he was on top form for that night's op.

Don MacLean was not, perhaps, the easiest person to make friends with, and that may well have been a character trait that he also extended to the fair sex. One of the WAAFs at Hemswell said to Gwyn one evening, 'Gwyn, isn't Don MacLean the navigator on your husband's crew?'

'Yes,' Gwyn replied, 'he is. Why do you ask?'

'Because,' said the WAAF, giving Gwyn a certain look, 'he's like a bull in a china shop!'

It would seem that Don's approach had not been overly subtle, which probably sums him up pretty well.

If there were ever any problems within the crew, Joe was the one to sort them out. There were very few times when disagreements arose, but he always resolved them quickly.

There was no point in dragging out an argument or letting any wounds fester – we relied on each other too much for that. By and large, we all got on very well and it showed in the way we went about our task. When the special ops training started in earnest, we were more than ready for it.

The first training flight was on 9 April and from then on the activity was relentless. All we knew was that the coming attack was to be at low level. Very low level. We were training to fly at 100 feet, not just on the approach to the target but for long periods of time. We flew during the day to begin with, and I loved every second of it. We started off as low as 300 feet, then we were down to 200 feet, then 100 feet. For an aircraft the size of a Lancaster, we thought 100 feet was incredibly low – 100 feet is less than the wingspan of the Lanc. Then we were told that we had to go lower, that we would be bombing from just 60 feet. Not all of us were entirely happy about this. We were used to being up at 10,000 feet, maybe 15,000, where you could see nothing but clouds below you until you got over the target. Being so close to the ground wasn't everybody's cup of tea, but I found it absolutely thrilling. It was dangerous and required great skill from the pilot. At 10,000 feet you can bank into a turn and afford to lose a few feet while you're doing so. If you do that at 60 feet you might well bury a wing tip into the ground or into a tree trunk, and then we would all have had it. I had no worries about Joe doing anything like that, so I could simply enjoy that immense feeling of speed. This was like the best part of take-off, but faster, at twice the speed, and for hours on end. I would see something coming in the distance and then we'd be over it in a flash. If I looked straight down, it was all a bit of a blur. The ground was just whooshing past. It was all very exhilarating. From his seat in the tail, Dave Rodger complained that there was no time to see what was coming until it had gone!

The training flights started off during the day but we would soon be flying low at night as well. The transition from day to night flying was handled by simulating darkness. The Perspex in the cockpit and in my office was covered with blue film. We then wore tinted glasses that were a yellowish-brown colour. We only ever had a couple of Lancs that were adapted with the tinted windows, so the crews had to take turns using these aircraft. When you disembarked into bright daylight and took off the glasses, it was pretty harsh on your eyes and some took to wearing sunglasses until they got used to the glare.

We had day after day of low-level flying on trips where it was specified that the flight time should not be less than three hours. Usually it was four or five hours. Sometimes we were up twice a day. My job changed quite a bit. I was no longer acting as a gunner but was helping out with navigation en route to the target. I had to spot landmarks and call them out to Joe and Don, sitting in my office with a map identical to the one Don was using. Some of the navigators liked to have their route on a long strip of map between two rollers so that they could unroll the map, following their course as they went along, but Don didn't agree with that. He liked to have the full map so that he could see where we were if, for some reason, we should stray off course. If you strayed off course on a thin strip of map you might not be able to find your way back onto the strip again.

Our routes would take us all over England, locating checkpoints to make sure our navigation was spot on, before ending up at the Wainfleet bombing range in the Wash, off the coast of Lincolnshire, for a low-level bombing run. We would take off from Scampton, fly to Shrewsbury, then Bromyard–Haslemere–Malmesbury–Wainfleet, straight into a low-level bombing attack, then home. We bombed using 25lb smoke bombs. We hadn't a clue as yet what type of payload we would be carrying on the actual op, or even what the target would be. Between 9 April and 15 May, we flew 27 different training flights.

It was full-on, flat-out training. Hedge-hopping our way across the country in a way that would previously have landed us in serious hot water. Low flying and 'buzzing' villages in a Lancaster were things that seriously upset the locals. They were the sorts of thing that crews would do and then scarper before anyone could take a note of their aircraft's number. What we were doing had once been taboo, but now we were being ordered to do it! Farmers complained that their cows were being put off their milk by the low-level bombers; there were stories of parade grounds on far-flung airfields being left in turmoil when we flew over; and we had real fun near the village of Sutton Bridge, not far north of Wisbech in Lincolnshire. There's an old swing bridge over the canal there but before you reached it there were electric power cables strung across the route. The challenge was to fly under the cables and then pull up to clear the bridge. That was great. It wasn't scheduled but everyone did it. It was a great buzz. We were young and I suppose a bit stupid.

One of the things that did concern me, having come from a farming background, was when we flew one of the routes that took us over the Spalding tulip fields. As we went over, the poor old tulips were just flattened. The slipstream and prop wash just blew them over, breaking the stalks. It must have cost a lot to compensate the growers for their crops. I hope they got their money.

Then, on one trip, we were on our way home from Wainfleet, barrelling along at, as I recall, not much more than 60 feet (it might have been a little higher but certainly not over 100) when I got the shock of my life as another Lanc flew underneath us! I was close enough to see their tail gunner waving. Joe was livid, yelling over the intercom, 'Jesus Christ! Who was that bloody idiot?' Leave aside the fact that one slip from him might have meant that we collided, being caught in his prop wash set up turbulence that Joe really didn't want at such a low altitude. I'm sure that Dave must have seen him coming, but if he did he kept quiet. Knowing him, he'd have thought it was a bit of a laugh. Joe certainly didn't see the funny side and wanted to know who the nutcase was that had flown underneath him. It was Les Munro. He denied it at first, probably because he could see that Joe was far from happy about it, but later admitted, 'It might have been me.'

Once we had got used to bombing from such a low level, it was explained to us that on the actual op we would have to drop the bombs a precise distance from the target at an exact height. To help us get the distance right, we had to make our own special bombsights by creating a triangle from plywood, with sides of a certain length and a nail sticking up from each of the two corners at the base. We were told that there would be markers on the target, and if we held our bombsight level and looked with one eye, when the nails were on the markers we would be at the correct distance from the target. So we set to work and made our own bombsights. After a while, some of the bomb aimers abandoned their triangular wooden sights and instead marked vertical lines on the Perspex nose

The New Recruit.
Johnny aged 19.

Johnny's Parents.
Charles Johnson and Ellen Johnson in 1901.

Sister Lena and Brother Bill in 1917.

A Farmer's Boy.
Johnny aged eight in Langford.

Early Salvation.
Lena in the early 1940s.

Schoolmates.
Lord Wandsworth College, 1939.

Newly Promoted Sergeant.
Johnny and Hamid, post Air Gunnery School in spring 1942.

The Happy Couple.
Johnny and Gwyn's Wedding Day (Lena far left and Nell far right).

The Morgan Family.
From left: Eunice, Nell, Johnny, Gwyn, David, John.

Chuck-Chuck Nose Art.

Joe McCarthy sitting in
the pilot seat.

The Team.
Q-Queenie crew and ground crew, April 1943.

Marbles on the Terrace.
Barnes Wallis and family in early bouncing bomb experiments, April 1942.

The Canadians.
From left: Dave Rodger,
Don MacLean, Joe
McCarthy, Bill Ratcliffe,
April 1943.

The Crew.
From Left: Johnny Johnson,
Dave Rodger, Len Eaton,
Don MacLean, Joe
McCarthy, Bill Ratcliffe and
Ron Batson, April 1943.

Reculver Trials.
Guy Gibson low-level bombing trials, May 1943.

Upkeep Intact.
The bomb failed to explode after AJ-E crashed in Germany, 16 May 1943.

'The American Dambuster' by Mark Postlethwaite.
T-Tommy 30 feet over the Sorpe dam on the tenth attempt.

Fond Memories.
Johnny with a Lancaster, East Kirby, 2008.

Proud Father and Son.
School athletics champion,
Singapore, 1959.

Fancy Dress.
A party at the Officers' Club,
RAF Changi, 1959.

Avro Shackleton MK1.
A similar aircraft to VP 254 B, which crashed into the South China Sea
in early December 1958.

Back to the Office.
East Kirby, 2010.

The Last Supper.
Gwyn, Johnny, Jean and Pip Mounfield at the Raffles Hotel, Singapore,
the night before departure.

Family Celebration.
Gwyn, Johnny, children, partners and grandchildren celebrating their fiftieth
wedding anniversary, Bristol, 1993.

Old Man and New Stars.
Johnny and The Red Arrows, RIAT Fairford, summer 2008.

Lap of Honour.
Johnny at the Goodwood Revival, September 2013.

Old Friends.
Johnny and Mary Stopes-Roe, Kinema in the Woods, Woodhall Spa, May 2008.

Old Comrades.
Johnny and Les Munro, a fellow Dambuster, at the RAF Scampton Ceremony,
May 2008.

The Johnson Family Leader.

cone, with strings of a set length running from the lines back to their eye. They then aligned the marks on the Perspex with the posts at either side of the target, claiming that they could hold that arrangement steadier than the wooden version. It was accepted that this method was perfectly valid.

We were also told that we would have to fly at precisely 60 feet (to begin with we were told 100 feet) at a set speed, later confirmed as 220mph. Our regular altimeters couldn't cope with giving us an accurate indication of 60 feet, and finding a way of maintaining that height at night over water was a real problem. The story in *The Dam Busters* film has it that Guy Gibson was at a show in London and saw the spotlights coming together on the chorus line on stage, inspiring him to suggest using a spotlight system on our Lancs. That was total bulls***. It was an Air Ministry boffin called Lockspeiser who designated the positions on the aircraft to fit the two Aldis lamps, which would shine downwards and converge at exactly 60 feet. The lamps were switched on by the flight engineer.

So now it was just down to practice. It was very much a team effort. The navigator was looking through the side panel and saying up or down, depending on whether or not the lights were converging. The flight engineer was watching the speed very carefully and the bomb aimer was giving instructions – right or left – to keep the aircraft on the correct approach. The gunners were keeping a sharp lookout (and would be heavily engaged over the Mohne dam), and the pilot was assimilating all the incoming information. Three different people talking to him at the same time. The lining up was the thing we concentrated on most. It was easier to adjust the speed and the height, but the approach had to be spot on. We practised this day after day, night after night. They had constructed a couple of poles on the bombing range at Wainfleet to represent the marker features that we were told would be at the target. On the approach at Wainfleet, I would have my triangular bombsight to my eye, lining up with the poles, and would be calling out, 'Left, left … Right …' and then eventually, 'Bombs gone!' The whole squadron was doing the same thing. Not all at the same time, and not all on the same route. The other major practice areas were the Derwent dam, the dam at Uppingham Lake, which was the codename for Eyebrook Reservoir, and Colchester Lake, which was the Abberton Reservoir.

We were all baffled about what the big op was going to be, especially when the modified Lancs began to arrive. The first one came at the end of the first week in April and it caused quite a stir. My initial reaction was: 'My God, do these things actually fly?' The first thing you noticed was that it looked like it had had its guts ripped out. There was no bomb bay, just two strange prongs poking down. And there was no mid-upper turret. The deflection fairing that prevented overenthusiastic mid-upper gunners from shooting off the tail, drilling an engine or blasting the cockpit was also gone, leaving these Lancs with a completely straight back from the astrodome at the rear of the cockpit all the way to the rear turret. Ron would be flying in the front turret, with me confined to the bomb aimer's space. They had fitted special stirrups for him to rest his feet in so that he wasn't constantly kicking me in the back. As more of these strange Lancs arrived, we did more and more of our practice runs in them until finally we received our own, Q-Queenie, which was swiftly adorned with a version of Joe's Chuck-Chuck nose art.

There was a lot of talk about our training being aimed at attacking U-boat pens or battleships. Maybe we were going for the *Tirpitz* again. Practising bombing runs over water certainly made it clear that water was going to play a part in some way. And, of course, we still knew nothing about the weapon we were to be carrying. As I remember it, that was not revealed to all of us until the night before the raid, when Barnes Wallis showed us a film about his 'bouncing bomb' and explained how it worked. Some of the pilots had seen the bomb a few days earlier and some had even dropped dummies filled with concrete. The splash caused by one of those caught the underside of Ken Brown's Lanc, ripping off some of the fuselage panels.

At his film show briefing, Wallis was afforded the utmost respect by all of the crews. We knew that he was a designer and engineer of enormous talent and ingenuity. He had designed the Wellington bomber and, although we didn't know it at the time, he had also produced designs for a massive 'Victory Bomber' with six engines, capable of delivering a bomb weighing more than 22,000lb from an altitude of over 40,000 feet. His purpose in proposing such an aeroplane was to destroy the dams that were vital for supplying power to Germany's munitions factories, and to release water that would cause havoc in the industrial hinterland downstream. His presentation to the assembled crews, however, was solely about the development of the bouncing bomb. There was no mention of dams.

For over a year, he had been working on the idea of some kind of missile or mine that could ricochet across the water, avoiding the torpedo nets that protected the dams. The months of experiments, trial and error had finally culminated in the successful deployment of the bouncing bomb known as 'Upkeep' just two days before Wallis's presentation to us. There were, in fact, two versions of the bouncing bomb – Upkeep, to be used by 617 Squadron, and the smaller Highball bomb for the Royal Navy, which was intended to be used against large ships. It had taken a huge amount of persuasion and perseverance by Wallis to generate support for the project amongst the High Command, not least to convince Bomber Harris that he should release some of his precious 'shining sword' Lancs and their crews when he needed every aircraft he could get his hands on to pursue his onslaught against the German cities. In fact, I don't think Harris was ever really persuaded, just overruled by the Air Ministry. He was highly sceptical about the operation, and even when it was over he cast doubts over its effectiveness.

Wallis explained to us why the bomb had to be dropped from just 60 feet, why it had to be back-spun at exactly 500 revolutions per minute (rpm), and why it had to be dropped at a specific distance from the target. What the majority of us still did not know was what and where the target was. We were to find that out the following day, 16 May 1943, when we were finally briefed for Operation Chastise.

# CHAPTER 7

# SMOOTH LANDINGS AND THE DAMS RAID

'Pilot to crew. Dropping below 10,000. Off oxygen.' That was the message from Joe that we had all been waiting for. It was like a kind of code, really. Obviously, what he was saying was that we were now at an altitude where we didn't need to be breathing oxygen, so we could switch it off and unfasten our masks. As a code, however, what we took it to mean was 'Time for a smoke!'

Of course, it was strictly forbidden to smoke in the aircraft, but, after a long and stressful trip, a cigarette really hit the spot as we approached the English coast. In the summer, the sun might just be starting to rise and as we got closer I could see the fields of Lincolnshire far below. Nearly home.

After a raid, there was no need for radio silence. Scampton could talk to Joe direct, using VHF voice communication, not Morse code, letting him know what to expect over the airfield – early morning mist, haze or cross-winds. We were now appearing on British radar screens again and the operators on the ground could issue instructions, helping to guide us in or directing us into a holding circuit. We were now steadily descending and Bill was checking the fuel situation. If we had enough to keep us airborne, we would join the circuit over the airfield, waiting for our turn to land. If there were a few of us arriving at roughly the same time, damaged aircraft were given priority and those with wounded aboard were brought in first. Once he had permission to begin his approach, Joe scrubbed off some height in a long turn, and lined us up with the runway.

With the throttles eased back, the engine note calmed to a slightly less intense roar. Bill threw the lever on his left to lower the landing gear and checked the warning lights to make sure the wheels were locked in place. We were now doing 150mph, dropping to around 110mph as we made our approach to the airfield. Crossing the boundary of the field, the speed was dropping even more, but now that we were so much closer to the ground, it all looked like it was whipping past beneath us pretty fast. There was a brief, floating feeling when Chuck-Chuck's wings trapped a cushion of air beneath them just before the wheels touched at around 95mph. On grass, there would be a bump, possibly a little bounce if we touched down on a slight hump. On a hard runway, the tyres would complain a little more, giving a bit of a squeal and then rumbling away as they rolled over the concrete. The engines were now really throttled back, their roar dropping to a relieved growl, sounding happy to be given some rest after their hours of hard work. The tail settled down onto its wheel and we gently slowed to taxiing speed.

Coming home in the winter, things were very different. I didn't have much of a view of anything over blacked-out

England and would be peering out into the dark, looking for the airfield identification beacon. Len would pick up a radio signal that led us in towards the airfield, but it was the airfield beacon that told us we were home. The light blinked at us out of the blackness, signalling the airfield's Morse code identification letters – AL for Woodhall Spa. It was always good to get the right airfield and, without the beacon, not too difficult to mistake nearby Coningsby or Bardney for Woodhall Spa. Nobody wanted the embarrassment of trying to land in the wrong place without a very good reason. A flare path illuminated the runway, the flares burning at regular intervals either side of the landing strip. They didn't light up the runway, but merely showed Joe where it was. By the time we were really close and I could see patches of grass in the pools of light thrown out by the flares, we were almost on the ground. Landing in the dark, Joe had to feel his way down until the wheels touched. Some pilots were famous for their heavy landings, bouncing the 18-ton Lanc like they were landing it on pogo sticks. Joe had a far lighter touch and, when we came back in good shape, he always set us down without any drama.

In the dark, the biggest headache was the weather. While we had been away, the conditions might well have changed dramatically. Torrential rain could put a grass runway out of action, making it too soft to be used, but the biggest nightmare was fog. If our airfield was fogbound, we would have to be diverted elsewhere. If the fog was spread over a wide area, then that could mean some extra flying time. If they had the fuel, crews could be sent as far away as Scotland, where there was generally less of a fog problem, but we were normally pretty lucky in this respect and our diversions were closer to home.

The trouble with fog was that it didn't always stay in the same place. An aircraft could be diverted to a field that was clear, only to find that it was fogbound once they got there, and by that time the fuel situation could be getting very serious. Aircraft were lost, having survived the trip to Germany and back only to run out of fuel somewhere over England. Crews were told to point their aeroplanes (not always Lancs) towards the sea and bail out while they were still over land.

One of the solutions to the fog problem was FIDO – Fog Intensive Dispersal Operation. Certain airfields equipped with FIDO could take redirected traffic by clearing the fog from their runway. FIDO basically consisted of pipes that ran either side of the runway. The pipes had valves and burners at regular intervals so that, when fuel was pumped along the pipes, it exited the burners as a fine spray. A Jeep carrying a long burning torch was then driven down each side of the runway, igniting the fuel to create two long walls of flame bracketing the landing strip. The flames burned with an intense heat that dispersed the fog, although burning the fuel produced smoke, which caused its own visibility problems. A FIDO dispersal could use as much as 100,000 gallons of fuel – a costly operation in wartime Britain – and, once the fuel was gone, the fog could easily close in again. While it was working, however, the flames could be seen from miles away. It was an incredible sight, a bit like descending into the fires of hell – not a position any of us ever wanted to find ourselves in. Nevertheless, FIDO undoubtedly saved many aircraft and many lives.

Thanks to skill, professionalism and our great good luck, we weren't involved in too many dodgy landings, and while Joe taxied Chuck-Chuck to our dispersal area, I could feel the tension starting to drain away. We were back. We had made it ... again. With the aircraft parked, Joe and Bill shut down the engines and ran through their 'switch-off' procedures. Outside, I could see some familiar faces examining the outside of the Lanc. The ground crew were there, checking for any problems, any damage, any battle scars that would need to be repaired. They could see me clearly in my office. There was a nod or a wave or a quick thumbs up while I waited patiently for Bill to get up and fold away his seat. Then we made our way back through Chuck-Chuck's gloomy interior to the crew door.

Outside, standing near the tailplane, we lit up another fag while we waited for the crew transport. Dave and Ron stretched their arms and legs, having had the most cramped journey sitting in their turrets. I had more room than most, but there was still a bit of stiffness to be shaken out. We all swayed slightly, still feeling the movement of the aircraft in our bodies, and we all talked far too loudly. The engines were shut down, the noise was gone, but our heads were still full of it, our ears still drumming away to the beat of the four Merlins. Many Lancaster crew members, myself included, would end up with 'Lancaster ears', leading to hearing problems in later life. The engine noise that I loved so much was, after all, a din of industrial proportions and we had no real protection for our ears.

There was time for a few words with the ground crew before the transport arrived and our cigarettes were stomped out on the grass, joining the butts we'd trodden out earlier before boarding. We were now headed for the debriefing session, which, like the briefing we had attended before the trip, was usually quite routine. But there was one particular briefing that was anything but routine ...

When the call came over the airfield tannoy on 16 May 1943 for 'All 617 crews to the briefing room', there was a real sense of excitement amongst all of us heading for the two-storey building. Some say the call came around 6.00 pm. I remember it as being much earlier. No matter – it doesn't affect the way things actually happened one way or the other. The point was that now we were finally going to find out what all of this low-level training malarkey had been for. We were going to find out about the target. We knew what the weapon was all about, we knew that it was to be carried externally, and we knew that those strange prongs dangling down beneath the special Lancs were Upkeep's mountings, but what we all really wanted to know, after all the speculation, was where we were going.

The pilots and navigators had already had their briefings but had been sworn to secrecy. They said nothing to the rest of us. Security was incredibly tight. Wireless operators had also been informed about radio procedures and had spent the afternoon on a closed Morse buzzer circuit (not actually transmitting), practising sending the Morse messages they would need to transmit to let the Operations Room know which aircraft had dropped their bombs and whether they had been successful or not. I remember us crowding into the room and I remember thinking that this was the most high-powered briefing that I had ever attended. Barnes Wallis was there, Guy Gibson was there, Gp Cpt Whitworth (Scampton Station Commander) was there and Air Vice-Marshal Ralph Cochrane (Commander of 5 Group) was there.

The charts were on the wall but there were also models on tables, carefully crafted miniature replicas of hills, lakes, forests, buildings and dams. The models were of the Mohne and the Sorpe reservoirs (the Eder model hadn't been finished on time) and at last the penny dropped. We were to be attacking dams. That was what all the practice over reservoirs had been about. Barnes Wallis spoke first. He and Gibson were to do most of the talking, with Cochrane saying a few words at the end, and it was Wallis who explained why we were attacking the dams and why Upkeep was the weapon to do the job.

For years, even before the war began, strategic planners had recognised that attacking the German dams, especially the Ruhr dams, could have a devastating effect on the country's industrial capability. The water held in the reservoirs would burst through a badly damaged dam and unleash havoc on Germany's industrial hinterland, destroying power stations, sweeping away roads and bridges, rendering canals (an integral part of the country's transport network) useless, and flooding towns, factories and farmland. The problem was that hitting a dam with a bomb big enough to breach it was nigh on impossible. High explosives dropped from high altitude could not be targeted accurately enough and even a direct hit from a bomb landing on top of one of these massive structures would only put a dent in it. The damage would be repaired quickly. The dams needed to be hit below the waterline on the reservoir side for a bomb to have any real effect. Torpedoes might have done the trick if they had been powerful enough, but nets and booms protected the dams, preventing anything in the water from getting close.

This was where the bouncing bomb came in. When dropped from precisely the right height at exactly the right distance from the dam, it would skip across the obstacles in the reservoir, hit the dam and then roll down the face. Once it had sunk to a certain depth, the water pressure would trigger the detonators and it would go off like a depth charge. All of our training now made perfect sense. Wallis also explained why we had been put through such an intensive training programme. There had been no time for a long, drawn-out schedule either for the development of Upkeep or for us to practise because the dams had to be hit when they were full, the optimum time being mid- to late May. From the moment the raid – Operation Chastise – had been given the go-ahead, there had been just 12 weeks to finish designing and testing the bomb; to establish the spin speed, altitude for release, air speed and range; to build or adapt the special Lancs required to deliver the bomb; and to recruit and train crews capable of pulling it off. It had been a remarkable achievement to get to this point.

Guy Gibson took over the briefing to explain the attack plan. We were to be divided into three groups. One group of nine was to fly with Gibson to the Mohne and Eder, the second group of five was designated to the Sorpe, and the third group of five would act as reserves to be directed as required. We were allocated to the Sorpe and, when it was explained what the attack on this dam entailed, our assignment came as something of a disappointment. The Sorpe was a different kind of dam. Its construction meant that using the bombing technique for which we had trained simply wouldn't work. Rather than attacking at right angles to the dam and bouncing the bomb along the surface, we were going to have to fly along the top of the dam and drop the bomb as close to the middle as I could judge it. There would be no spinning and no bouncing, yet the Upkeep bomb was still the best weapon available to us. With an overall weight of 9,250lb, it was packed with 6,600lb of Torpex explosive. Torpex was far more powerful than the Amatol that was used in our giant cookie bombs.

So, we had to deliver our Upkeep with pinpoint accuracy, from very low level, never having practised this method at all. During his part of the briefing, I am convinced that I heard Barnes Wallis say that it would take six bombs to crack the Sorpe. If we managed that, the water pressure would do the rest, splitting the dam open.

The Sorpe group, our lot, was to take off first, just before 9.30 pm, with Joe flying the lead aircraft. We were called the 'Second Wave' but we would be leaving first because we had furthest to go. Flying individually, our route was to take us out over the North Sea until we hit the Dutch coast over Vlieland, one of the Frisian islands. We would then turn south-east and come in over the Ijsselmeer, a massive inland lake that had been part of the Zuiderzee until it was sealed off by a huge dam in the early 1930s. From there we would head on across Holland and into Germany. The dams were not as far away as Berlin, Nuremberg or Munich. As the crow flies, they weren't as far as the north of Scotland, but to get to the dams we had to skirt round the heavily defended German industrial heartland. We would rendezvous with the others near the target area, although the different groups were headed for distinctly different targets. The idea was that splitting us up would keep the Germans guessing about the intended targets and leave their fighters covering the wrong areas. Because we were a small force, they might even think that we were diversionary raiders and leave us alone, waiting for a main massed bomber group to appear. Our Second Wave comprised five aircraft piloted by Joe, Bob Barlow, Les Munro, Vernon Byers and Geoff Rice.

Gibson's 'First Wave' was to leave at 9.39 pm, taking off in formation, three at a time, and remaining in flights of three until they reached the target. We were, remember, taking off in good visibility – fading daylight – and there would be a good moon to help us with navigation. The First Wave was to fly south-east, cross the Wash then overfly Norfolk and Suffolk, leaving the English coast somewhere around Southwold. They would hit the Dutch coast at the Scheldt estuary and then head east. The five reserve aircraft, the 'Third Wave', were to leave just after midnight either to attack the primary targets of the Mohne, Eder and Sorpe, if they had not been breached, or to hit the secondary targets of the Lister, Ennepe and Diemel dams.

We needed the full moon to see where we were going and to see the targets clearly, but we would be flying very low to avoid being spotted and to try to avoid radar. The whole briefing took about an hour and a half, with Gibson doing most of the talking and Cochrane rounding things off by wishing us all luck. I think that our crew was to have far more than our share of luck that night.

I have always found it strange that the Sorpe was not given more attention in the planning. We now know that, with only four or five days to go, Wallis had severe misgivings about whether the method of attack that had been practised so assiduously would work against the Sorpe dam. Because of the earthen construction of the dam, he finally decided that the bouncing bomb would not be effective and Cochrane decided that it would need to be attacked in a different way. Why was it that this decision was made so late in the day? The specific construction issues of the Sorpe had been well known for some time and destroying this target would clearly have had a much more devastating effect on the German industrial complexes of the Ruhr than breaching the Eder dam.

It may well be that Wallis and the others were concentrating so hard on the bouncing bomb and getting it ready on time that not enough thought was given to the specific problems that the Sorpe would throw up. It also seems strange that the Sorpe crews were only briefed on the method of attack on the actual day of the raid. At first, I thought that 'the powers that be' had decided that this would be a simple attack and it was not necessary to have anything more than a cursory briefing session. It now transpires that they realised that the alternative form of attack wouldn't be quite as easy as they had thought. The Sorpe dam needed more experienced crews in the attack force and, the day before the raid, our crew and Les Munro's crew were transferred from the First Wave to the Second Wave. That may well have been our first stroke of luck, given the hot reception Gibson and his crews were given at the Mohne.

After the briefing, we had a meal of bacon and eggs, which was eaten in a far quieter atmosphere than usual. There was a complete ban on talking about the raid, although it was impossible to hide the fact from anyone not directly involved that something was up. Gwyn knew. One of her friends at Hemswell came off duty early and, when Gwyn asked why, she was told: 'We've all been stood down. Nobody's flying tonight from anywhere except Scampton. They're locked up tight. They must have a big do on.' Of course, I couldn't talk to Gwyn. No one could leave the base and no one could make any private phone calls. Gwyn said that she heard the aircraft taking off that night and that she heard them coming back in the early hours of the morning. She couldn't count them all out and count them all back, but she said she knew that I was safe. That was something in which we both always had unshakeable confidence. Neither of us ever thought for a moment that I wouldn't come back.

While we waited for the off, some of us just stooged around, killing time. Some went back to their rooms and wrote letters – the letters that would be passed on to loved ones if you didn't make it. I wrote many letters to Gwyn during the war, sometimes I was writing almost every day, but I never wrote one of those 'last letters'. There was never any point. As far as I was concerned, I'd be back at base in a few hours, so writing a special last letter was a waste of time. I know that Hoppy Hopgood wrote a letter that night. Later, as they made their way to their aircraft, he told Dave Shannon that, if he didn't come back, Dave should find the letter and destroy it. He might have written something about having misgivings about the raid and then decided that he didn't want it going to his family. He wouldn't have wanted them to think that he had set off feeling anything but entirely confident about the operation.

Once we were kitted up, we piled aboard the crew transports for the run out to the dispersal area. At this point, it all felt pretty much like a normal raid. Then we saw our special Lanc, Q-Queenie, sitting looking black and menacing on the grass with this strange bomb hanging underneath her like a giant oil drum. With a few minutes to go before take-off, a red flare went up and the first two waves started their engines to warm them up. We were to be first off, leading the Second Wave, but it soon became clear that we had a major problem. Glycol was leaking from the starboard outer engine and there was no time to fix it. Q-Queenie was going nowhere that night. Joe was furious. 'For Christ's sake!' he shouted. 'Everybody out and let's get over to the reserve before some other bugger does and we don't get to go!'

Earlier that day, another Lancaster, T-Tommy, had been delivered and made ready for the raid, including being 'bombed up'. It was the only reserve aircraft on standby for this raid. We all exited Q-Queenie in a big hurry, carrying everything that we would need and dashing towards a nearby truck that would rush us over to T-Tommy. Unfortunately, Joe got his parachute release caught as he clambered out and he was running to the truck with his chute billowing all around him. As a native New Yorker, Joe could call on a fair few choice turns of phrase when the need arose, and the air was turning blue by the time he clambered into the truck. I don't think any of the parachute packers ever had the nerve to ask him for the 2/6d.

When we got to T-Tommy, Don immediately reported that there were no compass cards on board. The compass card is an essential piece of kit for navigation purposes. A compass points to magnetic north but can be affected by the metal in the aircraft, causing it to deviate slightly. When the aircraft is being prepared by the ground crew, they will work out the exact amount by which the compass is out and a compass card will be marked up as a kind of calibration for the navigator to use to correct his calculations in flight. Because the bomb load can also have an effect, the ground crew has to prepare a second card once the payload is aboard. Each aircraft, therefore, needed two compass cards for each trip – one for the navigator to use when we were fully loaded on the outward journey, and one to use on the way home once the bombing run was over.

Joe rushed to the flight office in a state of high tension, where he was met by Chiefy Powell who scampered off to find the correct compass cards. When he came back with them, he noticed that Joe had no parachute and said that he would fetch him one. Still very 'hyper', Joe's response was that he didn't need a parachute and would go on without one. Chiefy Powell then had a quiet word with Joe, advising him that he needed to calm down, 'Otherwise you're going to make a complete pig's ear of this whole job.' A new parachute was duly delivered and Powell handed it to Joe, saying, 'Your parachute, sir,' in a tone that no NCO would normally dare use with an officer – as though, in fact, he were issuing an order. Joe took the parachute and, noticeably calmer, headed back to the aircraft. In the meantime, Dave Rodger had enlisted the help of the ground crew to make some minor alterations to his rear gun turret. This involved ripping out a large piece of Perspex to improve visibility, just the way that he wanted it.

While all this had been happening, everyone else had gone. Bob Barlow had taken off first at 9.28 pm, followed at one-minute intervals by Les Munro, Vernon Byers and Geoff Rice. Then the First Wave had gone, taking off in threes. The Lanc is a big aircraft, and it was quite a sight to see them go off three at a time, thundering down the runway in formation like Spitfires or Hurricanes. I'd never seen that done before, and never saw it done again. Quite why Gibson decided to do it that way that night I have no idea.

We eventually took off last (apart from the Third Wave reserve aircraft), just over half an hour late. Given everything that happened to those who went before us, the delay may well have been another instance where luck fell in our favour. The two waves of aircraft were supposed to cross the Dutch coast at the same time, although 120 miles apart. Our route was to take us north of the island of Texel, which was known to have ferocious flak defences. Unfortunately, depending on the state of the tides, Texel could look very much like Vlieland, which was less heavily defended and where we were aiming to make landfall. This was where the first disaster was to strike the Sorpe flight. It is thought that Bob Barlow's Lanc took some heavy flak crossing the coast. Other reports have it that they hit high-tension electricity cables. It may well be that they suffered a combination of the two. In any event, they came to grief near Haldern in Germany, at around midnight. The bomb did not explode on impact and the Germans were eventually able to work out what this new secret weapon was.

Les Munro also ran into trouble on the Dutch coast. The squadron records state that: 'Aircraft was hit by light flak at Vlieland on the way to the target, which put the intercom out of action and forced the aircraft to return with his load to base.' One of the crew said they were over Texel. Another said they were hit by a flak ship. Whatever happened, Munro's plane was severely damaged. There was no intercom between the crew and no way of communicating with other aircraft in the flight, let alone with base. The compass had been demolished and to all intents and purposes they were defenceless against night fighter attack. Munro decided that there was no point in continuing. They really had no option but to turn for home.

Following Munro was Vernon Byers. Squadron records rather grimly simply report: 'Missing without trace.' It is likely that Byers too was hit by flak off Texel. There is some suggestion that, having cleared the coast, Byers climbed to get a fix on his location before being hit and crashing into the sea. There were no survivors.

Geoff Rice was the fourth aircraft in the flight. He had successfully crossed the North Sea on course. Flying very low, he had to rise up to clear a sand dune then dropped down again. Moments later, his flight engineer noticed that the altimeter reading was zero, but before he could say anything there was a violent jolt and a horrendous crashing noise. In a remarkable piece of airmanship, Rice managed to pull up immediately but not before the plane was awash. He had struck the water with such force that the impact had ripped the bomb from its mountings, damaged the rear fuselage and deposited the contents of the Elsan, along with a flood of water from the Ijsselmeer, in the rear turret. Needless to say, his gunner was far from happy at having almost been drowned. With no bomb on board, there was no point in continuing and Rice returned to base.

This, however, was not the end of Rice's problems. Because of the damage to the aircraft, including to the tail wheel, which had been bent up inside the fuselage, Rice called for an emergency landing at Scampton and, with the crew in crash positions, he began his approach. As he did so, another Lancaster flew directly underneath him and proceeded to land. It was Munro. With no communications, he had no alternative but to go straight in without warning anyone. Later, both would have to explain themselves to Gibson, an interview that provided an interesting reflection on Gibson's management style. He is reported to have sympathised with Rice, saying that he himself nearly suffered the same fate. His comment to Munro was a curt: 'You must have been too high.' Les was not impressed, to say the least.

Of the five aircraft designated to attack the Sorpe, we were now the only one still operational, although we hadn't a clue about that at the time. We had made up a good deal of time but we were still running around 20 minutes behind schedule when we approached the Dutch coast. We had seen the sun set over England as we crossed the sea but we now had a good moon and, according to my map, we were bang on the aiming point. Having had four Lancasters come over in the last 25 minutes or so, the gunners in the flak batteries were on high alert and, even if they weren't able to see us coming, they must have been able to hear us. They would have recognised immediately the distinctive sound of the Merlin engines. They gave us a warm welcome, with Ron and Dave responding in kind, but we were so low that we were gone before the gunners on the ground could get a proper fix on us. There were two sand dunes on our track and Joe simply ducked down and flew straight between them. With that, and with a little help from some trees, we avoided the worst of the searchlights and flak. Joe remembers seeing night fighters above us at about 1,000 feet but they apparently did not notice the lone bomber scurrying inland at treetop height. Either that, or they simply weren't interested in coming down so low. At our height, they would have no room to manoeuvre, no room to alter their line of attack, making them ideal targets for Dave and Ron. They would not have known that we were missing our mid-upper turret and were therefore far less of a threat.

Guns and fighters were not so much my problem on the Sorpe trip. What I needed to concentrate on was spotting landmarks and calling them out for Don. Everything seemed to be hurtling towards us very fast, but it was amazing how much I could see. It was all shades and tones of grey, the moonlight draining almost all of the colour out of the landscape, but I could still make out canals, roads, churches, houses, trees. Everything that we needed to see.

Concentration was key and everyone was playing his part. Joe never took us above about 100 feet or below 200mph, with Bill coaxing every last morsel of performance out of the Merlins to try to make up time. Having warmed up the flak crews crossing the coast, Ron and Dave were now on the lookout for potential trouble. In the front turret, Ron was also keeping his eyes open for obstacles such as electricity pylons or cables. Don and I put all of our effort into keeping Joe on course while Len Eaton was trying to re-establish radio contact with base. He had lost communications shortly after take-off and Joe had told him not to note the correct time in his log book. In theory, losing the radio should have meant that we turned back.

Just south of Hamm, a city that we knew we had to avoid as its railway junctions and yards were a real flak nightmare, we were toddling along with a goods train running parallel to us. Ron asked Joe's permission to 'have a go' and Joe agreed. Ron opened up with his twin .303s. What we didn't know was that this was an armoured goods train with rather more than .303s on board. They started blasting back at us with a lot more firepower than we had banked on. Joe got the plane out of there but we knew we had been hit because we heard and felt the thump of the shell. Everything seemed fine and, wherever we had been hit, it wasn't affecting the performance of the aircraft, so we pressed on. What we didn't know was that the shell had passed right through the aircraft and had burst the starboard tyre, which was to give us a bit of a problem later. It also missed the starboard fuel tank by just a few inches. A direct hit would have been a disaster. Another example of luck playing its part?

Although it was misty on the way out, we did find the Sorpe. In the totally clear moonlight, it was an incredible sight. What we couldn't understand was why nobody else was there. We had made up enough time for us to have been able to see the others circling, taking turns to line up their bombing runs, but not only was no one else there, it was apparent that no one else had been there either. The dam was still completely unscathed. Why were none of the others there? The answer seemed horribly obvious, but there was no time to dwell on it. We still had a job to do.

Flying over the dam, what was abundantly clear was that our operational briefing had been a little short on detail. From the reservoir, the Sorpe dam looked about 700 yards wide and had hills rising sharply to around 1,000 feet on either side. High in the hills to the left (the west side) was the small village of Langscheid. The plan was to approach from the west, fly over the village and drop down to run along the length of the dam, lining up the port outer engine with the centre of the crest. I had to release the weapon at the centre point of the dam from about 30 feet and we would then pull up, turning to port to avoid the hills on the other side. The spotlights that we had rehearsed with were set to 60 feet and would have been no help whatsoever. T-Tommy, having been delivered to Scampton only that afternoon, hadn't been fitted with the lights in any case, due to a shortage of time. Joe really was flying by the seat of his pants and only he and I could judge where and when to drop the bomb.

The planners had considered this to be a relatively simple attack and we had consequently been given no chance to practise it. Anyway, practice would probably not have been able to take into account the problem of the church spire. In order to align T-Tommy with the dam, Joe had to take a route that had the spire slap bang in the way. In the end, he decided that it actually made quite a good aiming point for him. All he had to do was to come whistling in low over the top, a bit like buzzing Lincoln Cathedral. The good news was that there were no ground defences to contend with, so now all we had to do was deliver the Upkeep. Easier said than done. The plan was tricky.

Joe was going to have to fly the Lanc like a fighter aircraft. He had to line up this big, heavy, four-engined bomber with the church steeple, pass as low over it as he could and then dive several hundred feet at around 180mph, levelling off at 30 feet above the top of the dam. We would be racing along the top of the dam at only the height of the average house and I would have to bomb on an aiming point less than 350 yards from where we levelled out. From the time we started to dive, we would have little more than seven seconds to decide if we were lined up correctly. If the bomb fell over the open side of the dam, it would be useless. Joe would then have to pull up very rapidly and turn in time to avoid smashing into the hillside that was fast filling his windscreen. And, although we had good visibility, we were doing this at night.

Now, it was all down to Joe and me. Bill would be keeping an eye on his gauges; Dave and Ron would be looking out for fighters, which could be arriving at any moment. Surely someone in the village would have reported our presence by phone? Len and Don just had to keep their fingers crossed. Joe circled the Lanc over the reservoir and we came in over the village, thundering low over the church steeple and diving towards the dam. But we were not properly aligned and I called, 'Dummy run.' We pulled up, circled round and had another go with the same result. Nine times we came in and nine times we aborted the attack. It was bloody difficult getting down to 30 feet above the dam from that height, particularly with the steeple in the way. Getting down on exactly the right line was even more of a challenge. If Joe wasn't satisfied he just pulled up and left me to call 'dummy run'. You can imagine that I wasn't the most popular person in the plane at that point.

Sitting in the rear turret, Dave Rodger was getting the worst of all this. He could not see what was coming, but he could feel the aircraft diving, running level and then, without warning, pulling up sharply. Because he was furthest from the aircraft's centre of gravity, every movement was exaggerated for the rear gunner. In a tight turn, a steep dive or a harsh climb, Dave had to put up with a G-force that made his life very uncomfortable. It was hardly surprising after the sixth or seventh dummy run that we heard Dave's voice grumbling from the tail: 'Will somebody please get that bomb out of here!' Joe later said, 'I had a real easy target but I couldn't get down low enough to let the weapon go. The crew was getting upset and the bomb aimer was being cursed for not letting the damn thing go. He was going to put it right where he wanted to and later pictures showed he put it right in the centre.'

I realised that the crew morale was not good at this point but I also knew that we had to do it properly. We all wanted to drop the damn thing, but none of us had risked our lives to get here only to then make a total mess of it. It would simply never have even entered their minds to think: This is bloody silly – just drop it and we can go home. The bomb had to go where the bomb was supposed to go.

On our tenth run in, both Joe and I were satisfied that we were right on track. I pushed the button and called, 'Bomb gone!' And from the rear turret was heard, 'Thank Christ for that!' As we pulled up and away, Dave Rodger now had the ringside seat. He said, 'God Almighty,' as the explosion threw a fountain of water up to about 1,000 feet. 'Jesus – that spray has come right into the rear turret. Not only have I been knocked about all over the place by you buggers, now you're trying to drown me!'

Joe wheeled us around and we could all see the effect. By the time I could see the spray, it was falling back onto the dam, but it was still very high. Once the water had settled, however, it became clear that the dam had not been breached. We had scored a direct hit and had caused some crumbling of the crest over a length about 20 feet wide, but one bomb clearly was not going to be enough. Don gave Joe a course and we turned for home, elated that we had hit the target but disappointed that we hadn't done more damage. Barnes Wallis had been right – it would have taken five or six hits to burst the Sorpe.

Our return journey took us directly over what had been, until 20 minutes earlier, the Mohne dam. The only way I can describe it was that it looked like an inland sea. There was still water pouring down the side of the dam and running out into the valley. It was simply amazing. We obviously took some satisfaction looking down on this. It was clear that the attack on the Mohne had been a huge success. There was no point trying to map-read over this area. Any features that I might have tried to pick out were now submerged. There was nothing to see but water. I was very glad that we hadn't been diverted to attack either this or the Eder dam because, in the rush to change aircraft at Scampton, I had forgotten to bring my special, handmade bombsight with me!

We still had two and a half hours of flying to do, mainly at low level, across enemy country before we were safely home. Shortly after leaving the dams area, we could see searchlights and a hell of a lot of flak going up straight ahead of us, all of it aimed at somebody else. That shouldn't have been happening. We were not supposed to be here. A quick discussion between Don and Joe established that we were way off course, somewhere over the city of Hamm in the north-east part of the Ruhr. We had blundered into one of the very hotspots that we knew we should have been trying to avoid. Joe circled round to try to take us out but by then we were over the huge railway marshalling yards with searchlights and flak gunners, who had woken up to the fact that we were up there somewhere, methodically searching the sky for us.

Don MacLean couldn't understand how this had happened. It has been speculated that he was using the wrong compass card and Don has always been the one who has been blamed for us straying over Hamm. People make mistakes, and in this instance Don was not the only one who had buggered it up. I was sitting there with maps in front of me. I was supposed to be locating landmarks to check that we were on course. Why hadn't I noticed that we were heading for Hamm? The truth is that I haven't a clue. I don't know what was going through my head right then, but it couldn't have been anything to do with map-reading. I was as much to blame as Don for us ending up over Hamm – but Joe was the one who sorted out the situation.

Knowing that he might not be able to trust his compasses entirely, Joe decided that we were going to go home the same way that we had come in, covering familiar ground to avoid getting lost again. He pointed T-Tommy towards the distant Ijsselmeer. Taking this route was, in itself, a risky business, but first we had to get away from Hamm. Joe took us down over the railway yards so low that the searchlights and flak guns couldn't come down low enough to pick us up. He was weaving his way over huts and signal boxes with even the trackside signal pylons looking unnervingly close. It looked like one of the signal arms could easily reach up and touch us. I could see all of this coming towards us. Dave Rodger saw it all vanishing into the distance. His voice broke in from the rear turret, 'Jeeeeez .... At this height they don't need flak! All they have to do is switch the points!'

The problem with taking the route back over the Ijsselmeer was that by now the moon was in a different position in the sky and it would make it easier for us to be spotted over the water, even if we were skimming the surface at less than 100 feet. We went out fast. This time around, Bill made absolutely no objection to Joe pushing T-Tommy as hard as he liked. There was no caution about saving fuel or preserving the engines. We hammered home across the water as fast as T-Tommy could take us. Bill later took a lot of teasing about pushing his engines on the run over the water, but no one cared too much about it at the time!

One flak gunner had a pop at us as we crossed the coast and managed to get close, but we left Holland behind without further incident. At around 3.00 am, when we were only a few minutes away from Scampton, 5 Group Operations Room received a signal from Len – 'Goner' – the code word to signify that we had attacked the target but not burst the dam. They should have had that message almost three hours earlier and I really don't know why they didn't get it sooner. I assume that Len was still having communications problems right up to the time when we were almost home. Had he been able to send it sooner, maybe some of the reserve Third Wave could have been directed to the Sorpe, but the way things worked out that probably wouldn't have made any difference.

It wasn't until we were coming in over Scampton, with the darkness fading in a pre-dawn light, that we discovered we had a problem. Bill lowered the undercarriage, checked the warning lights and glanced out to take a quick look. It was then that he spotted that the starboard tyre was flat, punctured when we were hit during the armoured train incident. Down in my office, any kind of tricky landing was going to be an unpleasant experience, but, as usual, Joe didn't seem at all perturbed. He put T-Tommy down as gently as a baby and we settled into a lumpy taxi. Home at last. It was 3.23 in the morning, five and a half hours after take-off.

We were collected from dispersal and went straight into a debrief with an Intelligence Officer, running through the highlights of the trip. Others had commented on the ammunition that had been loaded into the guns – 100 per cent tracer. They said that it had looked terrifying and that they were sure it had put the fear of God into the flak gunners. Joe disagreed. He reckoned that it was too showy, made us an easier target and gave our position away. Details aside, our part in the raid was now over and we were able to start finding out how it had gone for the others.

Shortly after midnight, the reserves had departed without any specific targets. They were briefed to approach the dams area by the southern route and the original intention was that they would be used to attack the Mohne and Eder if those had not been successfully breached. In the event, Flt Sgt Ken Brown was instructed to attack the Sorpe, as eventually were Plt Off Burpee and Flt Sgt Anderson. For whatever reason, Plt Off Ottley and Flt Sgt Bill Townsend were sent to the Lister and Ennepe dams respectively. Quite what was to be achieved by single attacks on these latter targets is a mystery to me.

Ottley was the first to leave, at nine minutes past midnight. He was heard to acknowledge his diversion to the Lister dam and then the squadron records state simply: 'No further trace.' Ottley's Lanc was hit by an intense flak attack near the dreaded Hamm and went down. In a remarkable escape, the rear gunner, Sgt Tees, was thrown clear on impact and survived. He was to spend the rest of the war in hospitals and prisoner of war camps. In later years he recalled that Ottley had just begun to brief the crew on their target when 'a hell of a commotion' interrupted him. They had been pinged by searchlights and hit very badly. Tees remembered Ottley saying, 'Sorry, boys, we have had it.' There were two explosions – first the port tank and then the bomb itself on impact. All other members of the crew were killed instantly.

Plt Off Burpee followed Ottley from Scampton and he was also officially recorded as 'missing without trace'. Eyewitness reports from other crews in the vicinity said that Burpee had made a fatal navigational error and strayed off course. His track now took him over a German airfield near Tilburg in Holland, where he was hit by the ground defences. His fuel tanks exploded, as did the weapon when they hit the ground.

Flt Sgt Ken Brown was directed to the Sorpe. After an eventful trip, dodging a number of flak attacks, he eventually found the dam. By now it was shrouded in mist but Brown decided to make the same approach as we had earlier. He made six or seven runs before the bomb was dropped and his successful hit produced pretty much the same result as we had achieved. The dam wall was crumbled in part but the structure remained largely intact.

Flt Sgt Bill Townsend received orders to attack the Ennepe dam. He described his flight over Holland and Germany as 'very, very nasty'. At one stage, showing the incredible airmanship that all these young pilots possessed, he actually flew along a fire break in some woods below the treetops to avoid the flak. Reaching what they thought was the Ennepe, but was probably the completely different Bever dam, they found it covered in thick mist. They ran in three times to no avail, unable to get the correct line and altitude. On the fourth attempt they let the Upkeep go and, bouncing correctly, it exploded some 50 yards short of the target. By now it was after 3.30 in the morning and on the return flight it was daylight as they passed over Holland.

The last aircraft in the reserve group was piloted by Flt Sgt Anderson. Dodging flak over the Ruhr, he had been forced off track and experienced navigational difficulties. He had been directed to the Sorpe but in the misty conditions he found it hard to identify landmarks, let alone find the target. With dawn approaching, and still north of the Ruhr, he decided to call it a day and head for home. The squadron report says that he 'was unable to reach target, due to mist in the valleys, mine returned to base'. He touched down at Scampton at 5.30 am, three minutes before Ken Brown landed. Anderson was castigated by some crew members for taking an 'easy option'. Others were more generous in their assessment of his problems. Typically, Gibson was not impressed and Anderson and his crew were posted off the squadron the next day.

In the final event, of the eight aircraft in total designated to attack the Sorpe, only two got through. Three were shot down and three returned unsuccessfully. Barnes Wallis had said that it would take the combined effect of five (or was it six?) bombs to breach the dam wall. The 'Gods of War' decided that this was not going to happen and the Sorpe survived, bloodied but not mortally wounded.

Elsewhere, however, the night had turned into a massive success for 617 Squadron. At shortly before 3.30 am, just as Brown was delivering his attack on the Sorpe, the first of Gibson's flights was returning home. Flt Lt David Maltby was the first down at 3.15 am, shortly followed by Flt Lt Mickey Martin. Maltby was to be the hero of the hour as it was his attack on the Mohne that finally breached the dam, although Young's weapon had started the process.

Millions of words and hundreds of hours of film have been given over to the attacks on the Mohne and Eder dams, and in the context of this book I have no wish to regurgitate the entire story all over again. But brief highlights are important because the Dambuster legend revolves totally around this success – and rightly so, because what Guy Gibson and his flight achieved demonstrates the virtues of all of the aircrews involved in Operation Chastise. Some were simply more successful, and some enjoyed a good deal more luck, than others.

Gibson took off at shortly after 9.30 pm together with Hopgood and Martin. They were followed in swift order first by Young, Shannon and Maltby, and then by Maudslay, Astell and Knight. In rather typically English fashion, this was to be the 'batting order' in terms of the attack. Experiencing the same navigational difficulties that had beset so many of us, Gibson's flight continually drifted off course and had to reset. The outward journey, however, was relatively quiet until they were close to the dams area, when they were attacked by light flak, suffering no material damage.

The second flight shared a similar experience, although Shannon received one minor hit. As the first six aircraft circled the Mohne dam in clear moonlight, the briefing on the defences was verified. The dam was well defended by a number of light flak guns, three of which were positioned in such a way that the attacking aircraft would have no alternative but to fly directly towards them on the final approach. Gibson decided to make a reconnaissance run and, having done so, despite the defending gunners, pronounced his confidence that they could perform as briefed. He then led the way, flying directly into the very hot defences. He had a good set-up, but the bomb was released a fraction early, exploding marginally short of the target.

Waiting until the target area was clear of spray, Gibson called up Hopgood, his number two, and instructed him to make his approach. Having witnessed Gibson's run, the flak gunners were now ready, but there was no other way in. They would simply have to fly straight into the defences. An intensive barrage rose up to meet Hopgood and the Lancaster suffered several hits. In the mayhem, the Upkeep was launched late, with the net effect that it skipped over the dam wall. The plane was now ablaze and Hopgood struggled to gain height in order to allow his crew to bail out. It exploded at about 500 feet. Remarkably, two crew members did survive despite bailing out at such an impossibly low height. This they did by pulling the ripcords before exiting the aircraft. Both Plt Off Burcher, the rear gunner, and Flt Sgt Fraser, the bomb aimer, would be POWs for the rest of the war. Many years later, John Fraser's daughter, Shere, married Joe McCarthy's son, Joe Jnr, and both remain my good friends to this day.

Next to go was Mickey Martin. By now the crews were in no doubt about what they were facing. Throughout all of our training, none of us had ever had to face this kind of intensive fire from ground batteries. It was at this point that Gibson's courage and qualities of leadership became truly evident. Ordering Martin to attack, he decided to fly slightly ahead and to the right of him, with the dual objective of drawing defensive fire and allowing his gunners the opportunity to give the dam defenders something to think about. Martin was also hit but suffered no severe damage and released his Upkeep. This shot was also slightly short and a little left of the target.

Young was called up and, as he approached, both Gibson and Martin flew in with him to distract the gunners. Young's attack was just about perfect, the bomb hitting and exploding exactly as Wallis had prescribed. As they waited for the spray to subside, there was much expectation that this was it. But it soon became evident that the dam was still intact.

Four of the nine Lancasters had now attacked the dam without success. Maltby came in, again supported by Gibson and Martin on either side. As he approached the dropping point, Maltby noticed that the 'crown of the dam was already crumbling' and that there was 'a breach to the centre of the dam'. He decided, however, to attack as planned and dropped his Upkeep as required. There was no immediate indication of success but, as Gibson called up Shannon to go in, they saw that this part of the mission had been achieved. The crews shared an immense sense of elation as they witnessed water pouring through a large breach in the dam wall. Gibson told Shannon to stand down and they circled, watching the result of their work with awe. Gibson, never given to understatement, described it as 'a tremendous sight, a sight which probably no man will ever see again'. Thousands of tons of water poured into the valley below, sweeping everything before it.

Cutting short the celebrations, Gibson sent Maltby and

Martin home and proceeded on the short flight to the Eder with Shannon and the remainder of his team. Young also attended in order to take over from Gibson in the event of the leader going down. Navigation again proved difficult given the early morning mist that was beginning to form and the plethora of small lakes and rivers that were in the area. Eventually, the Eder was identified and the attack route was determined. This was not going to be easy. The Lancasters would have to fly over a castle, drop down 1,000 feet and take a sharp turn to the left. Rising up over a short spit of land, they would then have to drop down again to the required 60 feet for the run in. The only piece of good news was that the dam was, to all intents and purposes, undefended.

Shannon was called up and was the first to go. He made three or four runs but was finding great difficulty in getting to the correct height after this complicated approach. Telling him to have a rest, Gibson ordered Maudslay to attack. He also had a couple of dummy runs without success and Shannon was brought back to try again. After two more abortive attempts, he eventually was satisfied and the drop went to order. After waiting for everything to settle down, it was clear that the dam was still intact and it was Maudslay's turn again. His bomb was dropped too late, skipped and exploded as it hit the parapet wall, severely damaging the aircraft. In one of the most poignant moments of *The Dam Busters* film, Gibson asks Maudslay if he is 'OK' and hears a faint voice reply, 'I think so. Stand by.' He was never heard from again. Henry Maudslay was shot down as he struggled towards home, hit by flak near Emmerich on the Rhine.

Gibson then called on Astell to make his attack and received no reply. What Gibson did not know was that Bill Astell had crashed over an hour and a half earlier on the way in. He had collided with an electricity pylon and high-tension cables north of the Ruhr, none of the crew surviving the crash.

With just one Lancaster left, Gibson now turned to Les Knight. After one dummy run, and after learning by watching the attacks of Shannon and Maudslay, he made a perfect run in, dropping the Upkeep on target. It hit the dam wall pretty much in the centre. Gibson, watching from above, later said, 'It was as if a gigantic hand had pushed a hole through cardboard.' The Eder dam had gone.

Just as the Sorpe wave and the reserves lost four crews, so was Gibson's First Wave to suffer four losses. Having lost Astell on the way out, Hopgood and Maudslay went down over the dams (or shortly after), and there was to be one more fatality on the way home. Again, the squadron records are inaccurate. Reporting on the loss of 'Dinghy' Young, they say, 'Eder dam and back to the Mohne when the attack was finished. He was not heard on R/T after this, and is believed to have flown over Hamm on the return journey and been shot down there.' In fact, Young made it all the way to the Dutch coast. Flying over the heavily defended area of Ijmuiden, he was hit by flak and crashed into the sea just off the coast. There were no survivors.

Shannon arrived back at 4.06 am, Gibson landed at 4.15 am, shortly followed by Knight at 4.20 am. The stragglers from the reserves all landed between 5.30 and 6.15 am. And Operation Chastise – the Dams Raid – was over.

## CHAPTER 8

# THE DEBRIEF AND A RETURN TO THE SORPE

After most other raids, we were still talking too loudly when we bundled into the debriefing room. We'd left Chuck-Chuck way out at dispersal, but we could all still hear her engines throbbing in our ears. It took some time for that to settle down. At the debrief we gathered round to be offered a mug of tea with a tot of rum in it. I declined the rum, but the tea went down a treat, especially if it came with a biscuit or two.

Then it was down to business. We tended to be interviewed as a crew, one crew at a time, with an Intelligence Officer, often a WAAF, firing questions at us over our tea, biscuits and cigarettes. There were routine, set questions to be asked about the journey to the target, the flak and night fighters along the way, whether we found our way there without too much difficulty ... that sort of thing. As far as the bombing itself was concerned, they needed to know if the PFF had marked the bombing area clearly and if we managed to drop our bombs on target. Had we seen any other aircraft being hit? Did our gunners engage any enemy aircraft? Lots of notes were taken, presumably so that they could piece together everything that had happened on the raid and work out what might have happened to some of those who didn't come home.

Usually the debrief didn't take too long. You couldn't really skip over the details, but we were all exhausted and keen to get off to bed. The worst thing was if you had landed away from the airfield for any reason. If you were miles away, in Cornwall or somewhere, you'd scrounge a bed for the night and fly home the next day, but, if you were close by, they would stick you on a truck and send you back to Scampton. We might have had five or six hours in the air and then have to spend an hour in the back of a truck before sitting down to the debrief when all we really wanted to do was to get to bed. That was a pain. Once we were finished with the debrief, I might try to see if there was any food on the go, but I usually headed for bed. You could count on being dog-tired after an op and, although it could take a while to wind down enough to get to sleep, bed was the best place for me. We would be up again later that morning and, although we were unlikely to be back on an op that night, we might well be doing a training flight or an air test later in the day. There was no thought of that right now, though. Just relax and hit the hay.

Depending on what time we had arrived home, I'd be up for breakfast the following morning. During the winter, we could leave as darkness fell in the late afternoon and be home again well before midnight, landing in darkness. That allowed for a good night's sleep. In the summer, we would take off far later as it wouldn't be starting to get dark until nine o'clock at night and we would be home early in the morning, often as dawn was breaking. That meant going to bed when it was light, which felt odd, but fatigue meant that I could usually nod off before too long. Most of the time I would be able to get by with a few hours' sleep and be up and at it bright and early. That, after all, was the way it had worked when I was growing up back on the farm – early to bed during the dark months and late working when there was enough light.

The morning after a raid, unless you had the day off, there wouldn't be that much to do. You could hang around the crew room, take a look at that night's Order of Battle once it had been posted or any other daily orders when they were pinned up. If you were lucky, there might also be a newspaper or a copy of *Tee Emm* magazine lying around. This was always good for a laugh. It was full of stories featuring Plt Off Prune and his antics – cautionary tales about not forgetting your parachute, the importance of punctuality and why a low-level pass over the airfield could be a bad idea. There was a serious message behind all of the moralising, and *Tee Emm* also included a lot of training articles. It was, after all, an official Air Ministry publication, *Tee Emm* being short for Training Memorandum.

When we weren't on ops, there were generally training routines to run through. These might involve low-level bombing flights, high-level formation bombing, even air gunnery practice, but, if I could wangle any time off, my absolute priority was always to get off the station and go to see Gwyn.

After the Dams Raid debrief, there were mixed emotions on the base as the crews arrived back. In the early morning light, the Lancasters limped home to Scampton and a reception where there was jubilation amongst the commanders. The raid had, after all, been an outstanding success. Signals and telephone calls rang out through the night, reporting this great triumph of British inventiveness and courage. There was some celebrating and a few beers drunk. Joe was happy to down a beer or two with some of the others, and who could blame them? It had been quite a night. There was a lot of talk about the way the dams had burst and a lot of people hanging around, waiting to see who was coming back.

The ground crews examined the aircraft as they came in, no doubt amazed that some had made it back. Geoff Rice's Lanc must certainly have left them scratching their heads. In the Sergeants' Mess, the WAAFs who served breakfast had been laying tables, ready for the returning crews. When they were told that eight of the aircraft had been lost – 56 of our boys who wouldn't be coming home – some of them simply burst into tears.

For me, after the debrief and with the adrenaline that had carried me through the trip now draining away, I was exhausted. I didn't wait up, as some did, until it was absolutely clear who hadn't made it. There wasn't anything that I could do about that. We had made it back and, as harsh as it sounds, that was what mattered most. We had done what was asked of us, we had done it to the best of our ability, and we were all still alive. It didn't do to dwell on thoughts of the faces missing from the mess. We had survived and now it was time to move on. The scratch squadron's 'one big op' was over and done with. Those of us who were still around had to think about what came next, but Operation Chastise wasn't done and dusted quite yet – not by a long chalk.

The Air Ministry and its PR operation swung into action.

BBC radio reported the success of the raid early on the morning of 17 May, announcing that 'The Mohne, Eder and Sorpe dams have been attacked. Two dams were damaged and heavy casualties were caused among the civilian population by the resulting floods.' Over the next week, national and local newspapers provided massive coverage with reports of the success (some somewhat overblown) accompanied by photographs from the Air Ministry. The general public was absolutely jubilant. Here was a major military success for the country, an attack that struck right at the heart of Germany. Given that this was the spring of 1943 and we had now been at war in Europe for three and a half years, the British public needed some heartening news. Rommel had been kicked out of North Africa, but Britain was still sitting just over 20 miles from Nazi-occupied territory and it's hardly surprising that there was such a positive reaction. Now they had something to celebrate. There can be no doubt that this was a massive boost to public morale.

The RAF top brass and their political masters joined in the euphoria wholeheartedly, almost falling over themselves to send each other congratulatory messages. Even Churchill, addressing the American Congress the following Wednesday, was able to use the success as part of his statement of British resilience and determination to succeed. Buckingham Palace was equally buoyant and Bomber Harris was called in to receive the congratulations of the King and Queen. You can only smile when you think of how Harris handled that audience. He had been thoroughly opposed to the attack and, even after the dust had settled, continued to question whether it had all been worthwhile.

The senior officers involved were very quick to give each

other a pat on the back, but, to begin with, there were few plaudits coming in the direction of the aircrews. The ground crews received practically no mention whatsoever. There was one amongst the aircrews, however, who received a great deal of attention – Guy Gibson. He was highly praised, and quite rightly so, for his role in leading the operation. Our losses were quickly glossed over, hardly mentioned by anyone.

It was left to Barnes Wallis to express the most balanced and considerate view. He made his feelings clear in a letter to Ralph Cochrane:

*It is impossible to find words adequately to express what one feels about air crews. The gallantry with which they go into action is incomparable. While the older generation of Air Force officers may not be called on to carry out actual attacks in person, the spirit of their juniors must proceed from their thought and training and in praising your crews I would like to add thanks which I feel are due to you as one of the senior officers of the Air Force, for the outstanding generation of pilots which your example and training has produced.*

*Will you please accept the deepest sympathy of all of us on the losses which the Squadron has sustained. You will understand, I think, the tremendous strain which I felt at having been the cause of sending these crews on so perilous a mission, and the tense moments in the Operations Room, when after four attacks I felt that I had failed to make good, were almost more than I could bear; and for me the subsequent success was almost completely blotted out by the sense of loss of these wonderful young lives. In the light of our subsequent knowledge I do hope*

*that all those concerned will feel that the results achieved
have not rendered their sacrifice in vain.*

Wallis felt deeply saddened by the number of lost crews. We
all felt it, too, but Wallis wasn't like us – he blamed himself
for their deaths. He was a technical wizard, his tenacity and
belief in the dams project had made it possible, but he wasn't
hardened to the news of young men dying, news that filtered
into most Operations Rooms in Bomber Command every
night. As the first casualty reports came in on the night of the
raid, he was almost inconsolable. I had always admired him
for his remarkable talent as an engineer, and his compassion
made me respect him even more. I don't believe that he ever
really got over the shock of so many crews being lost on the
raid. I remember him with great affection and I was proud to
be invited to attend a number of reunions with a great man.
I am also glad to say that I am friends to this day with his
daughter, Mary.

We may have been better equipped to cope with the Dams
Raid death toll than Barnes Wallis, but I found that there were
other things that could get to you, little things that niggled you
in unexpected ways for no apparent reason. The night after the
raid, I was sitting on a bus with Gwyn. We were going to the
cinema in Lincoln. The other passengers were chattering away
about the good news from the RAF that had been all over the
front pages that day. Their babbling really got under my skin. I
leaned over to Gwyn and spoke as quietly as I could.

'God, I wish they would shut up about it,' I said.

'Why?' she asked.

'Because that was us,' I told her.

'That was you? On that raid?'

I just nodded. She looked incredulous for a second, then saw the look on my face and didn't say another word. Gwyn knew me. She knew I didn't want to talk about it and that because of security I shouldn't talk about it, so she didn't press me. Quite what she told her friends in the WAAF quarters later that night, I have no idea, but I suspect it was a story told with some pride.

We couldn't talk in any detail about the bomb, which was still a 'secret weapon' that might have been deployed against other targets, but, if you were 617 Squadron aircrew, you enjoyed a degree of celebrity that had its own rewards. Because I used to go to Hemswell to see Gwyn even if she was on duty, I was there so often that it got to the stage where the guards in the guardroom knew me by sight. They knew that I was there to visit my wife, who worked in the telephone exchange, so I would cycle over and be waved through the main gate without any trouble. Then, one evening, a new guard on the gate started to question me about who I was and where I was going. He disappeared into the guardroom to ask the duty corporal if I should be allowed in and I heard him getting a proper mouthful in reply. 'You can't talk to him like that! He's one of the Dambusters and he's here to see his wife!' I never had any trouble after that.

The celebrations rolled on. On 27 May, the King and Queen visited Scampton to meet the crews and congratulate them personally. There is a wonderful photograph of 'Big Joe' towering over a much shorter Queen Elizabeth. It was quite something for us to be meeting the King and Queen. We were all still mere youngsters, after all, with Dave Shannon celebrating his twenty-first birthday the day that we all lined up on parade for the royal couple.

On 22 June, we were in royal company once again when there was an investiture at Buckingham Palace. The King was in North Africa so it was Queen Elizabeth who presented the medals. Following Gibson's well-earned Victoria Cross, the other recipients were introduced in strict alphabetical order. Thirty-four medals were presented. All the pilots (with the exception of Rice, Munro and Anderson, who did not complete the mission for one reason or another) received the Distinguished Service Order (DSO), apart from Ken Brown and Bill Townsend who were Flight Sergeants. As non-commissioned officers (NCOs), they were not entitled to receive the same medal as commissioned officers. They received the Conspicuous Gallantry Medal. Other crew members received the DFC, if officers, or the Distinguished Flying Medal (DFM), if NCOs. I was awarded the DFM and was absolutely petrified when my name was called out. Gwyn was there watching but, even with her moral support, the thought of receiving a medal from the Queen scared me rigid. I marched forwards, doing my absolute best to keep it crisp and smart, terrified that I was going to slip, trip or otherwise make a complete twit of myself. The Queen could obviously see how nervous I was and simply smiled and spoke quietly and calmly to settle me down. Don't ask me what she said – I haven't the foggiest! Neither do I know how I responded. It was totally nerve-racking, but a very proud moment.

That evening, Vickers hosted a party for the officers while I made my way back to Scampton by train with Gwyn and the other non-commissioned crew members. Many drinks had been drunk, although not by me, and on the way home some of the others had run out of cash. They gratefully borrowed money from Gwyn in order to carry on celebrating. The loan was never repaid, nor was it asked for. 'They probably forgot all about it,' was all that Gwyn said when recalling the moment some years later. 'They were completely bladdered.'

After the war, historians began to analyse the material impact of the Dams Raid on the German war effort and some started to cast doubt on its value. It became perhaps even fashionable to challenge the results. At the time of the raid, on the German side, Albert Speer (Hitler's Minister of Armaments and War Production) inferred that the impact was modest. Hitler's deputy, the Luftwaffe chief Hermann Goering, was not so sure. Hitler was said to be very concerned, particularly about water supplies. He was equally vexed that the Luftwaffe was apparently incapable of defending the dams. Certainly, the German High Command was appalled that the RAF could mount such an attack, successfully executing a precision strike in the heart of Germany on targets that they thought were impossible to hit.

The critics point out that the dams themselves were repaired five months after the event, but they were not fully operational as they took some time to refill and the Germans were careful forever afterwards to keep them below maximum capacity in order to prevent any subsequent attacks having such catastrophic consequences as the original raid had done. It also required a massive reallocation of manpower and resources to complete the rebuilding. A recent television programme suggested that transferring thousands of men from working on the construction of the Atlantic Wall defence system to rebuild the dams made a significant contribution to the success of the D-Day landings in June 1944. The defence systems of all of Germany's major dams were upgraded and fortified with troops – troops who could have been usefully deployed elsewhere. The effect on German industrial production was clearly overstated by our Air Ministry in 1943 but it was significant, and little is made of the devastating effect of the flooding on the agricultural output of the fertile valleys that felt the full effect of this man-made tsunami. There is no doubt that food production was severely hampered.

And so the arguments continue for and against the raid. But why? Why are people still playing numbers games to denigrate or justify Operation Chastise? What do they really hope to achieve? The raid was deemed a success at the time and that's what really matters. What do the revisionist historians think they can contribute? These people make me bloody angry. If I were ever to meet one, I would have to hope that someone would hold my hands behind my back. I have only two questions for them. Were you there? And do you have any idea of what it was like? Not just for us, the ones who flew on the raid, but for the general public in Britain. You can argue over lost industrial production and the time it took to restore the dams until the cows come home, but you can't ignore the fact that we were taking the war to the Germans and giving people from London, Coventry, Birmingham and Glasgow something to cheer about. You can analyse by how many percentage points German steel production dropped due to the dams being destroyed but you can't measure the benefit of the lift in morale amongst the general public, the politicians, the troops and the military commanders in Britain. People were happily chattering about the raid in pubs and on buses. We, as a nation, had given the Nazis a 'bloody nose' and it felt very good.

The other and, perhaps, more difficult argument is always that the losses were too high a price to pay for what was achieved. How can this be truly evaluated? The percentage loss rate for this particular raid was huge. If you discount the three aircraft that came home without having been able to make an attack, we lost eight out of our 16 attacking planes – a 50 per cent loss rate. Only three of the aircrew from the downed Lancs survived – 53 were killed. By any measure that was devastating, but every night far larger numbers, in terms of aircraft lost and aircrew killed, were being experienced in raids over the German cities. In March 1944, more than 90 aircraft were shot down in one disastrous raid on Nuremberg. You can't calculate any kind of 'cost efficiency' when it comes to human lives – and, remember, we were all volunteers. We knew what we were getting into and we chose to fight our war this way.

After the war, on returning to his native Canada, Ken Brown joined in the 'anti' argument. He claimed that the losses were not worth it. A great deal has been written about the raid and I think that Brown's own personal accounts always seemed to be a bit exaggerated, somewhat on the 'flowery' side. When he started mouthing off in Canada, criticising the raid, the powers that be got hold of Joe McCarthy and told him to shut Brown up. This he did, and, knowing Joe, he would have done so in no uncertain terms.

It is a tragedy that so many young men died on the raid, but I refuse to believe that they gave their lives in vain.

In 2008, I was invited by a television production company called Atypical Media to take part in a film with Simon Parry, an aviation historian, on behalf of Channel 5 and the History Channel. All of the 617 Lancaster aircraft that had taken part in the raid had been accounted for in terms of their final resting place, whether at their crash sites or where they were scrapped after the war. All, that is, with the exception of ED 825, T-Tommy. We never flew in her again, but she was reconfigured as a normal Lanc and flown on operations by new crews. T-Tommy was known to have crashed over northern France in December 1943 but precisely where, no one was sure. The bodies of the crew members had been interred in a small village cemetery at Méharicourt near Amiens in northern France, but no wreckage of the aircraft was discovered after the war. Neither had it been possible to piece together the last minutes of the flight.

A film crew led by TV producer James Cutler and director Cy Chadwick was to cover an archaeological dig in search of T-Tommy's last remains. Simon Parry's book *Spitfire Hunters* gives an excellent account of this operation, which did indeed unearth some remains of the aircraft and enabled the team to work out how it had crashed. What is clear is that both this aircraft, piloted by Fg Off Gordon Weeden, and another flown by WO Bull had been detailed to drop munitions to the French Resistance outside the town of Doullens in the Somme region. They were both shot down. It has never been fully proven but the locals believe that the Maquis had been infiltrated by the Gestapo and the Germans were pre-warned about the drop. There are many cases where in-fighting between different factions of the French Resistance during the war led to betrayals, so it's not beyond the realms of possibility that this is what brought about the demise of Weeden's and Bull's Lancs. Certainly, a flak train had been moved into the town at the last minute and this accounted for both aircraft.

James Cutler had invited me to witness the dig, take part in the filming, and provide any insights that might be of value. He had also organised a civic reception for me, hosted by the mayor and all the old local resistance fighters, complete with full flags of honour and the town band. In an exhausting 36 hours, we gave speeches, made presentations, laid a commemorative wreath and enjoyed an excellent lunch. We also made a sorrowful visit to the graves of Gordon Weeden and his crew, accompanied by Weeden's nephew – also called Gordon – who had flown over from Canada to be part of the event. It is only with hindsight that I realised how important this trip was for the larger Weeden family. For the past 65 years, all they had known was where he had been killed. They wanted to know how he had died and what exactly had happened. Did that knowledge make any difference? Yes, it did. Gordon Weeden's story had an ending that everyone could understand and come to terms with.

The bulk of the wreckage had been removed during the war but the archaeologists turned up some interesting artefacts, including a decent-sized piece of Perspex which was from the bomb aimer's 'blister'. I found that quite fascinating. I had looked through that piece of Perspex in May 1943 over the Sorpe dam. The member of the dig team who had found the Perspex had spent many hours cleaning it up and was apparently hoping that it would be autographed by everyone, serving as a nice memento of his trip. Unfortunately, nobody told me that. I thought they were presenting it to me as a gift, so I said, 'Thank you very much,' and pocketed it. They must all have found it too embarrassing to ask for it back! I still have it somewhere …

The point of this digression into later years and northern France is that, although it hadn't been part of the original filming schedule, James Cutler decided that he wanted to take me on a visit to the Sorpe dam and to get my reaction to seeing it for the first time in 65 years. I would also have the chance to meet some of the local people who had stories to tell about that night in May. Over the years, I had been asked many times to talk about the Dams Raid and I had generally been able to give a very straightforward, hopefully accurate, account of what went on. For many of those years, I would still have been serving in the RAF, and I have no doubt that my version of events was quite 'military', a bit like a written report, without too much unnecessary detail and no real emotion. That was how they liked things to be done in the forces, and, given my upbringing, that kind of reserved approach suited me just fine. I didn't want to display any feelings about the raid – I didn't really want to have any feelings about what we did during the war. Remorse, regret, sympathy, sorrow – all far too awkward. That was to change quite a bit on the trip to Germany.

In the film *The Last Dambuster* (the title refers to the aircraft, not me), I found myself walking along the Sorpe dam on a spring afternoon with my grandson, Richard. I had never had any doubts about what we had done – I still believe that it had to be done – but it was a powerful feeling to be there with Richard and to realise that, not so very long ago, I had actually dropped a bomb on that very spot. It was all so calm and peaceful, with families taking a walk in the sunshine and small boats sailing on the reservoir. I surprised myself when I turned to Richard and said, 'To look at it now, you wonder why we ever went to war.'

Cutler's researchers had found a German couple, Marianne and Gunther Bortelsmann, who live near the spot where Warner Ottley crashed on his way to the Lister. For years they have tended a memorial that they created at the crash site. I was very touched by their incredible kindness. No one forced them to maintain this lovely, simple memorial in the countryside. They did it out of respect for the brave young men who died there. Gunther had lived in Berlin as a child and his family had been trapped in their cellar when their house was bombed and collapsed on top of them. Can you imagine the horror? Buried alive as people clawed at the rubble for hours to try to dig them out. There were plenty of families in Britain who suffered in the same way, of course, but Marianne and Gunther's attitude to their experiences was a revelation to me. They told me that they didn't hate the British or the RAF. 'It was Hitler we hated,' Gunther said. 'He was the cause of it all.'

The same outlook was shared by Hans Durvald, to whom the film crew introduced me the following day. He had been in the Hitler Youth and was just 15 years old when he manned the flak gun that finally shot down Henry Maudslay's stricken Lanc over Emmerich as they struggled homeward from the Eder. We were a bit wary of each other at first but we chatted over a beer and a glass of wine and he showed me the medal he had been given for shooting down the Lanc. He said that he wasn't proud of it and that 'sitting in front of you now I have no hatred for you as my enemy'. He also said, 'I know who started the war. I know it was Hitler who started it. Today I can't believe how we were seduced by him.'

A visit to Astell's crash site was accompanied by a graphic account from a local historian, who showed me a particularly unpleasant photograph of the crashed Lanc and the charred bodies of the seven aircrew lying nearby. I saw the electricity pylon that they had crashed into, standing just as it must have done all those years before. The crew must have known that there was nothing they could do. They were too low. There was no way they could bail out. In those few seconds they must have known they were going to die.

Finally, the production team took me to the Mohne Dam Museum where the curator showed me photographs and film footage of the devastation. Someone there told me how he had attended the funeral of 20 local village folk who had been on the periphery of the damage. The trip made me think about things that I hadn't ever allowed myself to consider before. It was an emotional experience and that, of course, is what the film people wanted to highlight. They were pleased to be able to film me looking out over the sunlit, rolling countryside below the Sorpe dam and telling Richard that I was glad that we hadn't burst the dam and destroyed all of that. In the mood of the moment, it was easy to say that I was glad that we hadn't wreaked death and destruction on that tranquil valley, but that's a notion that I can afford to harbour now, knowing that we defeated Hitler and with the war so far in the past. At the time, I had no qualms whatsoever about destroying the dams or the consequences – or, for that matter, anything else that we did during the war. In the film, I told Richard, 'You are in it to fight. You don't get emotionally involved. If you become emotionally involved, you don't fight.'

I remain immensely proud of what we achieved on the Dams Raid, immensely proud to have been part of Joe's crew and of 617 Squadron. I believed then that what we were doing was helping to win the war and I believe that now. If you dropped me back into 1943, I would not hesitate to do it all again.

CHAPTER 9

# NORTH AFRICA AND THE LEMON RAFFLE

So that was it. We had done our 'special op' with 617 Squadron and it was all over. We were given a week's leave – a week to rest, relax and take stock. We had all done our 30 trips and were due to be assigned to other duties for a while before we went back on ops again … only it didn't quite work out that way. We had done a very proficient job on the Dams Raid, possibly showing ourselves to be too proficient for our own good. The media loved us. They loved the fact that there was an elite RAF bomber squadron that was capable of pulling off what the Germans thought was a 'mission impossible'. Their readers, listeners and newsreel audiences couldn't get enough of 617 Squadron, and the RAF High Command was quick to recognise that fact. They realised that the British public needed to know that 617 Squadron was out there giving Hitler a poke in the eye, so the idea of us being together just for one special op was quickly forgotten. Disbanding the Dambusters was unthinkable.

We would probably all have gone back on ops again eventually, so when we were told that 617 Squadron was to remain as an operational unit, but reserved as a 'Special Duty Squadron', it didn't take much to persuade us that we should stick with it. As an elite unit, we would no longer be expected to fly the regular trips to Germany but would train to attack specific targets, sometimes carrying 'special weapons'. We would no longer have to take part in Bomber Harris's all-out assault on German cities and industrial centres.

Once all of the celebrations and junketing were over, it was back to work on 29 May. In the following weeks, we flew training missions day after day. We flew high-level formations, low-level formations, low-level bombing runs and endless low-level cross-country jaunts. We flew almost every day, sometimes twice a day, on continuous low-level, cross-country flying and bombing exercises. On 9 June, one cross-country trip took us out over the North Sea and I spotted a dinghy in the water, with two airmen in it, waving for help. Clearly, they had ditched and there was no sign of their aircraft. They looked in reasonably good shape, but we had no way of telling how long they had been in the water and the North Sea is not somewhere you want to be bobbing around in a flimsy emergency dinghy, even in the summer months. We radioed their position back to base so that they could alert the nearest Air Sea Rescue unit and then tried dropping supplies to them. We used our own ditching supplies, some of them going out through the bomb bay and the smaller stuff down the flare chute. God knows how much of it they actually managed to retrieve from the water, but the pair of them survived. We had a message from a Beaufighter squadron a couple of days later to say that they had made it back. They sent a few beers as a thank you.

Our first operational trip came on 15 July when we were detailed to attack a power station at San Polo d'Enza in northern Italy. We had been to Italy before, but this trip was to be slightly different. With North Africa firmly in Allied hands, we were to fly there after we dropped our payload, heading south across the Mediterranean to land at Blida airfield in Algeria. There we were to refuel, rearm, have another load of bombs slotted into Chuck-Chuck's belly, and, once we had had time to rest, bomb Italy again on the way home.

It all started out like any other op. We took off around half past ten at night and flew south across Europe to the target, which lay just beyond Parma. Conditions were hazy when we arrived, difficult for accurate bombing or to verify exactly where all of the bombs went, but we saw six of our 14 bombs straddle the target, blue flames rising as they exploded. The only real problem was that we were bombing from very low down – no more than 800 feet. These were 500lb bombs and they could spread their destructive power over a wide radius, but I didn't expect that to include my office! A chunk of shrapnel from one of our own bombs thumped into the fuselage, giving me the fright of my life. It lodged in the seam where the Perspex of my bomb aimer's 'blister' joined the nose of the aircraft. Had it been a couple of inches either side, it would probably have come smashing straight through, but, with folded metal and Perspex forming structural reinforcement in that precise spot, it stuck there like a dart in a dartboard. Somebody up there was looking after me – another stroke of luck to add to my tally!

There's no note in Joe's logbook of us having been hit by our own munitions. There was no major damage, so it wasn't an incident worth noting – that would have been his view.

You can't argue with that, really, but not everyone got away so lightly. Les Munro was bombing from 1,300 feet (above us, for a change) and was peppered by shrapnel that damaged his bomb aimer, Jim Clay's, office and burst one of their tyres. Nobody was hurt but it made their landing at Blida a bit tricky.

Having bombed the power station at 3.55 am, it was almost four hours later by the time we were coming in to land at Blida. What a sight that was. I had expected North Africa to be just as it was on the newsreels at home where we saw tanks rumbling along in clouds of dust and grimy troops in parched landscapes – nothing for mile after mile but sand dunes and scorpions. Blida was nothing like that. It was full of colour. We came in over the beautifully blue Mediterranean and the wide plain that stretched from the beaches on the shoreline to the foothills of the Tell Atlas mountain range was green with fields and groves of citrus trees. There was obviously plenty of water here – it even snows in the mountains in winter – but, not too far to the south, the dry wastes of the Sahara Desert could be glimpsed. This was like nothing I had ever seen before.

Even though I was, by then, quite a well-travelled young man, nothing that I had experienced in the United States or Canada could possibly have prepared me for Blida. They, after all, spoke English, after a fashion, and even the Americans' strange accents were somewhat familiar from the Hollywood movies we had all seen at the cinema. The mixture of French and Arabic that we heard in Blida was totally alien to me, but I was fascinated when we left the base to visit the town. We did, in the end, have plenty of time to take in our surroundings because the weather closed in and delayed our departure. By the time we were able to leave and an Italian raid could be rescheduled, we were to have been in Blida for eight days.

This, of course, gave us the chance to visit the markets where we mingled with the crowds and, although it always comes with difficulty for us Brits, we did our best to haggle for goods, as was the local custom. In Blida there were restaurants where there was wine and fresh food of all descriptions available in abundance, especially vegetables and fruit, unlike in wartime Britain where the austerity of rationing was still the order of the day. So what we bought in the markets was fruit, not to eat there and then but to take home. I brought back a box of lemons that I sent to the ward sister at the hospital in Basingstoke where I had had my hernia operation. You couldn't get lemons for love nor money in England, so they were a highly prized commodity. She had moved on from Basingstoke to one of the hospitals in Padstow but I had a letter saying that the box had been forwarded to her and that they had raffled the lemons, raising a fair sum of money for the hospital.

Aside from the markets, the town of Blida was also a revelation. With elegant buildings from the French colonial era nestling amongst those with a more Arabic flavour, there was something to marvel at around every corner. And everywhere you went, you could see the four minarets of the Al-Kawthar mosque. Although there were gardens laid out among the barrack blocks and administrative buildings, the airfield at Blida was a huge, flat open space. At over 600 feet above sea level, the wind swept across it relentlessly, drying the sun-baked ground and making this the dustiest place in the area. The buildings and the hangars were modern but, while airfield buildings the world over can tend to look much the same, there was no mistaking that we were in North Africa. Many of the doors and windows, even on the building that housed the control tower, were a typically Arabic 'keyhole' shape – a tall rectangle below a wider, rounded top.

Blida airfield was a busy place, with Coastal Command running maritime operations from there, and all sorts of aircraft that we weren't used to seeing could be spotted outside the hangars. There were RAF Hudsons, Wellingtons, Bostons and Marauders as well as some US Army Air Force machines such as the Airacobra. There were also a few fairly old and decrepit-looking French types standing around.

Even the heat was different to what I had experienced in Florida. In Blida the climate was dry and warm as opposed to the heat and humidity of America's 'Sunshine State'. Of course, I ate well when I was training in America and the same was true in Blida, apart from one thing – rice pudding. In the Sergeants' Mess they used to make rice pudding in huge steel trays and it was pretty revolting stuff. It was like eating rubber and everybody hated it. Why, then, would some joker want to steal an entire tray of the stuff and smuggle it out to a Lancaster being prepared for its homeward journey? The answer was that the rice pudding wasn't going all the way home ...

On 24 July, we finally left, heading back across the Med to bomb the docks at the Italian port of Livorno, detailed as Leghorn in our orders. Apparently the town has also, historically, been known as Legorno, leading English people to call it Leghorn. It was almost one o'clock in the morning and again we had haze over the target, making accurate bombing impossible. Nevertheless, we managed to locate an oil storage dump north of the town and I pressed the button to release a 4,000lb cookie, four 500lb bombs and a tray of rice pudding that had been loaded into the bomb bay. I still have visions of some poor Italian running to take cover from the bombs, only to be hit on the head by a tray of rice pudding ...

While we were dropping a dodgy dessert on the Italians, Bomber Harris was unleashing a savage attack on Hamburg. Codenamed Operation Gomorrah, the plan was to raze the city to the ground. There were good reasons for choosing Hamburg, both political and tactical. It was also an easy target from an operational planning point of view, relatively close and easy for navigation. Harris, as already mentioned, came in for a lot of criticism over his tactics for the carpet bombing of German cities – but not at the time. As the aircraft of Bomber Command wrought havoc, the feeling was very much that the Germans had done it to us and this was payback time. That's how we all felt as aircrew. The fact that we were better at it than the Germans simply meant that we were winning. This was war, and in any sort of fight, if you don't hit harder than the other man, you lose. With hindsight, I can appreciate the arguments people make about Bomber Harris's campaign against the German cities. I understand that it might never have demoralised the German people to the extent that they simply gave up. That didn't work in British cities, after all – in fact, the 'Spirit of the Blitz' made people more resolute than ever. Why should the Germans be any different? And it may well be that the German High Command would never have caved in as they saw city after city being flattened, but that's not entirely the point either. Harris was aware that destroying German industry was a tall order, so destroying the cities and making it impossible for the workers to get to the factories was a way of supplementing the strikes on the factories themselves.

There is no doubt that the campaign caused massive suffering. On the night of 24/25 July, 800 bombers were sent to Hamburg. A further 700 attacked on 27/28 July. On this occasion, the result was one of almost complete devastation. The hot, dry weather provided perfect conditions for the incendiary bombs to create an unholy firestorm in a city with an abundance of wooden buildings in closely packed streets. Ultra-high temperatures allowed the fire to consume everything that lay in its path and over 40,000 people were reported to have been killed that night. Not content, Harris sent a further 700 aircraft on the night of 29/30 July. The civil defence forces, already overstretched, simply could not cope and the devastation of Hamburg was complete. In addition to the dead and dying, over one million people left the city to seek refuge elsewhere.

None of this makes Harris a monster. He did not plan or execute his strategy alone, and he had the total backing of, amongst others, Winston Churchill, who was very much in favour. After the war, of course, when some people started to pour scorn on the bombing campaign, Harris was left to carry the can, but, whatever his detractors may have thought about him, we backed Butch Harris all the way.

If Germany still had to be battered into submission, the Italians were approaching the end of their war. Mussolini had been overthrown towards the end of July and the new Italian government was about to sue for peace with the Allies. In an attempt to secure the support of the population for an Allied invasion, leaflets were to be dropped on the major Italian cities. Codenamed 'Nickel' raids, 617 Squadron took the lead role. On 29 July, nine Lancs set off to scatter leaflets over Milan, Genoa, Turin and Bologna. We were the only crew detailed to 'bomb' Bologna, but, with extremely hazy, moonless conditions, we couldn't be sure of our target and went to Milan instead.

You couldn't really say that you ever looked forward to an op, but this one was a bit different. We were dropping leaflets, not bombs, and from Milan we flew on to Blida for the second time. We were due to fly out after two days, but Chuck-Chuck earned us a few extra days by needing some repairs. Les Munro and his crew were also 'stranded' at Blida. We eventually flew out on 3 August, cruising west along the Mediterranean coast to Ras el Ma in Morocco where we spent a couple of nights before heading back to Scampton.

It was this trip to Blida, I think, from which there later emerged a story about a Canadian soldier pleading with Joe for a lift home. He had a month's leave, but it would take him two weeks to get to the UK by ship, at which point he would have to turn round and come back again. As the story goes, Joe eventually said yes and the Canadian was smuggled aboard at Blida, then smuggled off the base when we got home. I think that the rest of the crew must have been really good smugglers, especially since they would have had to get him out of the aircraft and then back on board again when we stopped off at Ras el Ma, because I don't remember seeing any unauthorised passenger. Mind you, given the way that I used to confine myself to my office during a trip, there is just a slim chance that the story might be true …

While we had been away on our extended tour of North Africa, there had been big changes back home at Scampton. Guy Gibson had been posted to 'temporary duty' – 617 Squadron had lost its famous leader. Gibson was to accompany Winston Churchill to Canada, where he was to attend a high-level conference at which he met the American president, Franklin D. Roosevelt. The whole exercise was a massive propaganda campaign and Gibson gave interviews for the media and made speeches, and a lecture tour took him all over Canada and the United States. Apart from the propaganda exercise, I think that the High Command wanted Guy Gibson off operations. What they didn't want was for him, the leader of the Dambusters and holder of the Victoria Cross, to be lost in action. That would be very bad for morale. Far better that he be sent off to do a bit of flag waving. It was a wise decision because, as he later demonstrated, if Guy Gibson was left to his own devices, there was no way that they would be able to keep him out of the action.

What Gibson's enforced absence meant to us was that we had a new Commanding Officer, Sqn Ldr George Holden. He was a bit of a strange choice, because Holden came from outside the inner circle of 5 Group leaders and I really don't remember that much about him. He was the skipper of one of the crews on the Italian raids that landed in Blida but none of us really had much of a chance to get to know him well. He was killed a few weeks later on the most disastrous night in the squadron's history.

The Dortmund–Ems canal is a 270-kilometre waterway linking the industrial area of the Ruhr with the sea port of Emden. It had significant strategic importance as a transport link for German heavy industry and as such had long been considered a prime target for Bomber Command. On the night of 14/15 September, nine crews from 617 were sent to destroy the canal but bad weather caused their recall and the mission was aborted. They did, however, lose one of the central characters of the Dams Raid when Sqn Ldr David

Maltby and his crew were lost in mysterious circumstances on the way home. They crashed into the sea off the English coast, and it has never been established whether this was as a result of human error or a technical malfunction. Only David Maltby's body was found.

The following evening, eight crews returned to the attack with appalling consequences. Five out of the eight were lost, including Holden, who was shot down over Germany on the outward journey. He had four of Gibson's Dams Raid crew members on board. The raid also claimed another of the Dams Raid stalwarts when Les Knight died in the most selfless fashion. With two port engines out of action and the aircraft almost uncontrollable, Knight jettisoned his 12,000lb bomb and gained enough height for the crew to bail out. Left alone, he tried to crash-land the Lancaster but died in the attempt. Two of the crew were captured but five made it back home after being supported by the resistance. Two crews who had been selected initially for 617 Squadron but did not take part in the Dams Raid, those of Flt Lt Wilson and Plt Off Divall, also perished, having been hit by flak. Flt Lt Allsebrook and his crew also fell victim to the flak gunners. Rice could not find the target owing to the poor visibility and jettisoned his bomb over Holland before returning. Only Shannon and Martin found the target and attacked, neither successfully.

By a strange quirk of fate, Joe McCarthy was sick and could not fly that evening. He acted as duty officer and could only listen to the news of the carnage as it came in. If he had been fit, there is no doubt that Joe would have gone on the raid, but, even if he had, I wouldn't have been with him. I was away on a Bomb Leaders' Course at Manby at the time, the Bomb Leader being the one who assessed other bomb aimers and signed off their logbooks. With Joe sick and me gone, our crew was stood down for that raid – yet another stroke of luck that kept us out of harm's way. We were, however, all pretty cheesed off with what happened. Joe and some of the other more experienced pilots had reservations about the raid. They thought it was a suicidal task and should never have been undertaken. I think that Holden was all for the raid because he was out to show that he was as good as Gibson – he wanted to make his mark on the squadron. No one can doubt his courage but it may well be that his judgement was clouded. As it was, the toll of casualties among the 617 'originals' was beginning to mount at an alarming rate. Having been formed at the end of March 1943, less than six months later 11 of the 17 pilots and most of their crew members were dead.

Following the disaster of Dortmund–Ems, 617 regrouped. Mickey Martin took over temporarily as squadron commander and replacement crews were posted in to begin training. We were now based at Coningsby, and had been since a couple of weeks before the Dortmund–Ems raid. A few weeks earlier, the squadron had been notified that we would be relocating because Scampton was at last going to be upgraded from grass runways to concrete. Apart from the Dortmund–Ems raid, there wasn't actually that much flying from Coningsby at first because poor weather conditions meant that operational duties were light all through October and November. I returned from the Bomb Leaders' Course in early November. It was to be an eventful month for me – one of the best ever.

Our new squadron commander was Wg Cdr Leonard Cheshire, who took over on 10 November. For some reason best known to the RAF at the time, Cheshire had had to accept a reduction in rank from Group Captain in order to be able to lead 617. He was in many ways the opposite of Guy Gibson. No less courageous or tactically astute, his personal character meant that he endeared himself to the squadron personnel immediately. He was friendly and approachable, taking time out to talk to all ranks. Outside the Officers' Mess, very few people in the squadron had had any genuine affection for Gibson and Holden was cut from similar cloth. Cheshire, on the other hand, was a complete breath of fresh air. He was, quite simply, the best commander I ever served under.

And there was another new arrival to look forward to. Later that month, we discovered that Gwyn was pregnant. As a result, according to the regulations at the time, Gwyn was required to leave the service immediately and she went home to Torquay. Our time together would now be restricted to occasional visits when I was on leave. Then, on 29 November, just a week after my twenty-second birthday, there was further cause for celebration. I was promoted to Pilot Officer. Still not drinking, I didn't do much celebrating. The pay rise would certainly come in handy with a baby on the way, but I also had to buy new uniforms and formal mess kit. There was, of course, a significant 'up' side in terms of my living conditions. I now joined the Officers' Mess with my own room and a batman – a 'skivvy' who would clean my kit and bring my morning tea. Gwyn had plenty of other things on her mind at the time, but I knew she was proud. It was, after all, quite something to be an officer's wife. She was a coal miner's daughter and had married a poor boy from the Lincolnshire farms. We were now taking a step up in the world. In future years, when things had settled down after the war, she would be going to formal dances, wearing ball gowns and long white gloves with pearl buttons. At times, she may have acted as though the whole promotion thing was 'all a bit of a drag' but the reality was that she was every bit as excited about it as I was.

On 9 December, our crew was seconded to 138 Squadron at Tempsford, along with the crews of Fg Off Weeden, WO Bull and Flt Lt Clayton and 16 ground crew. This squadron was a secret special operations squadron primarily concerned with supplying arms to the European resistance movements. On the night of 10 December, Weeden, Bull and Clayton attempted a drop in northern France without success. As I mentioned earlier, Weeden and his entire crew were killed. Bull was shot down but managed to survive with five crew members, only to be captured. Clayton returned to base, his mission unsuccessful. I have no idea why we were not required that night, but yet again luck was on our side. We were to try another such drop on 20 December but the weather was against us and we failed to spot any marker flares or lights on the ground. We had to abort. It may well have been that the local resistance had been largely rounded up by this time or had gone further underground to avoid detection. On the same night, Geoff Rice was shot down returning from a raid on Liège. He was the only survivor and managed to contact the local resistance but was eventually captured, becoming a POW. Another 'original' had gone.

While the rest of Bomber Command kept up its almost nightly attacks on the German cities, 617's attentions were now to switch to industrial production sites and weapons installations in France. And things were not going well. An attack on the V-weapons site at Flixecourt failed due to poor marking by Pathfinder Mosquitoes. Missions to an armament site at Liège and another V-weapons site at Abbeville were abandoned because of bad weather. We returned to Flixecourt on 30 December. The squadron reports show many pilots claiming that the 'target was hit provided marker flares were correct'. Again, the markers were off-target and the site survived. We were becoming increasingly frustrated by the lack of accuracy from the Pathfinders. The average bombing error was only 95 yards, with no bomb further than 150 yards away from the markers – that's pretty good going from 14,000 feet at night but it wasn't good enough. Cheshire, ably assisted by Mickey Martin, who had long been held as one of the best pilots in Bomber Command, particularly at low level, would tackle this issue himself.

In the autumn of 1943, 617 had been re-equipped with the SABS – Stabilised Automatic Bomb Sight. This was a huge improvement on the Mark 14, as it was able to calculate more accurately the variables that affected targeting and, once it was set on target, it released the payload automatically. On the Flixecourt raid, however, it wasn't only the PFF target marking that didn't go entirely to plan. We were dropping a 12,000 pounder and the bomb duly released on target, we felt the usual bump as the aircraft lost weight, and I looked down to see the bomb falling. Part of my job was to go back to the bomb bay and visually check that the weapon had dropped and the bomb bay was clear – only on this occasion it wasn't. This dirty great bomb was still hanging up in the bomb bay. The bomb that I had been tracking must have come from another aircraft and the bump we felt was probably from an explosion. I called upstairs, 'We still have the bomb, Joe!' 'Jeeesuus!' came the response. I wasn't too happy about keeping this thing on board. Don MacLean wanted it jettisoned. Getting rid of it would probably have been the sensible thing to do, but Joe had other ideas. 'No way!' he said. 'Either the instruments man is a shit or the bomb aimer is a shit, and I aim to find out which it is!' So we returned to Coningsby with a 'live' 12,000lb bomb on board. Fortunately for me, it was the 'instruments man' who was at fault. The bombsight had been changed on the afternoon before the operation and had been set for manual release, whereas the standard practice was to use the automatic release function. No one had even told me that there was a manual release on the SABS. I found out that it all depended on which socket below the bomb aimer's panel the sight was plugged into. That was very useful to know when it came to training others in the use of the SABS. There was considerable relief in the Officers' Mess that evening, but I wouldn't have liked to be that 'instruments man' when Joe caught up with him.

The New Year brought yet another move for the squadron, this time to Woodhall Spa, where I had the opportunity to stay in the famous Officers' Mess, which is now the Petwood Hotel, scene of the annual 617 Squadron reunion. Still concentrating on the V-weapons sites in northern France, we attacked Pas de Calais with some success on the night of 21 January. However, a return trip four nights later did not increase the damage. The weather was poor for flying and so operations were at a reduced level, but, with new crews constantly arriving, wherever possible training continued.

Cheshire and Martin had been working on a more efficient way of marking bombing points. They had decided that the best way to achieve this was to effectively 'glide bomb' the Lancaster, releasing the markers at a low level after a shallow-angled descent towards the target. They had tested the theory unofficially and were pleased with the results. On 8 February, they put it to the test operationally. In an attack on an aero engine factory in Limoges, Cheshire made low-level passes over the works to warn the workers to get out. This is a classic demonstration of Leonard Cheshire's humanity and it is doubtful that Gibson would have thought this necessary. On the fourth approach, he dropped incendiaries onto the factory roof. Martin followed the same tactic. The remaining 10 Lancs then bombed from 11,000 feet with great success. There were no casualties. Apart from an unsuccessful return to the Anthéor viaduct, February operations were effectively ruled out by the poor weather conditions.

If February had been snow-bound and quiet, 617 returned to the skies over France with renewed venom in March. Between 2 March and the end of that month, we flew nine separate missions, including four between 15 and 20 March. Using Cheshire's new marking system, we set about obliterating the heavy production factories in France.

March 2th BMW engine factory, Albert
March 4th Aborted attack on Saint-Étienne caused by bad weather
March 10th Bearings factory, Saint-Étienne
March 15th Aircraft factory, Woippy (aborted – bad weather over target)
March 16th Michelin rubber factory, Clermont-Ferrand
March 18th Powder factory, Bergerac
March 20th Explosives works, Angoulême
March 23th Aero engine factory, Lyon
March 25th Return attack on Lyon

The new marking system was working brilliantly, so much so that, when Cheshire asked for a faster, more agile Mosquito to make the task simpler, Harris not only responded enthusiastically but decided that 617 would now act as the marker squadron on multi-aircraft attacks. The first real test of this new strategy took place on the night of 5 April. Nearly 150 aircraft from 5 Group were despatched to an aircraft repair factory in Toulouse. Cheshire led the attack in his Mosquito and the remaining Lancasters obliterated the target. The evidence was clear. With accurate marking, even the less well trained were able to hit their targets much more successfully. On 10 April, we had similar success on a signals equipment depot at Saint-Cyr. Of the 25 aircraft taking part, 20 reported 'aiming point obtained'.

However, the Saint-Cyr raid was to be the last operational trip for Plt Off G. L. Johnson DFM. I had now flown enough ops to complete a second tour and it was pointed out to me that it was time to call it a day. I hadn't given any thought to leaving the crew. There was still a war on, after all, and we were now getting very good results hitting the Germans hard and very effectively. It was Joe, of course, who took me aside and had a quiet word. He knew that Gwyn was due to give birth in only a couple of months. 'Look, Johnny,' he said, 'you must know that Gwyn is going to be very concerned. She's going to be worried that she isn't going to have a husband, that this baby will never have a father. You have got to give her a chance. Pack it up now.'

I had never considered for one moment leaving the crew. I thought that my place was with them, for as long as it took, but Joe made me see sense. He made me see that I now had other responsibilities apart from fighting. So, with much regret, I left. I didn't want to, but it was a question of facing up to what I had to do. As a pilot, I hadn't been up to scratch. As a gunner, I had never actually shot at anything except practice targets. As a bomb aimer, I had had my chance to hit back at the Nazis and had made a good job of it. Now it was time to see how I would cope as a father.

# CHAPTER 10

# FROZEN POTTIES AND CAREER SUICIDE

On leaving 617 Squadron, I was posted back to Scampton, of all places, as a bombing instructor. In January 1940, when I left Lord Wandsworth's, I don't think that I would have been able to tackle this sort of job. Even two years before, I would have gone a bit weak at the knees. The idea of standing in front of a group of complete strangers and talking to them all – all of them at once – would have filled me with dread. By now, however, in the spring of 1944, I had been trained, I had travelled, I had been instilled with the culture and the discipline of the RAF, and I had been to war. I was also a married man, with a wife who gave me the support and encouragement I needed to progress and improve. I had complete confidence in my own abilities with bombing techniques and procedures, so I knew that I had something to offer as an instructor, even though it was a completely different kettle of fish from when I was told to take a young lad aside in training camp and teach him how to march properly. I had a few qualms about handling the classes but thought I could do a decent job.

This confidence came in spite of the fact that I was still relatively uncomfortable in the company of people I didn't know. I was still teetotal and no more at ease with the drinking culture in the Officers' Mess than I had been in the Sergeants' Mess. I could see how some of them enjoyed letting their hair down with a bit of horseplay – people's trousers being thrown out of the window, that sort of thing. When I hear stories today about seven men – an entire crew – piling into and clinging onto a two-seater MG Midget for a trip to the pub, or motor bikes being ridden up to the bar in the mess, it makes me smile. That sort of thing was not unusual, but it wasn't for me. The camaraderie and sense of belonging that I felt as part of Joe's crew meant a great deal to me and I thoroughly enjoyed being accepted by them as 'one of the boys', having a laugh and a joke with those I regarded as my friends, but I didn't need to go wild in the bar to let off steam. I was, I think, quite self-reliant and still very comfortable on my own.

Becoming an instructor was to go a long way towards changing that. At first I simply told myself that I had been given a job to do, so I had better get on with it. If the RAF wanted me to be an instructor, then that's what I had to do – we were still in the middle of a war and I still had a contribution to make. I knew about the SABS and had used it in action. I had to pass on what I could of my experience to others. Then a strange thing started to happen. Not only was I standing in front of my peers, even officers senior in rank to me, and lecturing them on bomb aiming, I was actually enjoying myself while doing it!

I put a bit of thought into it, too. Shortly after arriving at Scampton, I persuaded the technicians to make me a dummy bomb aimer's panel – a mock-up that I could use as a teaching aid. A senior officer, a bombing leader, came nosing round one day, saw my dummy panel and said, 'That's a very effective instruction tool. We could use that at Wigsley.' Wigsley was just a few miles away and was the home of 1654 HCU (Heavy Conversion Unit), training crews on four-engined bombers. I objected to losing my panel, so I said, politely but firmly, 'I'm sorry, sir, but I had this specially made and need it for training new arrivals to bring them up to scratch. I need it here.' He didn't seem too put out and I felt quite pleased with the way I had stuck up for myself. What I didn't know was that he was also the postings officer and, rather than argue with me about taking my panel to Wigsley, he simply moved me there, panel and all!

It wasn't long afterwards that I received a phone call from one of Nell's neighbours in Torquay – the same one who had made our wonderful wedding cake. Gwyn had given birth at home in her mother's house – a difficult 72-hour labour culminating in an instrument birth. It was 10 days before I could organise leave and get down to see Gwyn and my newborn son. My first introduction to fatherhood did not go well. Unused to the sight of newborn babies, my opening remark of 'Doesn't he look funny!' was greeted by a hysterical reaction from my wife. She burst into tears and gave me a proper tongue-lashing. It was all a bit awkward for a while. I had just about evened things out after that blunder when I made yet another, bigger one. The next day, I went to register the new child. It was required by law that babies be formally registered in the days immediately following the birth, so I had to do this sooner rather than later. Unfortunately, Gwyn and I hadn't had much of a discussion about the baby's name, but, in my naivety, I didn't see this as a major problem. A name was a name, so, with Gwyn still under doctor's orders to take as much 'bed rest' as possible, I went ahead and registered the baby as Charles Morgan Johnson, to be known as Morgan. Charles was my father's name – a family name – and Morgan from the Welsh family surname. It all seemed perfectly logical to me ... I had a lot to learn about being a husband and a father.

Gwyn did not take well to the fact that her son had been named without her being properly consulted. She burst into tears and started shouting again. She wasn't at all fond of my father and didn't see what her maiden name had got to do with anything. Nell came racing up the stairs to find out what was wrong, demanding to know why I had upset her daughter yet again. She asked what the names were and, when informed, gave her seal of approval. 'Well, there now, that's lovely. A wonderful idea,' she said, before telling Gwyn to 'stop being so bloody silly'. Having Nell's seal of approval settled the whole matter. Had it gone the other way, life could have been very difficult for a while.

Gwyn and I travelled back to Lincolnshire together to a house where we had rented some rooms from a woman in the village of Saxilby, in the same street where one of my brothers lived. It was the first time that we had actually lived together in nearly 18 months, but it wasn't to last long. I couldn't make it home one evening, having been instructing aboard an aircraft that was diverted for some reason. Gwyn had had a really bad night. The baby was suffering from the after-effects of his inoculation and she had been up half the night trying to get him to sleep. The lights had gone out and she did not have the right change for the meter. By the time I got home the following morning she was, understandably, at her wits' end. She had had enough of Saxilby and we decided that she should go home and stay with her mother in Torquay. I went down to see them whenever I could get leave – not an ideal start to family life, but there was still a war on and that is how it was for many young couples.

My next major training job was instructing the newly formed Tiger Force on the SABS bombsight. Following the German surrender in May 1945, the Allies turned their attention to the war in the Pacific. The Tiger Force was to be a long-range bomber force formed from squadrons of the RAF and the Commonwealth air forces. They would be based on Okinawa, striking targets in Japan prior to the Allied invasion. They began painting their aircraft white. The Lancs looked eerie in white – like ghosts. Tiger Force was disbanded, however, following the bombing of Hiroshima and Nagasaki in August 1945 and the subsequent Japanese surrender.

In the meantime, we had found an end terrace cottage in the town of Louth. The RAF had no responsibility for whatever off-camp accommodation its married officers arranged for themselves and their families. If married quarters were to become available, there was a waiting list and seniority provided priority. We would have had to wait quite a while for married quarters. Officers could be put up in the Officers' Mess, but if you wished to cohabit then you had to find your own living quarters. There was an NCO living next to us in the terrace and he helped to organise it all. For the first time, we were living together in a home of our own and beginning to feel like a proper married couple.

When we first arrived, it was all a bit of a shambles. The living room was pretty small, roughly 9 feet by 9 feet, and the adjoining kitchen wasn't much bigger. The toilet was outside and so was the water supply. There were two small bedrooms. Morgan had one, we had the other, and by God it was cold in the winter. You had to get into bed half-dressed and gradually strip off as you warmed up. In Morgan's room there was a potty under his bed and quite often the contents were frozen. Took a bit of emptying sometimes. This tiny two-up two-down was to be home for three years.

We made some improvements. While we were redecorating the living room, we stripped off the wallpaper to find layers of newspaper underneath. We spent so much time reading the old papers that the decorating got a bit behind. We called the house 'Lovely Cottage' after the horse that won the 1946 Grand National, and knocked down the wall adjoining a little pantry to create a utility room, bringing running water inside to a sink there. The toilet had to remain as an outhouse. There was no bathroom as such, so bathing was in what we called a 'zinco', a zinc bath that we put in front of the fire and filled with water heated in a copper washtub. Later we made some further improvements. We had new neighbours, an NCO who worked for me called Chalky White, his wife and young son. We decided that these cottages needed a coat of paint on the outside so we borrowed a ladder from a shop down the road and did the job. When the landlord came round to collect the rent he remarked on what a great job we had done and reduced the rent by 5 shillings a week!

We were beginning to make friends in the town as well. One particular couple, Dave and Ann Blackall, had rooms in the local pub, the Boars Head, which was just on the edge of the cattle market. Dave had been a pilot but was leaving the service and the publican decided that he and his wife were getting a bit old to be running this particular pub, so they asked Dave if he would like to take over, which he duly did. He knew nothing about business but persuaded the local Lloyds Bank cashier to do the books for him. Payment was in beer. Friday was market day when the local farmers would come to town, do their business and retire to the Boars Head afterwards. When the pub shut, we would always come back to our cottage. The living room was so small that the last person in closed the door and put their chair in front of it. Dave would always bring a case of beer and a good time was had by all.

By this time, I was actually able to enjoy a drink or two. It was Gwyn who finally persuaded me that it might not be such a bad thing. Towards the end of the war, we had been walking home one evening after a visit to the cinema when she suddenly disappeared behind a blackout curtain. I quickly followed her and found myself in a pub – and it wasn't at all an unpleasant experience. I remember having a glass of brown ale but later decided that I preferred having a nice glass of wine or a whisky. I didn't much care for drinking to begin with, but eventually grew to enjoy it – sometimes a bit too much!

In September 1946, Gwyn gave birth to our second child, a daughter named Susan Elizabeth (after full consultation). I came home early one afternoon because Gwyn had said she wasn't feeling too good and it was obviously getting very close to Sue's birth. Gwyn had seen a pair of green shoes in a shop and had said how much she loved them. I went out in the pouring rain and bought this pair of wedges. Wedge heels were all the rage at this time. Susan was born without any of the drama Morgan had induced – maybe the green wedges helped – and mother and daughter were soon home in 'Lovely Cottage', where we were to live for another two years.

Those immediate post-war years were a difficult time for many people. Life wasn't easy. We had two small children and money was tight. Rationing was still the order of the day: 2 ounces of butter, 8 ounces of sugar, 4 ounces of bacon or ham, one egg and so on – these were our weekly allowances. Clothing, coal, petrol, soap, washing powder and all the things that today we fill the supermarket trolley with every week were in short supply. Sweets were limited to 12 ounces per month. No crisps, burgers, pizzas. No mention of child obesity either in 1945. Our 'Lovely Cottage' had no modern conveniences – no electricity, no central heating, no electric iron, vacuum cleaner, washing machine or dishwasher. Yet we were happy there. I had a wife who loved and cared for me. I had my own young family. No car. I hadn't got round to taking the driving test yet. The war was over and we were all safe. I had a job that I enjoyed and was good at, and I had a circle of close friends. Post-war Britain still had its problems, but, as far as I was concerned, I had never had it so good! Gwyn used to say that these were some of the best years of her life. Living standards have obviously improved a lot since then, but I am not sure that we are any happier.

The first of a series of changes came about when I was giving courses at RAF Manby. The station had been an air armaments training centre during the war and was to become the RAF Flying College. I got on well with the Flight Lieutenant in charge of my courses and when it came time for him to leave his job he put in a word for me with the commanding officer.

I was interviewed and then appointed as officer commanding the Bomb Leaders' Course.

In the Officers' Mess at Manby, a certain standard of etiquette was required. During the war, mess conduct was a rather haphazard, 'boy's own' affair, certainly for operational squadrons. The Station Commander at Manby, Air Commodore Spreckley, was keen to return to pre-war standards. He instigated five formal dining-in nights per week for resident officers and three per week for living-out officers. All permanent commission officers were expected to wear formal mess kit. Career officers in the RAF, as opposed to those on a wartime short service commission that was expected to last until the end of hostilities, held permanent commissions.

We learned a lot about proper etiquette in those years. If you knew the rules and knew how to behave, many of the functions were very enjoyable. This is when the officers' wives would wear ball gowns and long gloves, buttoned gloves that they would unbutton when they sat down to dinner, slipping them off their fingers so that they could handle the cutlery. Not all squadrons would have the same formality in the future, but we were well trained.

Being in charge of the Bomb Leaders' Course was a great job, but it wasn't to last. While I was at Manby, the RAF offered me a permanent commission. This was something that required a great deal of consideration. The problem was that they did not give permanent commissions to bomb aimers, so I would have to learn another 'trade'. I would have to become a navigator. This would mean training for 18 months with various moves to different training centres covering different parts of the navigators' course. And that meant that

Gwyn and the children would be in a state of upheaval for the foreseeable future and, since I wasn't entirely confident about my own aptitude when it came to the different areas of navigation, I knew that there would be a lot of stress and very hard studying involved if I were to pass the courses.

I have never been afraid of hard work, but the courses came with the added pressure that, should I fail to pass and should I be ineligible for a permanent commission, we were in trouble. The choice that the RAF was offering was accept a permanent commission or leave the service – that was the way the system worked. My dilemma was: what on earth would I do if I had to leave the RAF? I had a wife and family to support. We didn't exactly have an extravagant lifestyle, but I certainly wouldn't be able to maintain our standard of living if I went back to my old trade as a park keeper. Gwyn understood the problem entirely but didn't push me one way or the other. She knew that I was the one who would have to put himself through the wringer to pass the courses and simply said, 'You make your own choice – only you can decide.' I decided to go for it.

The first stage of my training as a navigator was at RAF Topcliffe in North Yorkshire. I left for Yorkshire ahead of the family but failed to find us all accommodation by the time Gwyn and the children arrived, which didn't make me very popular. We stayed in a hotel until Gwyn found rooms in a very large house owned by a wonderful old man named Tommy. He was absolutely great and went out of his way to make us as comfortable as possible. He had been through two fortunes, living a good life, and his wife had died some years before. I think there was something about Gwyn that reminded him of his own wife and nothing was too much trouble to make her happy. He would even cycle off to the local farm to get us eggs when she wanted them. His wife had had her own sitting room where she would invite her friends to tea. Tommy insisted that Gwyn used it in the same way and many a legendary tea party took place with Tommy playing the part of 'butler'. The only thing that remained slightly annoying was a huge grandfather clock in our large sitting room. The chiming was very irritating so I stopped it. But every time we went away he would reset it again. Eventually we had to move on as I progressed to the last phase of my navigator training. Tommy cried the night we told him. He was a lovely man.

I was next headed back to Lincolnshire again, ultimately to RAF Swinderby, where I would work on the next part of the navigators' course, but, until they had a slot for me on the Swinderby course, I was 'parked' on familiar ground at Hemswell, although with aircraft that were somewhat new to me. I was assigned to 100 Squadron, which flew the Avro Lincoln, a development of the Lancaster that had been introduced in 1945. It had a more powerful version of the Merlin engines and could carry much the same payload as a Lanc but was faster and could reach over 30,000 feet. We managed to get into married quarters at Hemswell, one of the old prefabricated jobs. Unfortunately, I, or rather we, didn't get on very well with the station squadron commander. He was rather fond of bringing in 'ladies of the night' for a bit of fun on a Saturday evening. On one occasion he asked Gwyn if the woman he had brought in could stay with us overnight. She replied, 'What! I wouldn't allow her to breathe the same air as my children.' I received a rather less than complimentary report on my stay there. I can't imagine why.

During the final part of my training at Swinderby, we actually stayed for six weeks with my father. He was living in a house in Collingham; he had married again and had outlived his third wife, to be left on his own in quite a nice house. It quickly became obvious that Gwyn and the old man were not going to agree about anything. At one point he even accused her of being a 'gold-digger', to which Gwyn replied, 'If I was a gold-digger, I wouldn't bother digging in this mine!' It's amazing that Gwyn put up with him for a month and a half, but, having left the decision about our future up to me, she was backing me all the way. I was getting stuck into the courses, determined to do my absolute best, convinced that the hard work now would mean that there were better times to come.

When I first arrived at Swinderby, the postings officer gave me a form to complete asking for my posting preferences. I chose RAF Chivenor in north Devon, as that was the nearest base to Torquay, where Gwyn would be close to her family. On successful completion of the course I was posted to Kinloss in Scotland. It would be difficult to find two RAF operational bases further apart in the UK than Chivenor and Kinloss. Originally the RAF had actually found me somewhere even further away from north Devon – Malta – but Gwyn was pregnant with child number three and her doctor refused to let her travel until after the baby was born. I was, therefore, transferred to the weapons training department at Kinloss. Nearly 18 months of training to be a navigator, the award of a permanent commission and promotion to Flt Lt, and it was back to weapons training – this time in the far north of Scotland. The RAF moved in mysterious ways, but again fate had taken a hand because this was to be the best posting of my career.

RAF Kinloss is situated on the Moray Firth. It is about 57

degrees north and John o'Groats is only 59 degrees north (can you tell I'd been training as a navigator?), so you can't go much further on the British mainland. Gwyn was convinced that we would all freeze to death away up there at the top of Scotland, memories of the bitterly cold winters in 'Lovely Cottage' still fresh in her mind. I went up to Scotland ahead of the family, as had become our custom, to get established before sending for them to join me. Gwyn and the children stayed with Nell in Torquay, who, when she saw a map and realised how far away Kinloss was, told Gwyn, 'You are not taking the children up to that foreign part.' Gwyn replied, 'My place is with Johnny and the children's is with their father.' In the end, with Nell distraught at the thought of never seeing her grandchildren again, Susan was left behind in Torquay for a while when Gwyn and Morgan headed north.

Nell needn't have worried quite so much. This was 1950 and travelling by train from Morayshire to Devon took only a day – leave at the crack of dawn and, if your connections worked right, you could be there by bedtime. It would be much the same by rail today. And we weren't living in a complete wilderness. Morayshire is a beautiful county. The weather can be unkind – it can be very cold and the wind and tides can be extreme – but generally Moray has an exceptionally dry climate with above average hours of sunshine. It was a favourite holiday destination for the Victorians, many commenting on their surprise at the lovely climate and early harvests. It has a lower average rainfall than Eastbourne. The coast comprises miles and miles of unspoilt sandy beaches, caves and cliffs. There are many old fishing villages and harbours, with Cullen Bay a renowned destination for dolphin watching. All due, I am told, to the Gulf Stream.

For a while we lived in the village of Findhorn and we enjoyed good summers on the long sandy beaches. I used to take Morgan, then about six or seven, out into the countryside to go rabbit shooting. I borrowed a shotgun from a local farmer and would bring home the kill, skin it and give it to Gwyn to roast. Delicious. We lived a little better here than we had done in our 'Lovely Cottage', but, like most of the rest of the country, we had yet to acquire a television set. These were very new but we did manage to watch Queen Elizabeth's coronation on a TV in a neighbour's house, in black and white, of course. It was still quite a spectacle and Gwyn was terribly excited.

For me, working at Kinloss became a joy. The station had begun life as an Operational Training Unit (OTU) for bomber crews in 1940. It was far enough away from the combat areas in the south to provide a safe flying area for crews in training, weather permitting, but they did, nevertheless, suffer a number of losses. Worn-out aircraft and crews being trained under pressure, with largely unpredictable weather conditions, combined to produce 60 accidents in 1940 alone. Aircrew arriving, for training could not have been heartened by the sight of many wrecked aircraft around the airfield. On one occasion, they might have seen a crashed aeroplane in one of the streets of Forres, the local town. The tide could catch crews out as well, making ditching in Findhorn Bay something of a lottery. At low tide it was a quagmire of wet sand and there are stories of high tides that could flood the Kinloss runway, making crews think that they had misjudged their landing. One crew apparently sent out a Mayday thinking that they had landed in the sea. They were launching their inflatable dinghy when they spotted the emergency crews driving along the runway to 'save' them.

By 1947, Kinloss had been converted to a School of Maritime Reconnaissance and I was originally assigned to oversee the bombing and gunnery courses. Shortly before my arrival, however, 120 Squadron came north from RAF Leuchars to make Kinloss their new home. The squadron had flown the B-24 Liberator during the war on anti-submarine operations and had re-equipped with the Lancaster GR.3 for the maritime recon role in 1946. In 1951, they were converting to the new Avro Shackleton, a direct descendant of the Lanc. The design of the Shackleton began during the war when there was a desperate need for long-range aircraft to hunt down the U-boats that were decimating the Atlantic convoys. The Liberator was an American heavy bomber that had been modified for this role with Coastal Command, producing impressive results – 93 U-boats were sunk by Liberators, with 120 Squadron claiming 19 of these.

Lancaster designer Roy Chadwick was called upon to produce an aircraft that would be able to 'loiter' over an area where submarines were operating, staying aloft for far longer than either the Liberator or the Lancaster GR.3 could. Submarines, at that time, could not remain submerged for very long before they had to surface to recharge their batteries and replenish the air supply for the crew. An aircraft that could hang around for hours on end had the best chance of spotting a submarine on the surface. The Shackleton was equipped with Rolls-Royce Griffon engines and contra-rotating propellers, each engine having two three-blade propellers that turned in opposite directions. These provided just as much 'pull' without the engine having to work so hard, saving fuel and giving the Shackleton greater endurance. It could hang around on patrol at 500 feet for hours, waiting to pounce on a sub as soon as it surfaced. The engines also produced a lot of noise pitched at a level that was later found to cause high tone deafness. The 'Lancaster ear' syndrome had now become 'Shackleton ear'.

At Kinloss, 120 Squadron was putting the new Shackleton through acceptance trials and, posted in as weapons leader, I was involved in a very intensive flying programme. It was almost back to wartime conditions. We had our own aircraft and our own crew dedicated to flying this one aeroplane on whatever trips were scheduled. These would mainly be endurance exercises – we once did a 23-hour trip. The point of the exercise was to fly the aircraft for as long as possible, with one crew and no spare personnel. Unlike heavy bombers, the Shackleton did have a rest area and a galley. The only problem with this was that you had to eat what was stored on the aircraft. On one occasion, the wireless officer was charged with preparing breakfast and he produced spaghetti straight from the tin, little worm-like strands smothered in cold tomato sauce. It tasted bloody awful and put me off spaghetti for years.

On another trip I was flying with the squadron commander, Wg Cdr Peter Farr, who lived opposite us and we were quite friendly. We were recalled to base early and on landing I was told that this was because they wanted another crew to finish off our trip. In fact, Peter Farr's brother, Derek, was a famous film star and he was in a film that was being shown locally. Peter wanted to go to see it, and we were invited as well. In 1955, Derek Farr was to star as Gp Cpt John Whitworth, Station Commander at RAF Scampton, in *The Dam Busters* movie.

While we were at Findhorn, child number three came along.

We had no telephone but there was an army engineering section stationed just up the road from our bungalow and I arranged with their commanding officer that when the time came I could use their phone to call for the doctor. When the time actually did come, I went to their camp very late at night only to be told by the duty orderly, 'I am very sorry, sir, but the telephone is out of order.' I jumped on a bike and cycled to the local village and the nearest telephone box to ring the doctor. By the time I got home, he was already there, and after a brief inspection he said, 'I think we had better get to the hospital pretty quickly.' With no time to call a taxi, he insisted on taking us in his new car. I am not sure what he was more worried about – Gwyn, the baby or the potential damage to his upholstery!

The third birth was the quickest of all and our second daughter, Jenny, was born in no time. It had been a busy night in the maternity section and there were no spare cots, so they took a drawer out of a dresser and turned it into a crib for Jenny's first night. We told her ever afterwards that she came out of the 'top drawer'. The sister midwife sat on Gwyn's bed after the birth and said, 'Do you fancy a fag?' Gwyn replied, 'No, thank you,' to which the sister said, 'Well I do,' and promptly lit up there and then. The two midwife sisters later argued about which one was going to accompany us home to make sure everything was all right. Sister Smith, who had actually delivered the baby, won, but the other sister came along too.

The three years in Scotland was a very happy time for us. We eventually moved into proper married quarters and we made many good friends. We had a very active social life, both military and with the locals. Scottish country dancing became a regular feature of evenings out. Mess functions were relaxed and plentiful. I had, by now, left my teetotal days far behind and one Christmas drinks session landed me in hot water. It was then the practice (and may well still be) for the officers and sergeants to serve the airmen's Christmas lunch and then repair to the Sergeants' Mess for a postprandial. Unfortunately, on one occasion, I rather over-imbibed and on returning home found the family Christmas lunch in the dustbin. The air was not only frosty but very blue. After taking a nap on the sitting room floor, I eventually persuaded Gwyn to come to the mess with me that evening, only to be met by a fellow officer who said, 'I thought Johnny was back on ops at lunchtime today, Gwyn. He weaved beautifully down the road.' I don't think his comment was particularly helpful.

The hours of Shackleton operations were occasionally broken by moments that would be regarded as madness today. The Wing Commander called me in one day and said, 'Come on, Johnny, we're going to drop some depth charges. They want to see at what range they can pick them up on their radar.' When I asked who else was going, he said, 'No one – just the two of us.' So there were just two of us in an old Lancaster. I acted as flight engineer for take-off, then went down to the bomb bay and dropped the depth charges, then climbed back up again to assist with the landing – all highly irregular, but fantastic fun.

On another occasion, the Territorial Army people wanted us to make a demonstration supply drop. The Wing Commander wanted me to do it and asked who I would like to take with me. I asked for Paddy Green, who, in addition to being a great character, was a very good pilot. I made a point of insisting that I shouldn't have to fly with one particular pilot. When asked why, I replied, 'Because he suffers from verbal diarrhoea. The man never shuts up.'

A few weeks later, the aircrews were complaining that the depth charges they were dropping after cross-country flying exercises were breaking up when they hit the water. They were supposed to drop them from less than 100 feet but they were releasing them much higher than that. I told them that they were dropping too high and they were adamant that they were right. So we loaded up with depth charges, some filled with TNT, some with sodium amatol. Paddy Green was the pilot again but the second pilot was the non-stop talker. As we took off, a voice came over the intercom, 'Second pilot to bomb aimer: I am off my mike now and I will keep it switched off.' Somebody must have had a word.

We started the exercise at 1,500 feet. This was the height that the crews were used to and, of course, the depth charges exploded on impact. As we dropped down there was inevitably less and less damage to the weapon. When we finally dropped from 100 feet or less, they worked perfectly. 'So that is your answer,' I told them. 'If you drop from the proper height, they will work properly.' They didn't appreciate this at all. They were not used to attacking from less than 100 feet and didn't like the idea very much.

When the time came for me to leave Kinloss, my next posting came less as the result of carefully considered career planning and more as yet another stroke of good luck. The Wing Commander Flying at Kinloss, Bill Deacon, had been posted to 19 Group at RAF Mountbatten in Plymouth as Group Captain Operations, and before leaving he told me, 'Get that bloody promotions exam passed and I will ask for you down there.' Plymouth was certainly a lot closer to Torquay than Kinloss, so I set about passing the exam that would qualify me for promotion to Squadron Leader.

Having passed the exam, I was initially posted to RAF St Mawgan, 19 Group's main operational base, but after a few months Bill Deacon made good his promise and I moved to Plymouth as an acting Squadron Leader and Group Weapons Officer. I was still heavily involved in flying duties, but now, if I was away for any length of time, Gwyn had her mother close at hand to help with the children, which was a big plus. I remember thinking that only a few years earlier I had been a lowly 'erk' on sentry duty on Plymouth Hoe. What a difference a dozen years had made.

As Group Weapons Officer, I was one of the judges at a Command Bombing Competition that was held just off the coast of Fowey in Cornwall. Different squadrons competed over a five-day period to see who could get closest to various targets. The other two judges were the Command Weapons Officer and the Weapons Officer from 18 Group. An Australian officer was also present as an observer. We watched from a launch as the bombers approached and made their attempts, assessing the crews' performances. During the lunch interval, we threw fishing lines over the side to catch mackerel. Anyone who has done any mackerel fishing will appreciate that this is not a particularly difficult task. During the day the wives and children would get together and in the evening the adults went on a pub crawl. Halcyon days.

Unfortunately, a substantive ranked Squadron Leader was returning from overseas and a job had to be found for him. I was bumped back to the old job at St Mawgan before being sent on the Senior Officers Administration Course at RAF

Bircham Newton in Norfolk. This was to be my fifth move in 15 months.

I wasn't quite going back to bloody Lincolnshire again, but I wasn't far away. Bircham Newton is just across the Wash, isolated a few miles from King's Lynn in the wilds of East Anglia. In early 1954, the weather was cold, wet and generally very unpleasant. It was not a desirable place to be. Nor was the Senior Officers Administration Course the most stimulating of experiences. It mainly involved learning the correct way to write official letters and the correct procedures to follow when involved in the kind of admin that the course title suggests. It was dull but it was a vital stepping stone towards a higher rank. Clearly, despite having required me to train as a navigator, the RAF had me marked down as a useful weapons man, suitable for further promotion.

The family moved to Norfolk in part. Morgan was at boarding school in Plymouth as Gwyn and I felt that, with so much moving around, he now needed some continuity in his education. The RAF helped by subsidising the school fees. Susan was having another temporary stay with Nell, but both she and Morgan were to join us for a short time. The course was for only a few weeks and we stayed in two rented caravans as there were no married quarters available. We used one caravan as living quarters and sleeping accommodation for myself and Gwyn, while the children had the other caravan. Gwyn had to take them to the camp hospital for a bath. It was far from ideal.

At the end of the course, everyone got their postings except me. I went to the course officer and asked where I was supposed to be going, and he said he would find out for me. He disappeared for a while, then came back and said, 'Ah yes. You are going to a Canberra conversion squadron and then you will go to the V Force training unit and then to a V Force squadron.'

The Canberra was a medium-sized jet bomber that had been in service for around three years. Like all jets, it was new and different, but it was seen as a huge success. In fact, it would become one of the RAF's longest-serving aircraft, the last of their Canberras retiring as late as 2006. The Canberra conversion squadron posting was to familiarise me with the new breed of jet aircraft and prepare me for the next stage, a transfer to the V Force. The V Force aircraft were the new jet bombers, and still top secret. The Vickers Valiant, Handley Page Victor and Avro Vulcan were highly advanced aircraft designed to drop nuclear weapons – with the Soviet Union as their primary target. When I was told that I would be joining the V Force, none of these aircraft had yet entered service with the RAF – none of them had even gone into production yet. Clearly, I was going to be moved around from one job or training course to another until these aircraft went into squadron service. In the case of the Victor, that didn't turn out to be until 1958. I didn't know that at the time, but what I did know was that there would be a lot of to-ing and fro-ing in the meantime.

I said to the postings officer, 'I don't think so. I have had five moves in 15 months and I think it is time I spent rather more time with my family. I need something more permanent.' As 19 Group's new Weapons Officer had not yet arrived, I was sent back to my old job to await my fate.

In Plymouth, I was called in to see the Air Officer Commanding about refusing the posting. He said, 'You do realise, Johnson, that this will probably have an adverse effect on your career.' I replied, 'Well, I am very sorry, sir, but I think I owe it to my family to have something more permanent before I start moving around again.' He looked me straight in the eyes and said, 'All right. If that is what you want.'

I knew what I had done. I was one of the officers that the RAF had picked out for promotion and, having assessed my skills and aptitude, they had planned my future. I was being offered the opportunity to follow a path that would lead to a higher rank and a potentially glittering career. I am sure that, if I had gone back after careful consideration and said, 'Sorry, I've changed my mind. I'll go to the Canberra conversion squadron,' then they would have slotted all their plans back into place. The trouble was that they hadn't consulted me about those plans or the path I wanted to take – and they were asking me to choose between my career and my family. In that contest, there was only ever going to be one winner.

I knew that Gwyn would balk at the thought of several more months, possibly years, of postings that would prevent us from living any kind of normal family life. We were still in our early thirties and had our whole lives ahead of us, which, for anyone else, might have meant seizing the opportunity to climb the career ladder. The price to be paid for accepting that opportunity, however, was simply too high. With Gwyn, I had been able to create a wonderful family, and along with that family came certain responsibilities. The children needed to have as stable a home life as we could give them. Gwyn did not want to carry on moving from pillar to post and neither did I. It was not good for the children and it was not good for us. How many more 'two caravan' situations might we have to put up with?

I have been asked many times if I felt that I did the right thing by rejecting the career plan laid out for me by the RAF and my answer is always the same – of course I did. I had always followed the service maxim 'Never volunteer for anything and never turn anything down', but in this instance I had to ignore it. I was not prepared to risk the things that I had always wanted most – a loving marriage and a strong family. I wanted to have my family around me, hear the laughter and the conversation, have discussions with my children about seemingly unimportant things – moments to treasure. I was determined to miss as few of those as I could.

In the future, I would be mentoring young men who would go on to be Air Chief Marshals with knighthoods, while I would remain a Squadron Leader (roughly the equivalent of a Major in the army or a Lieutenant Commander in the navy), but there would be no regrets. I had made my choice and I had to stick with it. It was the right choice, and the RAF still had a lot to offer, including the most exotic posting I would ever have …

# CHAPTER 11

# SINGAPORE, SWORDS AND MISSILES

My next move was to RAF Bridgnorth in Shropshire and No. 7 School of Recruit Training. The reaction of most of my colleagues was, 'Jesus, Johnny, Tech Command, Recruit Training School – what a bloody bore!' From my point of view it wasn't quite as bad as that because it would give me my first experience of man management. Up until then, all my work had been involved with aircrew or on operations. I felt that this would be good experience. We went up to Bridgnorth, managed to get into married quarters, and I started as a Flight Commander. We had an intake of over 200 individuals broken up into four flights, two flights per squadron. We had corporal drill instructors for each of those flights.

Shortly after arriving at Bridgnorth, my substantive promotion to Squadron Leader came through. When I went to see the Station Commander about it, he said, 'Well, A Squadron – the one you are on at the moment – is commanded by an acting Squadron Leader and Group have decided that

that post is to be upgraded to a substantive rank, so he is going to move over. Do you think you could make as big a mess of a squadron as he did?'

'I'll try hard, sir,' I replied, and took over in charge of training A Squadron. This turned out to be far more rewarding than I could have hoped. No two days were the same and I was managing the staff as well as being responsible for the recruits. By this time, the young lads coming into the RAF were doing their two years' National Service and, while most of them were perfectly decent young men, not all of them really wanted to be part of the military. This did cause occasional problems.

There was one incident when I was called from my office to deal with a recruit who, according to the NCO who had rushed over to fetch me, was 'about to commit suicide with his bayonet, sir!' When I got to the barrack hut and found the young man in question, he was clearly extremely upset and was, indeed, threatening to do himself some damage with a bayonet. For many of these young recruits, this was their first time away from home, the first time that they had been separated from their families. They were in a totally unfamiliar environment, caged up with a bunch of other young men who could be loud, boisterous, even aggressive. On top of that, they were expected to adhere to military discipline, obeying orders that came to them loud and fast from NCOs who were not the most sensitive or sympathetic souls. I talked to the young man with the bayonet. I knew what he was going through – I had been there myself many years before, lost and alone in a strange place. Slowly, I gained his confidence and persuaded him to hand over the bayonet. After that incident, we kept an eye on him and made sure that he wasn't going to get himself into such a state again. He finished his basic training successfully and went on to learn a trade, a credit to the RAF.

Not every problem had quite such a satisfactory ending. We had one young Welsh lad who was a complete disaster. He could do nothing right and wasn't interested in learning. Even laying out his kit for inspection was beyond him. He was disruptive and obstructive, and his corporal lost patience with him – corporals never really being renowned for their endless patience – and hung him from the barrack-room rafters by his webbing straps, leaving him dangling there to teach him a lesson and as an example to the others. The recruit complained about his treatment and there was a huge fuss. The corporal was court-martialled. I gave evidence at his hearing, describing the recruit as useless and the corporal as an exemplary NCO. He lost his stripes and was sentenced to 28 days in the glasshouse, later reduced to just seven. Within a few months, he had earned his stripes back again, while the recruit was caught stealing a watch, court-martialled and dishonourably discharged from the service.

Bridgnorth had been a good posting for us. The work was satisfying, the social life was fun and we had the family around us. Apart from anything else, I learned to drive there and passed my test (second attempt), as did Gwyn (first attempt), but in April 1957, with my time at Bridgnorth coming to an end, I went to see the Station Commander, who by that time was Tony Trumble, to ask about my next posting. I got along very well with Tony, and his wife was in charge of the camp wives' club, organising social events and suchlike, and had roped Gwyn in as secretary, so we were good friends with them. Tony had no idea about where I was supposed to be going next, but one of our officers had just been posted to the

Ministry of Defence in charge of Squadron Leader Navigator postings and Tony told me to give Mike a ring. It seems quite a casual way to organise your career, but, when you knew the right people, that was the way it was done. I gave Mike a call.

'Well, what sort of posting do you want?' Mike asked.

'Overseas would be nice,' I said.

'Hmm … when did you last go?' he asked.

'I've never been!' I said.

'Really?' said Mike. 'We'll have to sort that out, then. Leave it with me.'

A couple of days later, he got back to me and said, 'The only thing I've got is Officer Commanding maritime ops AHQ [Air Headquarters] Singapore, but it's not until October. In the meantime you can do the joint navy course.'

'I've already done it,' I replied.

'Well do it again, then.'

The posting to Singapore was confirmed in October and Gwyn wasn't at all happy about it. She really didn't want to go and was all for me going on my own, leaving her in England with the children. I argued that it would be a change of scenery, something completely different, and eventually persuaded her that it would be a good thing for the family.

We set off for Singapore on what was possibly the worst troop ship in service – the MV *Devonshire*. We did have an enjoyable six-week voyage, visiting fascinating places en route that before had just been names on a map – Gibraltar, Port Said, the Suez Canal, Aden, Colombo. The crew were predominantly lascars, which, we learned, was a name for any Indian or Malay serviceman. Most of them, as I recall, came from Goa. They were a good lot and cooked delicious curries. Another new experience. We dined with the ship's officers and other officers in transit, which was usually very pleasant, although the engineering officer was a thoroughly miserable character. As it turned out, he had plenty to be miserable about on the clapped-out *Devonshire* as the engines packed up in the Malacca Straits on the approach to Singapore and we suffered the ignominy of being towed into harbour. I suppose that's the good thing about a ship. If you lose your engines, it's not the end of the world, unless you're caught in a horrendous storm. That actually did happen to the *Devonshire* the following year, on her way back to England while crossing the Bay of Biscay. She sent out a Mayday call but then managed to get her engines going again.

I only ever remember a Mayday, or the equivalent request for an emergency landing, being sent out once when I was on ops. If a Lancaster lost all four engines, you'd had it, but it could struggle home with difficulty on just one engine. Almost as serious was coming in with two engines out – I remember Joe landing Chuck-Chuck with only two engines, both on the same side. He informed the control tower that we were coming in for an emergency landing and ordered us into crash positions, so I was up out of my office and sitting with my back to the main spar. It took quite some skill to fly a Lanc on two engines, even more to land it safely, but Joe put Chuck-Chuck down as light as a feather. He did, however, land to the side of the main runway – not a problem on a grass airfield – to make sure that, if it did all go horribly wrong, we wouldn't be blocking the runway for other aircraft coming in. That was the Lanc for you – reliable as the day is long and a dream to fly when it was handled by a pilot like Joe. Joe's son told me a story in later years about a time when a heavy flak shell burst so close below one wing that it flipped the aircraft over, with a full load of bombs aboard. Joe simply rolled it back onto an even keel and carried on. I don't think that I was with him on that trip. I'm sure that I would have remembered being thrown up onto the roof of my office! I don't believe that either of those incidents are recorded in any official documents that I have ever seen, but official records don't always tell the full story about everything.

When we eventually disembarked from the *Devonshire*, we went to the Grand Hotel where we were to stay until we could be allocated more permanent accommodation. I paid a visit to the Headquarters Far East Air Command to see the Group Captain Operations in order to find out when I would be starting work. He greeted me by saying, 'Good morning, Johnson. When are you going back to the UK?'

'I beg your pardon, sir,' I replied, 'but I have only just come out.'

'Yes, yes,' he said, 'but the job you have come out to do is being done away with in December – so what are we going to do with you in the meantime? I suppose you can sit in with our Weapons Officer, Bottom. Calls himself Botomme actually, would you believe. You can't possibly make as big a cock-up of this job as he has, so you can join him for the time being.'

For anyone who wasn't entirely used to the way that the RAF worked, this might all have been a bit worrying. No job for me to do? Had I brought my whole family all that way for nothing? I wasn't too concerned. These things have a way of sorting themselves out in the service. It was clear that there were changes afoot – and when changes are happening, having an experienced man on hand is never a bad thing. One of the changes involved 205 Squadron, which was re-equipping with Shackletons, having previously flown Catalinas and Sunderland flying boats based at RAF Seletar. The runway at Seletar, however, wasn't long enough to operate Shackletons, so the squadron was moving to RAF Changi in the east of the island. For someone like me, with a lot of experience on a Shackleton squadron, there was almost certainly going to be a job to do.

Changi was a busy place, with Transport Command Valetta, Dakota and Hastings aircraft competing for space with a few Bomber Command Canberras and now 205 Squadron's Shackletons. To operate the Shackletons effectively, what they needed was a Maritime Ops Room at Changi and, luckily enough, there I was, ready and willing to set it up. This became my new job and I loved it. We had to start from scratch. Even building up the complete sets of the maps we needed to cover the whole of the Far East area was a challenge, but I had some good people working for me and I was able to run the place the way I wanted it. I was responsible for Maritime Squadron operations as well as Search and Rescue in the Far East.

We moved into married quarters at Changi, where we had a large bungalow, although Gwyn didn't have to worry too much about the housekeeping because we also had two amahs, delightful elderly Chinese ladies who did all our household chores. We were living the sort of ex-pat, colonial lifestyle that we could only have dreamed of a few years before, and, given the welcome addition of overseas allowances, we were financially better off than ever before. Once we were settled into our own place, any misgivings Gwyn had had about the move to Singapore were quickly forgotten.

Maritime Ops involved a lot of training flights to prepare the crews for their role in searching for downed aircraft or ships in trouble. There were lots of operational flight exercises, most of them far out at sea, and we used operating codes that changed every day. We were at the height of the Cold War, after all, and the Soviets were listening to everything that we did, so new code sheets were issued every time we went out. Should one of our aircraft find an aircrew or ship's personnel in trouble in the water, they could drop 'Lindholme Gear' to them. This was a rescue apparatus developed during the 1940s that comprised five cylindrical containers. The containers were roped together, the middle one containing a nine-man inflatable dinghy. The Lindholme Gear would be dropped upwind of the survivors, with the dinghy inflating when it hit the water. The whole lot would then drift towards the survivors. Once they were in the dinghy, they could drag the other cylinders aboard – these contained emergency rations, medical supplies and survival kit. Hopefully that would keep them alive until a naval vessel could reach them.

We also flew anti-piracy patrols when the Shackleton would carry a liaison officer from the local police force. They would be looking for suspicious vessels and reporting their position so that the navy could try to intercept them and find out what they were up to. We later had a detachment on the island of Gan in the Maldives, where the RAF had inherited a base from the Royal Navy. Gan was used as a staging post for aircraft flying from the UK to the Far East but we were primarily there to mount anti-piracy patrols. The Search and Rescue role, however, was our most important function, never more so than when we had to go looking for one of our own aircraft.

On 9 December 1958, I visited the naval base to discuss a joint exercise with the Royal Navy, and when I got back I took Gwyn for a night out at the Officers' Club. We were enjoying the evening when a call came over the tannoy: 'Will Squadron Leader Johnson please report to the Operations Room.' I rushed over to the Ops Room to discover that one of our aircraft was missing. Shackleton VP254, piloted by Flt Lt Bouttell, had been on an anti-piracy patrol in the area of the Philippines and nothing had been heard of it since lunchtime. We started up the Search and Rescue operation but it was clear that Changi was too far away from the area where the aircraft had been lost, so we had to move our centre of operations to Labuan, off the coast of Borneo. We had become good friends with the base Medical Officer, Pip Mounfield, and his wife, Jean, and they remain my close friends to this day. Before we left for Labuan, Pip, knowing that we would be spending long hours on this job, gave me and the officer who was to act as my deputy some pink 'wakey-wakey' pills and some blue sleeping pills to counteract their effects when we could spare some time to rest. Once we got to Labuan, I took the first shift, organising the search aircraft while my deputy got some rest. When it came time to hand over, he was woken up, decided to take a pill to get him going, but took the blue instead of the pink and went straight back to sleep! I had no choice but to carry on directing operations.

For six days we searched for the missing aeroplane but could find no trace of it whatsoever. We were using other Shackletons from the squadron, we were using transport aircraft – Dakotas and Hastings – and we were even using an old Anson from one of the communications flights. It was the Anson that came back from a patrol on the sixth day to say that they had spotted a fresh grave on a very small island. There was a cross on the grave with B 205 written on it along with an RAF roundel and a red, white and blue striped symbol representing the markings carried on the tailplane of a Shackleton. There was no doubt that the grave was linked to our missing aircraft and a New Zealand navy frigate went in to investigate. They found just one body, that of the flight engineer, Flt Sgt Dancy.

There was a Russian supply ship in the area, not a spy trawler or anything like that, a genuine factory ship to which the Chinese fishermen would take their catches to be processed. We wanted to find the fishermen who had discovered this body and to find out why they had buried it as they did, offering a reward for information. A lot of information came back, but it was relatively simple to work out that which was of value from the stuff that was not. We eventually did find the fishing crew that had dug the grave. They said that they had been fishing in the area and had seen this aeroplane come along very low. Suddenly it went into the water. They had circled around but the only thing they could find was one body and, because it still seemed warm, they hauled it out of the sea. Had it been cold they would have left it. The man was dead, however, so they took the body to the nearby island and buried it. They were given the reward, which, as I recall, was fairly substantial.

There was much speculation about why the Shackleton had crashed. Although affectionately described by its crews, who loved the Shackleton, as '10,000 loose rivets flying in close formation', it was not an aircraft that was known to have any serious vices. With no wreckage to examine, however, it was impossible to work out exactly what had happened. The official board of inquiry stated that in the absence of any detailed information the most likely cause of the accident was pilot error. When the squadron had re-equipped, some of the flying boat crews had converted to Shackletons. The co-pilot on this trip was a former flying boat pilot and it is thought that, while they were involved in a low-level search run, he may have taken the Shackleton in too low, at a height that might have been fine for a Catalina or a Sunderland with their high wings keeping the props and engines well clear of the water, but that was fatal for the Shackleton. This was really the only explanation that made sense.

The navy brought the body back to Labuan and Doug Thomas, one of the Dakota pilots, was detailed to fly it to Changi, but this was the tropics, hot and humid, and the corpse had been in the ground for some time, so when he landed he said, 'My God ... the stink in that aircraft ... please don't ever ask me to do that again.' The whole crash incident affected everyone on the base and Gwyn was very much involved as far as the wives of the missing aircrew were concerned, doing her best to console as many of the wives as she could. The wife of the pilot had lost her second husband to an RAF crashed aircraft. There was a funeral service and that was the end of that dreadful episode.

By now it was just before Christmas and there was a mess party planned. After much discussion following the loss of the Shackleton crew, it was decided that this should go ahead. Once the search was called off, the rest of the squadron left Labuan to return to Changi and we, the operations staff, stayed behind to tidy up. We were told that they would send a Hastings back for us that evening, so we went to the mess for the first time since we had been there. We had a drink in the bar to start with, then went to lunch, and then we went to the NAAFI. Out there drink was even cheaper than in Singapore. Because it was nearly Christmas we stocked up on booze and at around eight o'clock the Hastings arrived. We went out to the aircraft carrying our bags of Christmas drink and, as I reached the top step of the rather tall ladder to enter the aircraft, I slipped, sliding right down to the bottom again … but, with great presence of mind, I held the bag upright and didn't crack even one of the bottles. When I got home I discovered that I had severely grazed my chest but that didn't matter – I had not lost any of the booze.

When we got back, the Christmas party was just about to get going but, having had very little sleep in the last 10 days, I was more than a bit tired. I got into my formal mess kit and lay on the bed. Pip and Jean Mounfield came to collect us, only to be told that I was asleep. Pip said, 'I'll fix that,' and went off to the hospital to fetch me a couple of 'wakey-wakeys'. He guaranteed that they would 'keep you going until three o'clock'. And they did. Just before three, Gwyn brought me home and put me to bed.

The Shackleton disaster aside, the work at Changi was so thoroughly enjoyable and the social side of things so much fun that there were times when I questioned whether we were achieving what we were really meant to be doing out there. When I thought about it seriously, I came to the conclusion that, yes, we were preparing ourselves for what we were tasked to do. We were providing a level of security for the area and we were on standby for all forms of search and rescue. They were a very interesting and fulfilling three years.

Singapore had many wonderful shops, particularly in Changi village, where there was a fantastic jeweller. Chang was a youngish man and we used to visit him to browse the items that he had on display, but Gwyn would inevitably say, 'Oh, come on, Chang, let's have a look at the valuable stuff you've got in the safe.' We would usually end up buying something from him and built up a very nice collection of bits and pieces, jewellery and watches. I remember that we had seen a tea service that we rather fancied in a shop in the city of Singapore but it was quite expensive. When we mentioned this to Chang, he said, 'Don't worry, I'll get it for you.' He did, and charged us trade price.

If ever the ladies wanted a new dress for a mess function, they would go down into the village where there were Malay ladies – some Chinese, but mostly Malay – who would make up the chosen material into the dress in a day. If they wanted shoes covered in matching material that was also easily done – all wonderfully good quality and very good value. For men, one of the things that was most popular was the sharkskin dinner jacket, which could be provided with equal efficiency. If you were having a suit or a pair of trousers made, one of the key questions was: 'Want a yip yon?' The answer would be: 'Yes, thank you – no buttons, just a yip.'

Because Morgan was sitting his O level exams (now called GCSEs), we were able to extend our stay in Singapore for six months, although we had to leave the married quarters. We hired a little house off the base and one Saturday afternoon I heard a band playing, so we went out to the garden gate and found that there was a Malay wedding reception going on in the kampong at the end of the street. We were invited in and it turned out to be quite a party! On another occasion, we went out on a Saturday morning, again having heard music in the air, and watched a Chinese funeral procession. They were filling up the hearse with all sorts of bits and pieces that they were going to bury with the individual, things that he might need in the afterlife, including fruit. The mourners were singing 'Happy Days Are Here Again', which seemed to us to be a rather odd song for a funeral, but, if they believed that the deceased was headed to a better place, it makes perfect sense.

At one point some of the boys from the grammar school, including Morgan, were going up to the Slim School in the Cameron Highlands during the summer holiday as part of the Duke of Edinburgh's Award scheme. The Slim School was for British forces' children and was named after Field Marshal Slim, who had commanded the British 14th Army in Burma during World War II. The D of E schedule at the Slim School included a three-day jungle trek. We went up into the hills at the same time and stayed at a small hotel called the Smokehouse Inn that was the nearest thing to an English pub I've ever seen abroad. The son of the landlord was the manager of one of the local tea plantations. He came down one night and said that the boys should not be allowed to go into the jungle as there were tigers about. 'One has already taken one of my planters,' he said. 'The slightest noise will attract one of these creatures.' We had a little bungalow in the grounds of the hotel and one evening we drove to another hotel to have dinner with some friends. We came back in the car, very much aware of the tiger stories, the dustbins at the hotel having been turned out by a tiger only the night before. I drove up to the bungalow and leaped out, leaving the car headlights full on while I opened the front door and switched on all the lights inside the house. Then I had to go and park the car, switch off the lights and walk back to the bungalow, constantly looking over my shoulder, expecting a huge tiger to pounce at any second. Needless to say, neither we, nor the boys, had any problems with tigers while we were there.

Apart from causing me to frighten myself half to death peering out into the darkness for tigers, Morgan's school was also responsible for a much-treasured and lasting friendship. Totally off her own bat, Gwyn had got a job as secretary to the headmaster of the Changi grammar school. One of the PE teachers was a very nice young woman called Ann and when a young officer called David Parry-Evans was posted to the squadron as a co-pilot, they met, fell in love and eventually David proposed. In those days, an officer had to be 25 before he could marry and they had to wait until David's twenty-fifth birthday, by which time he had been promoted to Flight Lieutenant and was the captain of an aircraft. Ann's parents couldn't get out to Singapore for the wedding, so she asked me to give her away. They were married in Singapore cathedral with the reception at the Raffles Hotel. This was a high-class wedding and they had a guard of honour, which meant swords. Ceremonial swords look great but they are rather valuable items of kit – difficult and expensive to replace if lost. The swords were FEAF (Far East Air Force) property and Gp Cpt Trumble, who had been Station Commander at Bridgnorth but had since been posted out as Group Captain Ops FEAF, knew just who to put in charge of them – his weapons man. When the arrangements for the wedding were being finalised and the question of swords came up, he said, 'Don't worry about that. Johnson knows about swords – he can take care of them. He'll be responsible for them.' Throughout the whole wedding, I never took my eyes off those swords. They were all handed back in good order afterwards.

We established a very strong friendship with Ann and David and we were delighted to watch David progress through a very successful RAF career. When we first met, he was a Flying Officer and I was a Squadron Leader. When I retired, I retired as a Squadron Leader. When he retired, he retired as Air Chief Marshal Sir David Parry-Evans. Rather a different result there but I was delighted for him. We made our different choices and followed our different paths. David deserved every promotion that he got, devoting himself to whatever job he was given. He was considered as the next Marshal of the Air Staff, but Air Chief Marshal Harding beat him to it. So he retired. He now lives in a quiet Gloucestershire village and we still stay in contact.

After three great years, I was ready to come home – it wasn't that I wanted to leave Singapore, but to me England is home, so that was where I wanted to be. Gwyn, the one who had not been at all happy about going out to the Far East in the first place, was not at all keen on coming back. She realised, of course, that we had no choice in the matter. We came back on the *Oxfordshire*, a new troop ship that was only three years old. In fact, the use of troop ships was to be phased out completely by the end of 1962, so, had we been travelling a couple of years later, we would have been given seats on an RAF transport aircraft. I don't know how I would have persuaded Gwyn to get on an aeroplane! As it was, we had a leisurely voyage home preceded by a lovely send-off. Pip and Jean Mounfield, who had become (and still remain) very close friends, came to our cabin for a quiet farewell and the grammar school headmaster had bought Gwyn a charm for her charm bracelet with the Lord's Prayer on it. A Shackleton flew past, dipping its wings in salute, as the ship left Singapore. It was an emotional moment.

Our first port of call was Colombo in Ceylon, now Sri

Lanka, then it was on to Malta. I got up for breakfast, leaving Gwyn in bed, and found an RAF accounts officer sitting at a desk handling currency exchange for those who wished to go ashore. It was Vernon Cavey, who had been a fellow officer at Bridgnorth. There was much hand shaking before I rushed off to fetch Gwyn and, once he had finished his business aboard the ship, Vernon took us ashore to show us around Malta, the beginnings of another lifelong friendship. Malta was a beautiful island and it did seem a shame that we hadn't been able to take the opportunity to stay there when I had been earmarked for a posting a few years previously, but such is life.

What concerned me now was my next posting and, had I known how that was to turn out, I wouldn't have been looking forward to seeing England again at all. Towards the end of my tour in Singapore, there had been a signal asking for volunteers for ground-to-air weapons training. That was considered to be the future career in the air force. For the second time, I went against the old maxim 'Never volunteer, never refuse' and volunteered for Guided Weapons training. When my posting came through, I could hardly believe it – back to bloody Lincolnshire! Hemswell again. And back to 97 Squadron, where my active service had begun 17 years earlier. The Guided Weapons course was mostly theory, a lot of code work, a detailed description of the Thor missiles and the procedure for launching, and so on. The Thor missile was massive, the biggest weapon that I had ever worked with, and I had now been responsible for pretty much everything, from swords upwards. The missile was 65 feet long and housed in a shed that, once the firing sequence started, rolled away on rails to expose the weapon. The missile then rose to the vertical position on its launch platform. Once it was upright, fuelled and ready to go, the rocket motor was fired. The whole launch sequence took about a quarter of an hour, and 18 minutes after that it would deliver its nuclear warhead to a target in Russia.

The missiles were American owned but deployed in Britain because their range of 1,800 miles or so made it possible for them to target the Soviet Union from Bomber Command's bases. Twenty RAF squadrons deployed Thor missiles at bases in Yorkshire, Norfolk, Suffolk, Cambridgeshire, Leicestershire, Northamptonshire and Lincolnshire. Bases were linked in groups for simultaneous launch, with Hemswell the main operations base for the group that included Ludford Magna, Bardney, Coleby Grange and Caistor.

Having just returned from a fantastic three years in Singapore, we went to spend Christmas in Torquay. We were on our way back to Lincolnshire the day after Boxing Day, 1960, and had reached Newton Abbot, only a few miles from Torquay, when we hit black ice. I was driving, with Susan in the passenger seat and Morgan and Jenny in the back with Gwyn, who had her feet up on a cushion behind Sue's seat. The car skidded, spinning straight across onto the other side of the road. Fortunately, there was no traffic coming the other way, but we smashed into a concrete bus shelter. The impact burst the fittings securing Sue's seat, which was pushed back onto Gwyn's feet, and at the same time the back door burst open and Gwyn was thrown out. Gwyn was clearly badly hurt and in a lot of pain. A nurse who was at the bus stop helped us summon an ambulance.

At the hospital, Susan had treatment for a cut on her face and Gwyn was taken off for X-rays that showed she had fractured her pelvis. That was going to mean a long spell of hospital treatment in Newton Abbot. Gwyn hadn't been there very long, however, when Pip Mounfield returned from Singapore. The doctor who was looking after Gwyn said to her one day, 'Who is this Dr Mounfield who keeps ringing up to ask about your progress? Was he at St Thomas's?' Gwyn said that Pip had been and the doctor replied, 'Good grief! I used to play rugby with the bugger.' Pip was soon able to arrange for Gwyn to be transferred to the RAF hospital at Nocton Hall, just the other side of Lincoln from Hemswell. I have to say that, while I had often been very critical of the railway system, I take my hat off to them for what they did the day that we transferred Gwyn by train. She was on a stretcher and wherever necessary they took the window out of the carriage so that they could get the stretcher in. Wherever we went there were people waiting to move this stretcher from one platform to another and from one train to another. They did themselves proud.

At Nocton Hall the orthopaedic specialist was Wg Cdr Griffiths. He was a super character and he settled Gwyn in properly. I used to visit her whenever I could, but I had to complete the course I was on and, of course, we had lost our car in the accident – it was a write-off. I went along to the local garage, which was owned by Henry Challons, a wonderful old man with a beard like Father Christmas, and his son Brian. Henry had a 1935 Rover 16 which he sold me for £35. A lovely old bus that was. We now had this big car in which Gwyn could stretch out on the back seat without any discomfort when she came out of hospital. We ran that car for quite a while. When Gwyn eventually came home, I got some leave in order to nurse her in the prefab we had as married quarters. One day, when we went up to Nocton for one of her outpatients' appointments, Griff said to Gwyn, 'I've got good news. You can get up and try to walk if you like.' I said, 'You're a bit late, Griff, she's been doing that for the last week!' There was no way that Gwyn was going to remain immobile for an instant longer than she needed to. It took a while to build her confidence enough for her to go out on her own or to drive by herself, but eventually she was right as rain again.

Gwyn being hurt and her period of recovery coincided with what was undoubtedly the worst job that I had in the RAF. There were three Thor missiles at Hemswell and three at each of the other four bases in our group. There were four groups, making a total of 60 missiles that could be fired from the UK. These were under 'dual key' control, meaning that they couldn't be launched without authorisation from both the UK and US High Command. This meant that, in practice, we could prepare the missiles for launch but only the Americans could 'push the button'. We worked with American Air Force officers in the Ops Room who, we were told, had been specially selected to get on better with the English than the Americans generally did. In fact, they were very pleasant to work with and we enjoyed their company. What I didn't enjoy was the work itself. It was the first time I had ever been on shift work – and it was the most awful shift system you could imagine. Two days from 8.00 am to 4.00 pm; two days from 4.00 pm to midnight; two days from midnight till 8.00 am the next morning. So your system got used to nothing. You didn't know if you were punched, bored or countersunk. After the midnight shift you got a sleeping day and a day off.

By this time we were living in my father's house. He had,

amazingly enough, married again in the ensuing years, his new wife and himself combining their funds (hers more than his, I suspect) to buy Guildford House in Collingham. Father's wife had passed away some years ago and he had died while we were in Singapore – I didn't bother coming home for the funeral. In his will, he had stipulated that the house should be split between myself and my brothers. Lena was left only the furniture. Given all of the years that my sister had devoted to him, that was simply unacceptable. I persuaded my brothers that Lena should be given the house to live in for as long as she wanted it, but it had ultimately become too much for her. When I was posted to Hemswell, I found Lena someplace more suited to her needs and we took over Guildford House. In the short term, what that meant was that my 'sleeping' days were spent working in the garden, which had long been neglected.

As a former gardener, of course, that at least offered a kind of stress relief for me because my working hours were spent sitting in the Ops Room at Hemswell on an eight-hour shift, hoping like hell that nothing was going to happen because that would mean that the balloon had gone up and the world as we knew it was about to end. There were occasional exercises from Group or Command and from time to time we organised our own exercises, but the majority of the shifts were spent working on the new codes as they came out each month and very little else. My smoking increased from 20 to 40 per day.

Towards the end of my time there, I was sent a letter from the Ministry of Defence to say that it was unlikely that I would receive any further promotion. That was the final straw for me. I was doing a job that I hated, I was not seeing my family as much as I wanted and I was now being told that this was the best I could expect from the service. I decided that I was going to apply for early release and leave the RAF. The question was, at the age of 42, how was I going to earn a living to support my family? The answer was really quite simple, but it wasn't going to be easy ...

# CHAPTER 12

# TEACHING AND THE TORY PARTY

There was a sense of déjà vu about what was now happening in my life. I had been through the same dilemma 15 years before when I had been offered a permanent commission. If I left the RAF, what would I do to earn a living and support my family? I had three children still at school and school fees to pay, although Morgan was shortly due to leave his boarding school in Taunton. Gwyn had a job at the local school, which helped financially, but for me to now become a gardener in a municipal park was even less of an option than it had been all those years before. One major difference now, however, was that I had a far clearer idea of how the skills that I had acquired in the service could transfer to civilian life. For the last 22 years, ever since I joined the RAF, I had been on one course after another, being instructed in a wide range of skills, from pilot training in Florida to the launching of a nuclear missile in Lincolnshire. I was never going to be a pilot and there isn't much call for missile launchers in Civvy Street, but the point was that I had been through many periods taking tuition as a student, and had spent just as much time giving tuition in my role as an instructor. I knew how people were taught and I knew how to teach. What's more, apart from my time spent with Joe and the boys during the war, working as an instructor was what I had enjoyed most. It was but a short step from there to deciding to become a teacher.

I came to this decision with Gwyn's full backing, of course. This would mean a big change for us, but she knew how unhappy I now was in the service and the shift work was very unsettling for the whole family, so she readily agreed to the change. Leaving the RAF was a seriously big step for me to take, but the time had come to move on.

While I was reasonably confident that I had something to offer as a teacher, I felt uncomfortable with the idea of going into a senior school, a 'secondary modern', to work with teenagers. After so long in the military, my idea of discipline would be so different from theirs that I was in no doubt that it would lead to many confrontations. I needed to work with youngsters who were more receptive, kids whom I could more easily persuade to do something that I wanted them to do, the way I wanted them to do it. So I opted to train as a junior school teacher and went for an interview at Clifton Teacher Training College in Nottingham. The principal there seemed a very decent sort and we worked out that, if I put in the work, I would be able to get through the three-year course in two years. He asked when I would be able to join them and all I could tell him was: 'In about six months' time.' I hadn't actually applied to the RAF for early release yet.

As it turned out, that didn't pose much of a problem at all. When I went to see the Group Captain about leaving, he said,

'You know, Johnny, if I had the guts I would do the same thing.' He clearly felt the same as me. The modern RAF was not the service that we had joined all those years ago and, for us, it was no longer a job that gave any real satisfaction. Gwyn knew how I felt and shared my concerns about leaving an institution that had been a huge part of our lives since the day we met, but it was time to bring that episode to a close. In September 1962, I ceased to be a serving officer with the Royal Air Force. It would be easier to say that I left the RAF, but that wouldn't really be true. In a number of ways, through the great friends that we had made, the reunions that we attended, and the memories of the good times we had had, the RAF would always be part of our lives.

On my last day in the service, there was a bit of a drinks do in the mess at lunchtime, with a crowd of my fellow officers giving me a send-off that left me rather the worse for wear. I was decidedly unwell after lunch – it wasn't perhaps the most dignified way to end my RAF career. When I left the service, I commuted part of my pension, taking it as a lump sum. This, along with the gratuity I received, was what we would have to live on for the next couple of years. Money was going to be tight, but we had been through all that before and survived. If we were careful, we could do it again. I used some of the money to buy a little MG Midget for Gwyn, although I ended up using it far more than she did, the car serving as my transport to and from college. College life was another absolutely new experience for me, where I had to absorb modern ideas about education that at first seemed utterly bizarre. It wasn't teaching as I knew it. They put a huge emphasis on using play as a method of teaching, encouraging teachers simply to give the children equipment and allow them to play with it, hoping that they would learn something in the process. Teaching, as I had always known it, seemed to be almost irrelevant. You guided the children into the subject but there was very little of what I felt was actual teaching. My other slight concern was that, because I was doing biology as my major subject, it felt rather out of place with junior teaching.

I accepted that the new methods were the way I would have to learn to teach children, at least until I got into a classroom and could do it my own way, and pressed ahead with the course. I found my fellow students really quite amazing. To begin with, I was a little apprehensive about how it would all work out, a 42-year-old mixing with 18-year-olds straight out of school, but it did work out – and it worked out extremely well. They would sometimes ask for my help because they felt I had more experience than they did, and I learned a lot from their youthful enquiry and enthusiasm. It was a good balance and we got on together much better than I had expected.

Practical experience in the classroom was part of the course and the college found two placements for me, leaving it up to me to find the required third. Jenny had just finished her junior school education at Highfields, a private prep school in Newark, and I went to see Keith Eggleston, her old headmaster, to ask if he could help with my third placement. He was happy to do so and I spent the final three weeks of the term on teaching practice at Highfields. When I finished there, Keith asked if I would be interested in joining them should a vacancy arise. I told him I would and then, having passed my exams, began my teaching career in an entirely different kind of school.

Once I had my teaching certificate, I was appointed to a state school in Newark. This was definitely a case of being thrown in at the deep end. I had a class of 46 C-stream 9- and 10-year-olds. I never actually had 46 in the class due to absenteeism, but there were usually about 40. They spent their first lesson with me sitting with their hands on their heads until they were all quiet, because without quiet we weren't going to do any work at all. They were a boisterous bunch and once, when I had gone into the classroom next door to ask another teacher about something, I came back to find two of them chasing each other around the desks. I caught hold of them and banged their heads together. One went back to his seat, the other shot straight out of the door and went home. I thought there would be a real fuss made over that, so I went to the headmaster at break time and told him what had happened. He simply said, 'Don't worry about it. When he gets home he will probably get a lot worse than that.' The absconder returned two days later wearing a pair of what were once sandals but were now falling off his feet. So I bought him a new pair of reasonable shoes to wear and this made it a little better between us. He settled in after that.

We had regular visits from the 'nit nurse', which were very essential for some of them, and a visit from the school inspectors one day. When I knew that they were coming, I thought I had best teach the way I had been told I should teach and got hold of a record player. I played the class a piece of music, telling them to close their eyes and listen to it. When it finished, I said, 'Right, now I am going to play it again and while it is playing I want you to write what is going through your mind. Write about what you think the music is telling you, what you think it is all about. And if you can't write it – draw it.' The inspector seemed suitably impressed with that and asked if I was having any problems. I admitted that I was.

'I have one lad,' I said, 'who writes utter nonsense, "Tan tan lobhed tan", that sort of thing. I have no idea what he means. Some of these kids can't read or write at all and I'm not sure how to mark their work.'

'Ah, yes,' said the inspector. 'You need to spend more time with these individuals. When a student wants to write something but doesn't know how to do it, he can come to your desk and you can write it for him and send him back to copy it out.'

'Fine,' I said, 'but what do I do with the other 45 while I'm dealing with that one?'

He just smiled and moved on to the next class. I never saw him again.

One of the children was the son of a scrap merchant. He had not the slightest idea about reading or writing but he was a genius at counting money – and we're talking about the old pounds, shillings and pence here, not the decimal stuff. Clearly, he had been handling cash almost as long as he had been able to walk. 'I may not know me letters, sir,' he said, 'but I know me money just fine.' I'm pretty sure he went on to do just fine as well. Not all of them would have done so. I felt sorry for some of them. There were children in these classrooms who clearly hated being in school and when they left junior school they had nothing to look forward to but another four or five years – half a lifetime to them – in a secondary modern. For them this was like a prison sentence and all they wanted to do was to 'serve their time' and get out into the adult world as soon as possible. To do what, who knows? Some of them may have changed along the way and started to take an interest in their education, but I think that the impetus for that would really have had to come from their parents, which, frankly, seemed highly unlikely.

Towards the end of my first year, I had a call from Keith Eggleston, asking if I would be interested in coming to work at Highfields prep. I jumped at the chance, and the change in the classroom experience was incredible. I went from teaching what could only be described as underprivileged children to those who had everything. That was the real difference – the gulf between the 'haves' and the 'have-nots'. I started with a class of just 10 nine-year-olds, a far easier number to handle, especially since their standard of behaviour and willingness to learn were of a different calibre entirely. There are always, however, students who need more care and attention than others.

One of my pupils was the son of a consultant at the local hospital for people with mental illness. He made a point of doing as little work as he could get away with. At the end of my first term, I wrote on his Christmas report: 'If David spent as much time trying to do his work as he does trying to get out of it, he would get on much better.' When his father, Dr Hunter, next saw the headmaster, he made a point of questioning him about the comment and the headmaster backed me to the hilt. 'What do you want to hear?' he asked. 'The truth, or some trumped-up rubbish that means nothing at all?' At the next parents' evening, I was introduced to a tall, gangling character who towered over me – Dr Hunter.

'Tell me,' he said. 'What have you done to David?'

'I'm not sure …' I said, feeling a little apprehensive. 'What do you mean?'

'Well, he no longer plays his radio at maximum volume,' said the doctor. 'He closes doors rather than slams them and he even holds out his mother's seat for her to sit at the table. I just wondered what you had done.'

'Ah,' I said. 'David and I have a new arrangement. I ask David to do something, and if he doesn't do it, I tell him to do it again, and if he still doesn't do it, I pull him out in front of the class and slap his legs.'

'Oh dear,' said the doctor. 'That's entirely against my teaching, but perhaps I should try it.'

He and I got on very well after that.

What I didn't know about David to begin with was that the Hunters had previously lived in Australia and, while they were out there, his mother had suffered a brain tumour. They came back to England for her to have an operation but the whole episode had left her with some disfigurement to her face. When she came out of hospital, as far as David was concerned, she wasn't the same mother who had gone in. That was really what was at the bottom of his problem. Once I knew that, I began to have a little more sympathy for him, cajoling him into doing his work rather than always being so inflexibly strict. He took more of an interest and we got along far better. He is now a qualified doctor like his father.

There were lots of lighter moments at Highfields. We had some very bright boys in the class, one of whom said to me one day, 'Sir, do you know where Edwinstowe is?'

'Yes,' I said. 'It's a town in Nottinghamshire.'

'No, sir,' came the reply. 'It's on Edwin's foot!'

I walked right into that one …

The essential difference between the pupils at the state school and those at Highfields was that the youngsters at Highfields wanted to learn. They were encouraged by their parents, their parents took an interest in their children's education, and they wanted to do well at school in order to do well when they left school. They were also competitive. Those who wanted to be top of the class worked hard to get there. That certainly wasn't what I had seen at the state school. From what I see of schoolchildren nowadays, that imbalance seems to have changed a great deal. That can only be a good thing.

While I was at Highfields, I did some evening work at Rampton Hospital, a hospital for 'bad men'. The hospital was established over 100 years ago when the Broadmoor facility in Berkshire became full to capacity and a new hospital was required to take the overspill. Rampton houses up to 400 patients who have arrived there via the criminal justice system and are diagnosed as requiring psychiatric treatment in a secure unit, as well as those who have been detained under the Mental Health Act. If they are in Rampton, then they have been deemed to pose a threat to the general public because of their mental disorders and violent tendencies. The hospital had advertised for a teacher to run horticulture evening classes and that suited me very well. It was quite a contrast teaching the middle-class children at Highfields during the day and the Rampton inmates in the evening. My Rampton students certainly put their instruction to good use as many of them worked on what was known as the 'Woodbeck estate', maintaining the grounds and gardens where the hospital staff lived.

In 1969, when I had been at Highfields for four years, Rampton applied to the local education authority to open an adult education centre. I decided to go for a job there and the fact that I had already been involved with the hospital stood me in good stead. Whilst teaching in Newark, I had also become interested in the problems of teaching children with learning difficulties. I was genuinely interested in this issue and took a great deal of satisfaction from working in this field. One of the qualities that the good Lord had bestowed upon me was that of infinite patience. A problem would take as long as it would take to solve and I was never frustrated by an apparent lack of progress. Rampton took me on and I moved from teaching children to teaching adults, neatly missing out the awkward teenage years. I had enjoyed my time at Highfields, but this was a new challenge, and a bigger pay packet, both irresistible enticements.

There was, of course, a criminal element at Rampton. Some of the patients were there because their lawyers had advised them that a period in Rampton would work out better for them than a long stretch in prison. I'm sure that some of them, who were by no means the smartest of criminal masterminds, actually didn't realise that they were going into Rampton at Her Majesty's pleasure, serving an open-ended term that would finish only when they were judged fit to be released back into society. Some of the patients, as far as I could see, hadn't a hope of ever seeing the outside world again.

I remember a teenage boy coming in as a patient. He had killed his friend's grandmother. He showed no remorse whatsoever for what he had done. He did not consider that what he had done was wrong. His friend's grandmother had refused to do something that he wanted her to do, so he had beaten her to death as she lay in her bed. He had a glassy stare and a blank expression – a walking, talking human body inhabited by a creature that was totally devoid of any kind of human emotion. As far as I know, he spent a long, long time in Rampton.

We had a few patients who, as well as their other conditions, suffered from epilepsy. They had to be watched very carefully because they could become extremely violent and, when they did, it was a question of making sure that you got them down and held them down until the fit passed, making sure that they were not a danger to themselves or to anyone else. There were always members of the hospital staff in the classrooms to handle that sort of thing. These were nurses, but they were really a cross between a prison officer and a nurse, Rampton being a secure unit. We all carried keys and you locked doors behind you as you progressed through the building – this was something that never allowed you to forget that Rampton was as much a prison as it was a hospital. There was a television documentary made about the hospital in the late 1970s that exposed violent mistreatment of prisoners, something that I found as shocking as any other TV viewer would. I had never seen that sort of thing happen in any of my classes, or anywhere else in the hospital for that matter. I would not have stood for it.

I taught general subjects at a fairly basic level, most of the patients having missed out on any kind of formal education, but I continued to teach my horticultural class on Saturday mornings, and this was where I saw the greatest rewards, not just for me but for the patients. I got to the stage where I was able to suggest to the authorities that I would like to take the horticulture group to a local garden centre to show them the commercial aspects of the sort of work that they were doing. I was aware that this would take a huge leap of faith from the 'powers that be', and there would certainly be some resistance to the idea. But, amazingly enough, they agreed. I read the riot act to my class, warning them that there would be severe repercussions if any of them misbehaved in the slightest, let alone if they had any thoughts about attempting to escape.

Hospital staff accompanied us – out of uniform – and everyone had a good look round. They all behaved themselves very well and I took them into the cafe for a quick cup of tea and a bun before we came back. I, of course, heaved a huge sigh of relief once it was all over, but it was obvious that the patients appreciated the opportunity to prove themselves and I was glad to have been able to give them that.

Not everyone thought that sort of thing was a good idea. Some seemed to believe that the patients at Rampton were 'spoiled'. They did have top-notch facilities there and there were those outside the hospital who thought that too much money was being spent on people who didn't deserve it. I wonder how much more difficult it might have been to control the patients, to give them the treatment and therapy that they needed, had they not had those facilities. There seems to me to be little point in putting people in an institution and leaving them to rot. If the role of Rampton is to punish people for their misdemeanours, so be it, but it is also there to help people who are, for whatever reason, not as fortunate as the rest of us. Medical care and education are essential parts of that process.

I had been working at Rampton for about three years when Balderton Hospital, which was much closer to where we lived, also decided to set up an Adult Education Unit. They advertised for a Senior Education Officer to run the department and I got the job – the fact that Dr Hunter was still the Head Consultant there helped in no small way in my securing the post.

Balderton provided care and treatment for people with many types of mental problems, some of which were the most severe that I had ever come across. If I could at all avoid it, I never went into the children's wards. I had difficulty in accepting that some of these poor youngsters should live their lives like they did. I know it sounds awful, but I have to say that I had a strong feeling at that stage that there was a real case for euthanasia. In the worst cases, those children had absolutely no chance of ever leading any kind of life. They were in no way aware of their surroundings. They would live and die in those wards, where they received medical attention, they received nursing attention and they were given food as they required it. I found their plight and the hopelessness of their situation very traumatic.

My main responsibility was to organise classes for the more able patients at the hospital. The classes were designed to help them acquire the skills that they would need to live an independent life, allowing them to go back into the community. It was really all about social education, teaching the patients how to take care of themselves. I had part- and full-time teachers, not a very big section, a staff of six. I was given a free hand to organise the teaching programme and I designed it in stages so that the patients progressed from basic housekeeping chores to learning about handling money, simple cooking and so forth. We had a kind of bedsit at the end of the section with its own kitchen, allowing us to stage lots of practical, hands-on teaching sessions. We would take them off-site as well, on little shopping expeditions when they could learn how to use the buses and build up some experience of the world outside the hospital.

Quite a few of them did go back into the community, living in accommodation that we organised for them. We realised that having people with impaired mental capability living next door might not go down too well with the neighbours, so part of the programme was to visit the neighbours before setting up the houses, asking for their help and co-operation. We invited them up to the hospital to see what we were doing, to meet some of the patients and to reassure them that anyone we sent to live outside was going to be capable of coping with everyday life. Eventually, we had 18 of our patients living in three council houses. I don't recall there ever being any problems with the neighbours and we visited regularly to ensure that the patients were doing what they were supposed to be doing and that things were going as smoothly as possible. Isn't it strange that when you involve people, when you engage them in what you are trying to do, you can receive far more support than you ever dared to hope for? The enterprise was judged to be a success. Some of the patients were able to move on from the monitored programme to live completely independent lives and that was the greatest satisfaction at Balderton – getting those people out into the community and giving them the chance to have a life outside the institution. It all seems very straightforward now, but this work took months of training and negotiation. It was a job where what others might see as small successes were actually huge victories.

I was at Balderton for 14 years and never once was bored, but I was coming close to retirement age. It was time for a change, not only for me but for the whole adult education section. It was time for a younger person to come in with different ideas, someone who could provide a fresh outlook. Every organisation can benefit from that from time to time. So I retired again, one year before actual retirement age. I was ready to ease back – however, I was not yet ready simply to let old age creep up on me.

For some years, Gwyn and I had been involved with the Conservative Party. Whilst living in Collingham, friends had encouraged us to join the party while I was still with the RAF at Hemswell. Strictly speaking, a serving officer in the RAF should not be affiliated to any political party, but in the beginning it was a social activity more than anything else and my RAF career was, in any case, drawing to a close. We became more involved when I was working as a teacher, as well as in the hospitals, and in 1975, when Margaret Thatcher became the leader of the Conservative Party, Gwyn was over the moon. She adored Mrs Thatcher. You can imagine her delight on 4 May 1979 when Margaret Thatcher became Britain's first female Prime Minister. Following Mrs Thatcher's speech to the Conservative Party Conference in 1980, Gwyn settled any discussions with me or the children simply by holding up her hand and saying, 'The lady's not for turning …'

When I retired, we moved down to Torquay to be closer to Gwyn's family – her father, brothers and sister, Nell having passed away by this time. We continued to be involved with the Conservative Party, and had been living in Torquay for a couple of years when I was persuaded to stand as a prospective councillor for Torbay council. Perhaps my service background helped to make them think that I would be suitable and, lo and behold, I was elected. It should be pointed out that, in those days, Torbay was a pretty safe Conservative area. I served mainly on the planning committee and eventually I became chairman of the local Conservative Association. It was a busy and interesting time made even more so by my dealings with Rupert Allason, our MP. He was a Euro-sceptic and in 1993 abstained from the vote on the Maastricht Treaty, which had become a motion of confidence. He disappeared and literally no one knew where to find him. There was a major rumpus. I lost count of the number of telephone calls that I had from the Conservative Central Office asking me where he was. How was I supposed to know? For the first time in my life the media was camped on our front doorstep, asking for regular updates on his whereabouts, to which my only response was: 'I have no idea.' When he eventually turned up, the party whip was withdrawn for a year. I was, together with some of my colleagues, very angry. I had met John Major at a couple of functions and I had a high regard for him. I may not have been completely on board with his European initiatives but that was the agreed party line and my expectation was that it should be followed. Individuals always, of course, have the right to resign if they feel strongly about an issue, but to abstain seemed to me to be a weak way out. I have talked earlier about how much I value loyalty and it seemed to me that we were being shown very little loyalty from our MP. A number of colleagues believed that there were good grounds for demanding his deselection, but it was decided not to pursue that course. On a personal level, I had lost a lot of faith in our MP and, when it came to the 1997 election, I, together with some others, decided that we could not work on his campaign. In the event, after several recounts, he lost by 12 votes to the Liberal Democrat candidate. Shortly afterwards I resigned as chairman, bringing my political career to an end.

Gwyn and I had a marvellous retirement in Torquay, at first living in a house in Goodrington that had a little path down to a large, sandy beach. Family would come every summer and our grandchildren loved it there. Getting them up from the beach for mealtimes or bedtime was always a battle of wills. The children never seemed able to accept that somehow Grandma would always win. The fine summer weather in Devon, of course, came as a welcome change from Lincolnshire. For Gwyn and me, this was a wonderful time in our lives. We were close to her family and we watched with pride as our own children's careers developed successfully, they married partners whom we liked very much and had families of their own. What more could we have asked for? All my life I had wanted a happy, tight-knit family, sharing in each other's success and helping each other in times of difficulty, and now here it was. In time, we moved to be closer to our friends in the centre of Torquay, to a very comfortable flat, which better suited our needs. It was easier for us to look after but we could still enjoy glorious views out over the bay, the town and Dartmoor beyond.

All my life, fate seemed to have been looking after me, but it was now about to deliver a hammer blow. Gwyn struggled with what appeared to be a bout of flu over Christmas 2003 but the medication she was prescribed seemed to be having little effect, and eventually hospital tests showed that she had cancer of the liver. The disease was quite advanced and it was not thought that she would survive an operation. There was nothing to be done but to let it take its course. The doctors gave her between six weeks and three months. We made a simple pact. We would treat every day as it came and consider every new day as a bonus. She was a fighter and we had another 18 months together. I nursed her at home for as long as I was able, taking her for walks along the coast in a wheelchair and trying to make what time we had left together as enjoyable as possible. The social services people were a huge help, as, towards the end, were the Macmillan nurses, and I will be eternally grateful for all that they did for both of us.

Ultimately, however, Gwyn had to go into a hospice, although she was there for only a few days. The children and I were with her at the end when she finally just peacefully drifted off into sleep.

I stayed on in the flat in Torquay, resisting all of my family's efforts to persuade me to move. There was something about being where Gwyn had been. I felt as though her spirit was still there and I found myself having conversations with her. If this sounds spooky, it shouldn't do. It seemed to me to be a most natural thing. I am sure other bereaved people feel the same way. But Torquay was a long way from my family and, however much I loved the apartment, it was a little isolated. I could go days on end without seeing anyone. Eventually, the pressure grew to the point where I knew it made sense to move. Jenny, two of her children and several great-grandchildren lived in Bristol, and she found a great retirement village hardly five minutes away from her house. So now, here I am. It is a lovely place to be, the support staff are first-rate, my neighbours are friendly and I have many visitors – children, grandchildren and great-grandchildren. Our thoroughly modern family enjoys a lifestyle that is a far cry from my early days back on the farm, and that is exactly what Gwyn and I always hoped and planned for. The family is without doubt our greatest achievement and I am hugely proud of all of them.

Around the family photos in my flat are various mementos from my time in the RAF, with paintings and models of the Lancasters in which I flew with Joe and the boys – Chuck-Chuck in her various guises and T-Tommy – taking pride of place. I find myself in regular demand to give talks about my time with Bomber Command and on the Dams Raid, or to attend functions with different organisations and charities, and I am happy to carry on with this as long as people want me to. I accept these invitations on behalf of my crew and all of the others who haven't been able to live as long as I have. I believe it is important that their memory is kept alive and the sacrifices that they made continue to be appreciated, even in the twenty-first century. I don't think it is right to dwell too much on what has gone – I believe in moving forwards. But, as we look ahead, as we make our plans for the future, every now and again perhaps we would be wise to think about the lessons we can learn from the past and those people who made it possible for us to be where we are today.

# EPILOGUE

Over the last 18 months, my father has led a whirlwind existence of media interviews, personal appearances and speaking engagements. His attitude is simple. If people are genuinely interested, he is very happy to speak to them. He very rarely says 'no' to anyone. Polite rejection is more likely to come from his immediate family as we try to manage his time, making sure that he doesn't overdo it. At the age of 92, he still seems to have considerable stamina and he loves being busy. Personally, I am astounded by the continued public interest in the events of 71 years ago and the genuine warmth of the reception he receives whenever he attends a function.

For him, the biggest event was in November 2012. In the late summer of that year he was quietly sitting having lunch in the dining room at Westbury Fields, the retirement village in Bristol where he now lives, when fate, which has so often turned events to his advantage, dealt him another lucky card. In his own words:

*A gentleman introduced himself as Terry Pendry and asked if he might join me for a chat. Terry and his wife, Sue, were visiting her godmother Brenda, who also had an apartment in the retirement village. Brenda had suggested that Terry may prefer to talk to me than listening to all the 'girl talk'. We had a great chat. He wanted to know about my war experiences and I soon learned that he had originally been a flat jockey and had later joined the Household Cavalry. He rose to be a Warrant Officer in charge of the horses and training and was eventually invited to run The Royal Mews at Windsor Castle, a job he has held for the last 19 years. Terry clearly has a great knowledge about and love for horses, a passion shared with Her Majesty, The Queen. She still rides out when 'at home' and he always accompanies Her Majesty, so they know each other well. At the end of our conversation he asked if I would like to come up to Windsor and have a look around. I was delighted to accept.*

As Terry drove home from Bristol, he thought to himself that the Queen might like to meet my father to hear the story of his wartime exploits with the Dambusters. He contacted Sir Richard Johns and asked his opinion. Air Chief Marshal Sir Richard Johns had a distinguished RAF career, initially with fast jets, rising to become Chief of the Air Staff between 1997 and 2000. On retirement from the RAF, Sir Richard had been appointed Constable and Governor of Windsor Castle, a post he held until 2008. In this capacity, he had come to know the Queen very well and he and Terry had also always got on well together. Sir Richard agreed that it might be a nice idea and said that, in the event of the meeting being arranged, he would be happy to be present. Several weeks later, when out riding one morning with Her Majesty, Terry mentioned the idea. The Queen agreed and once back at the castle a date was fixed for 10 November at 11.30 am.

'My first reaction on hearing the news was a mixture of excitement and almost total panic,' my father admits.

*My head went into a spin far greater than anything Joe McCarthy had managed to induce. What were the logistics? How do you greet the Queen? What was I supposed to say? All the angst was slightly tempered by the realisation that this was a huge honour for me. This would be an entirely private meeting. Totally informal. No civil servants or advisers, just two or three of us talking, just having a chat really. There was nothing in the training manuals that prepared you for 'a bit of a chat with the Queen' and it was only a couple of weeks away.*

*Terry and my family took care of the logistics and at 10.30 am on the dot, Morgan, his wife Lyn and I arrive at the castle. Terry and Sue live in a lovely grace and favour home in the Royal Mews. It is hundreds of years old and very cosy. Photographs of family and members of the Royal Household on horseback abound. They are a lovely couple, warm-hearted and very generous. We are invited to stay for a light lunch after the 'event'. Sir Richard arrives at pretty much the same time and over coffee I ask him if he knew Sir David Parry-Evans. This is an instant icebreaker as he knows David very well and we begin to share stories about our careers. Eventually, Terry says it is time to go and my nervousness returns. This is, however, somewhat alleviated by the look on*

*Morgan's face when he is told that he is coming too! This is a total shock to him and he is clearly more worried about making a fool of himself than I am.*

*We are met by a member of the Royal Household in full livery and told that 'Her Majesty will meet you in the Oak Room'. On the way up, Sir Richard briefs us on the simple protocols of how to behave and what to say when we meet. Her Majesty is waiting for us when we arrive and steps forward, holding out her hand for a firm but gentle handshake. She smiles in a kindly manner and, pointing to four chairs arranged in a horseshoe shape, she says to me, 'Come and sit next to me.' Protocol requires that private conversations with the Queen remain private and so it shall be in this case. Suffice to say that it was a wonderful occasion. The time simply flies by and soon the conversation comes to an end. Her Majesty stands, and as we bow and shake hands she says, 'That was most interesting. Thank you for coming to see me.' We are just bowled over by how gracious and friendly she has been.*

As we went down in the lift, my father had a little smile and gave a long sigh of relief. Terry said that the visit was a great success. 'Most audiences last 20 minutes, you got 40. She must have enjoyed it.' Really, 40 minutes? It felt like five. As we left the castle compound, a policeman saluted and a sentry snapped into 'present arms'. Terry drove us around the estate, showing off the farm, golf course, cricket pitch, riding tracks, stables and so on. He clearly loves his job. Then we returned for lunch and, over a glass of champagne, we talked about the meeting. Father looked totally at peace and very happy. In fact, he was quite tired as if all the adrenaline that had fired him up for the meeting had now vanished. After having had a final glass of red wine, it was time to go and we gave our profound thanks to Sir Richard and particularly to Terry and Sue.

The journey back to Bristol was less than two hours and Dad slept most of the way. As I left to return home, he gave me a big grin and said, 'That was probably the most memorable day of my life.' And with one or two obvious exceptions, it probably was. A couple of days later he told me that he was sitting quietly in his apartment that evening and all the old memories came flooding back. He said, 'I wonder what Joe and the boys would have made of it?' No reply seems necessary.

As we approached the seventieth anniversary of the Dams Raid in May 2013, everything seemed to go into overdrive. A large number of invitations and notifications of celebratory events began to arrive. Some were to be on a grand scale, others lower key but, to my father, no less important. Two invitations illustrate the point. On 27 April he was invited to speak to a local history society in Wellesbourne, Warwickshire. The week of 15 May included a programme of events in and around Woodhall Spa as part of the official 617 Squadron celebrations. Both were accepted with alacrity. The Wellesbourne invitation was from Dad's good friend Roger Wright. The local history group had arranged the event to raise funds for the Bomber Command Memorial Maintenance Fund and the Barnes Wallis Memorial Trust. Both charities are close to my father's heart and it was another opportunity to meet with Mary Stopes-Roe, Barnes Wallis's daughter, who has become a good friend over the years. Together with Mike Gibson (Guy Gibson's nephew), they all talked about their memories of those fateful days. The audience was about 140 people and a good time was had by all.

In contrast, the week-long programme of celebrations in Lincolnshire looked exhausting – so exhausting, in fact, that I arranged to accompany Dad for only half the week with his grandson, Richard, taking over midway. But our hero goes on relentlessly. The week opened with a showing of the famous film *The Dam Busters* starring Richard Todd. It was shown in a small cinema named 'Kinema in the Woods' that had been built in the 1920s just behind the Petwood Hotel. The cinema had been frequented by officers from various squadrons, particularly 617, who had used the Petwood as their Officers' Mess. It remains a wonderfully authentic cinema from those days, complete with red velvet seats, back projection and an organist who appears up from in front of the screen in a break in the movie while they change the reels. It was a black tie event, with current 617 Squadron aircrew present and a fly-past by the *City of Lincoln* Lancaster from the Battle of Britain Memorial Flight. After the screening, there was a reception for 175 guests at the Petwood. The next day, we were invited to lunch at RAF Scampton with the Station Commander and some of his staff. In the evening, there was a 'Sunset Ceremony' televised by the BBC. This was a particularly poignant moment for my father, who was accompanied by Mary Stopes-Roe and Les Munro, who travelled over from New Zealand. After a fly-past, the Lancaster slowly taxied forwards to come to a halt behind the RAF band as they played the famous Eric Coates' 'Dam Busters March' – there was, as they say, hardly a dry eye in the house. On the following day, there was a memorial service at Lincoln Cathedral. Saturday brought the 617 Squadron Association dinner and Sunday an altogether more relaxed, if still formal, dinner with the Battle of Britain Memorial Flight officers and guests at nearby RAF Coningsby.

Two weeks later, I took Dad to the RAF Benevolent Fund dinner in London. Here we met Air Chief Marshal Sir Stephen Dalton, who was shortly to retire as Chief of the Air Staff. Over dinner, Dad chatted happily away to Lady Anne Dalton, whom he described as 'a lovely lady'. As the evening drew to a close, Sir Stephen handed my father a handwritten note. It said 'RIAT July 20/21'. Neither of us knew what this meant at the time.

Two days later, Dad met John Sweetman, the author of *Operation Chastise*, which my father considers the definitive work on the Dams Raid. They have known each other ever since John interviewed Dad when researching his book and it was a simple meeting of two friends, but another date to add to Dad's busy schedule.

A few days after that, all became clear about Sir Stephen's strange note, as an invitation to the Royal International Air Tattoo at Fairford on 21 July arrived. RIAT is the world's biggest military air show, held every year in support of the RAF Charitable Trust Enterprises, and over 150,000 people attend over the weekend. Dad and I were invited. Our participation began with a formal dinner for the great and the good of the air forces from around the world. There was a moment of high drama at the hotel when we were changing into black tie for the dinner. My father cut his finger badly. Blood was pouring everywhere. I could only think, 'Oh no! He's only got one dress shirt!' I wrapped his finger in toilet tissue and ordered him to stand still with his finger well away from his shirt as I rushed to the hotel reception to get the necessary first aid equipment. With the wound dressed, we finally arrived at the dinner to be met by Sir Stephen and introduced to General Sir Nicholas Houghton, the newly appointed Chief of the Defence Staff. My immediate impression was very positive as he seemed more interested in talking about golf than anything else. Later, he delivered an extremely interesting and erudite speech on the role of the armed forces in today's political environment worldwide.

When we arrived at our table for dinner, the place names were all set out, but two retired Air Chief Marshals decided to change everything so that Dad could sit between them, and they spent most of the evening talking to him about his wartime experiences. The air show the next day was quite spectacular, young pilots from around the world throwing jet aircraft around the sky with huge skill and a lot of noise, helicopters showing amazing agility and large transport aircraft barrelling along the runway. The stars of the show were undoubtedly the Red Arrows – the RAF display team. Their performance was mesmeric and both of us looked on in awe at the pilots' skill. It is easy to imagine our surprise when, a little later, after they had landed and were mixing with the VIPs, their manager introduced herself and said to my father, 'I hope you don't mind me interrupting but the boys would love to meet you.' Dad posed for a photograph that remains in pride of place in Bristol.

One of the things I have found interesting over the last couple of years is the high regard that current serving aircrew have for my father and everything that he represents. It shouldn't be strange because he is, of course, an integral part of their history, but there is an affinity that somehow goes beyond that. For his part, he is extremely fond of the current members of 617 Squadron and gets on with them very well. He admires what they do and believes strongly that they are maintaining a very proud tradition.

Some weeks before RIAT, I had received a very gracious invitation from Lord March for my father and me to attend the Goodwood Revival. The Goodwood Revival is a renowned event held every September, celebrating the glorious days of motor racing in the 1950s and 1960s. It also includes classic aircraft. People wear period costume and it has become a major event on the social calendar of every car and aeroplane enthusiast. Lord March had decided to organise a celebration of the Dambusters as a centrepiece event and said that he would like my father to attend. Not knowing what to expect, we turned up on a very cold and windy day to be met by a delightful staff who immediately took us under their wing and briefed us. At the appointed time, we were driven in an old US Army Jeep onto the track in front of the main grandstand. There was a march past as the band played 'The Dam Busters March', a Spitfire flew a low pass along the track (the weather being too bad for the planned Lancaster) and Lord March gave a speech in memory of the Dambusters. We were then driven around the whole Goodwood circuit and everyone in the stands stood and cheered as Dad went by. I am told that the attendance was 40,000 people. It was a very emotional experience.

Two weeks later, Dad spoke at a dinner for cadets from the Gloucestershire Air Training Corps and, with no let-up in his schedule, October and November brought small private dinners with clubs of one kind or another, and a great trip back to Newark, his home town, to open a new art gallery and bookshop on behalf of Mark Postlethwaite, a talented aviation artist who has become a good friend. Then there was the end-of-season dinner with the Battle of Britain Memorial Flight at Coningsby. This was followed at the end of October by a week-long tour of Lincolnshire with Roger and Pat Wright, organised by Dave Harrigan of Aviation Heritage Lincolnshire (AHL). AHL is an interesting initiative by Lincolnshire County Council to promote tourism to World War II airfields in the county, including, amongst other attractions, a museum at RAF Scampton. Dad recorded an interview with Radio Lincolnshire, visited St Vincent's Hall, where 5 Group had planned the Dams Raid, and planted a memorial tree. The local historians were delighted as this was the first visit by a member of 617 Squadron since Guy Gibson took his final briefing there on 14 May 1943. He also visited RAF Digby and RAF Waddington for more receptions and museum visits.

Quite out of the blue, I received an enquiry asking if Dad would be available to take part in the opening ceremony of the Festival of Remembrance at the Royal Albert Hall on behalf of the Royal British Legion. Televised on BBC, this annual event celebrates the lives of those who have died or who have been severely wounded in the service of the country, as well as being a tribute to those still serving. Dad was very proud to have been invited and agreed instantly. By coincidence, this event was exactly one year after his audience with the Queen. In an incredibly moving opening ceremony, the RAF band played the quiet moments of 'The Dam Busters March' as my father walked across the auditorium flanked by two current serving officers of 617 Squadron. One carried the remembrance torch, the other read the dedication. Some 5,000 people rose to their feet to give a long standing ovation. It went on for so long that there was a delay before the officer could read his words. The ceremony was held twice on that Saturday, and the evening saw a repeat of the ovation they received in the afternoon. On this occasion, the Queen was present and, as I looked on, I wondered if she remembered their meeting the previous year.

Three days later, Dad was back at the Royal Albert Hall. On this occasion, he was the guest of honour at the Music for Youth prom. Included in this concert were 600 schoolchildren from around Lincolnshire, who, as a massive choir, performed the premiere of a piece called *Lincolnshire Skies*, a tribute to the Dambusters written by Lincolnshire-based composer Jonathan Nowell. Before they sang, a spotlight hit the balcony where we were all seated and Dad was introduced to the audience. Remarkably again, 5,000 people got to their feet and cheered to the rafters. After the performance, in a moving moment, he went on stage to thank the children and to say how proud he was of them – and how proud he is to be a 'yellowbelly', the affectionate name given to the people of Lincolnshire after the frogs found in the fenlands.

And so it goes on …

Describing all this activity is not to boast about my father's popularity but to make two points. At Dad's age, it would be easy to decline these invitations, big or small, grand or intimate gatherings. He has a ready-made excuse in terms of his old age. But that is not his style. He is delighted to play a part in the remembrance of his colleagues and what they achieved, telling their story to whoever wants to hear about it. He will never push himself forward but equally he does find it hard to say no. The second, and more important point, is the affection that is shown to him by the thousands of people he has talked to, briefly greeted, or just waved to in the last couple of years. And this is not purely a generational thing. I have seen him keep a sixth-form history class spellbound with his stories. He recalls with pride being asked by one enterprising junior school teacher to talk to her class of nine-year-olds who were doing a project on the war years. He asked for a briefing meeting beforehand to ensure that he pitched his words correctly so that they would not think he was talking down to them. Of course, his primary 'admirers' are of an older generation who remember those years first- or second-hand, but my father's story still resonates with a much broader audience.

Very importantly, he is the first to recognise that all of this attention is not purely about him personally, but is directed at what he represents. The Dambusters became a wartime legend that captured the public imagination and, as the last British survivor of that night, he represents all of them and what they achieved. There are many, many other stories of individual and collective achievements during World War II. Stories of extraordinary courage, of battles won in impossible situations, of acts of heroism against overwhelming odds. But the Dambusters remain high on the list of public affection. And that is what he will be remembered for, by the public at large.

I, together with all the members of our family, am enormously proud of Dad and it is an emotion founded upon much more than those wartime exploits. It is about things the public cannot know. As I have listened to him talk over the last few years, I have come to realise just what he has achieved from those humble and difficult early years. It is quite obvious to me that the two things he craved more than anything else were the love of a good wife and the warmth of a tight-knit family. With his innate stubbornness he fought for the first, a battle I think he considers more important than any other, and together they created the second – not just with the first generation but also with those who came after. And, whatever the odds, he was never going to let that go. I still find it extraordinary that in his early thirties he effectively walked away from a promising career because he wanted to spend more time with his family. Such an attitude would be very unusual even today.

Many of my father's other character traits contrast vividly with what has apparently become the norm nowadays. He would never dream of pulling the wool over someone's eyes, 'pulling a fast one' as he would say, in an attempt to make a quick buck or profit from them. He spent his life in the service of others and never expected any reward from it other than an 'honest day's pay' and job satisfaction. He is as honest as the day is long. He is generous to a fault, going out of his way to help in any way he can, financially or otherwise. He would never shirk a responsibility or blame others for his own mistakes. Through all the difficulties he and my mother experienced, they never, unlike so many in today's 'entitlement society', believed that anyone owed them anything. What they didn't have, or couldn't have, they would do without and they made the best of it. He created deep and loyal friendships that he would defend whatever the odds. None of these things was taught to him by his father. These were a set of values that he developed for himself, many of which were due to his wartime experiences. To 'discipline, respect and loyalty', which he believed in then and continues to hold dear today, you can add 'affection' and 'always believe in the best in other people'. And, yes, you can also add 'stubbornness' – if it matters that much, never give in. He is essentially a thoroughly decent man.

In today's world, my father might be considered something of an anachronism – a throwback to an old and, for many, irrelevant generation. For my part, I look around me and, watching the news or reading the papers, I sometimes wonder where did all these values go? Wouldn't we be better off as a society if honesty and common sense were still important virtues? Can't we learn something from my father and his peers? Strangely, society's apparent loss of basic human values doesn't seem to worry Dad. He is, for example, very supportive of young people today. 'Yes, there are problems – there will always be problems with some sections of any society,' he says, 'but most youngsters are decent and hard-working, honestly trying to do their best.' He will listen to the supposedly great and good pontificate or weasel their way through this issue or that and then look at me with a sardonic grin, shrug his shoulders and say something like, 'If that's the way it is, you just have to live with it and make your own way.'

And that's exactly what he did. He made his own way, helped enormously by some quirks of fate that occasionally gave him a very helpful push in the right direction. He has lived through a period of enormous change both culturally and in technology but, through it all, Dad has remained steadfast in his beliefs. He and the love of his life, my mother, created a successful and well-balanced middle-class family. They survived and they succeeded in a modest way. In the process, he has experienced more than I, and I suspect most of us, ever will.

As he looks back on those 92 years, does he feel content?

Does he feel fulfilled? Does he feel happy? You can bet your life he does. It's been a hell of a journey for a poor farm boy from Lincolnshire whose best friend was a pig.

# ACKNOWLEDGEMENTS

I have so many people to thank for helping to make this story possible. In particular, my children, their partners and my grandchildren for their unfailing love, support and encouragement. The Morgan family, who showed me in those early days what family life could be like, and particularly Dave and Margaret, whose support in recent years has been so generous. Thank you to those friends who over the years have always been on my side. Not just Christmas card friends but people who make you smile whenever you think of them. Pip and Jean Mounfield, Ruth and Vernon Cavey, Jack and Kate Batty. To Joe McCarthy Jnr for his continued interest and for being a constant reminder of the man who probably had the single most important influence on my life – his father. To the 617 Squadron Association who have shown their support at all times. More recently, Dave Harrigan and the team at Aviation Heritage Lincolnshire and Roger and Pat Wright, whose friendship is very important to me. To Terry and Sue Pendry, who made one of the most important days of my life possible.

In terms of writing this book, my son, Morgan, did most of the donkey work and listened to my endless ramblings over many hours together. Thank you to Mark Postlethwaite whose early encouragement helped to get the show on the road; Robert Owen, author and historian, for his authoritative help and advice; John Sweetman, author of *Operation Chastise*, which, in my view, is the definitive work on the Dams Raid and has been a constant reference work; and Gill Kelly and the Sternians' Association for their remarkable archive material on Lord Wandsworth College, which helped me recall those pivotal years. And to all those people who scrabbled around old photo albums to find the right pictures.

A particular thanks to Sara Cywinski at Ebury Press for believing that this was a story worth telling and her constant encouragement. And finally my great thanks to Rod Green, whose insight and creativity have been so instrumental in making it all 'come alive'.

# GLOSSARY

Rank Abbreviations

| | |
|---|---|
| Sergeant | Sgt |
| Flight Sergeant | Flt Sgt |
| Warrant Officer | WO |
| Pilot Officer | Plt Off |
| Flying Officer | Fg Off |
| Flight Lieutenant | Flt Lt |
| Squadron Leader | Sqn Ldr |
| Wing Commander | Wg Cdr |
| Group Captain | Gp Cpt |

# PICTURE CREDITS

Pages 1, 2, 3, 4, 5, 6, 7 (above), 8 (above), 11 (above left and right) and 13 author's own.

Special thanks to Mary Stopes-Roe (page 7 below), Rex Features (page 8 below), Imperial War Museum (page 9 FLM 2352 / HU 62922 and page 11 below ATP 17351B), Mark Postlethwaite/www.posart.com (page 10 above), Cliff Manners/ www.artisticuk.com (page 14 above), Goodwood Revival (page 14 below/Marcus Dodridge) and John Aron (page 15 and 16).